PRESTWICK IN THE 40'S

NEWSPAPER CUTTINGS FROM THE AYRSHIRE POST

Compiled by Ian Welsh

Kyle and Carrick District Leisure Services
Libraries and Galleries

Ayr 1992

Kyle & Carrick District Council
Leisure Services
would like to thank
Scottish Universal Newspapers
for their kind permission
to reproduce the material in this book.

PRESTWICK IN THE FORTIES

There has been a considerable revival of interest in the study of local history and this booklet is a small response to that revival. It owes much to the extensive coverage of local affairs provided by the Ayrshire Post in the 1940s and is a representative collection of articles, extracts, letters, public notices and adverts. The 1940s were turbulent, dynamic and formative years for all those involved and although the hardship of the war years was followed by the austerity of the post-war years, they seemed to be stamped, nonetheless, with the spirit of optimism.

1940 was the year when Britain became slowly acclimatised to being at war. Winston S. Churchill became Prime Minister, heading a National Government. It was the year of Dunkirk and the Battle of Britain. Seaside towns like Prestwick were used for the evacuation of the cities threatened with bombing. Sir Harry Lauder visited the Broadway and Sunday golfing was an issue which split the Town Council and became an issue for virulent debate. The Spitfire Fund was launched and Prestwick was lambasted for mustering only three ARP volunteers with one of them 84 years old!

By 1941, Bevan and Morrison, two prominent Labour politicians, had undertaken to look after the Home Front on behalf of the National Government and helped to usher in a period of full industrial employment and comparative freedom from industrial unrest. The German U-Boat campaign was hitting hard and Pearl Harbour sent shock waves across the Western world. Metal railings were biting the dust all around Prestwick, including the ones at the Bruce's Well, uprooted in aid of the war effort. In Boydfield Gardens, a Junkers 88 bomber was displayed. Target-bombing around the British Isles was causing considerable dislocation. As a result of one raid on Clydebank, a clutch of Glenburn miners came off their shift and headed straight for Clydebank to search for the missing relative of a colleague. To offset possible damage in Prestwick from incendiary bombs inhabitants were schooled in the art of the stirrup pump. At the Broadway, Sir Patrick Dollan came to speak to the "millionaires of Prestwick" about the blitzed people of Glasgow.

By 1942, Clement Attlee was deputy-Prime Minister allowing Churchill to devote his attention to executing the war effort. Throughout the country, American forces were finding themselves overpaid, oversexed and over here! The Beveridge Report which was to redraw the social boundaries in post war Britain was published. Nearer home, a public subscription was raised for the purchase of an ambulance to serve Prestwick and outlying areas while waste paper salvage, an early example of recycling was a major growth industry at Prestwick High School who collected a mammoth 14 tons of waste paper. This was calculated as being sufficient to supply the Services with 3,000 shell components, 18,000 shell-fuse components, 22,000 mine assemblies, 21,000 dust covers for aero engines, 15,000 boxes for aero cannon shells and 72,000 cutout targets.

Some of the more devastating casualties of the war, thus far, were occurring in the Russia of 1943 as Germany, having turned on its former ally, finally floundered at Stalingrad. Glenburn Primary school raised a commendable £1.5s for Mrs. Churchill's Aid to Russia Fund. The ability of towns to provide cheap nutritious and affordable food for workers was enhanced by the idea of British Restaurants and the Prestwick British Restaurant in the United Services Club in Templerigg Street, the 2001st in Britain, provided meals throughout the war. Lord Sherwood opened the road which crossed the runway. It was named after him but there were memories also of the older Glasgow-Ayr Toll road of 100 years earlier. Most seriously, there was local upset at the indiscretion of a BBC radio programme which gave details of Prestwick Airport's strategic role in the war. Prestwick Provost Dunsmore blasted the BBC claiming that it had put Prestwick "on the bombing map of Germany".

R.A. Butler's 1944 Education Act marked a milestone in attitudes to education and helped to create a consensus that would see British education through the next several decades. It was the year of D Day and on June 6th the allied forces landed on European soil. A feeling that the war was winding down was evident in Prestwick. In the Town Hall, the Citizen's Company was performing James Bridie's play Mr. Bolfry with a young actor called Duncan MacRae. There was concern about the gas lighting in Glenburn and Francis Pritty, Town Clerk, was addressing the WEA in the Broadway on Prestwick's role as a trans-ocean airport. He reminded his audience of Prestwick's role as a flying school which had turned out so many efficient flyers who, in turn, had played their part in the Battle of Britain. The year was clouded, however, by the killing of six year old Irene Haswell after a plane landed on houses in Hillside Avenue.

In 1945, election fever was in the air and the Labour party swept to power with a 150 seat majority. The atomic bomb was dropped with horrific consequences at Hiroshima. Within the Council Chambers, post-war housing was becoming the dominant issue but there were also discussions about schooling and recreational facilities for the post war period. D.F. McIntyre and the Duke of Hamilton had the Freedom of Prestwick conferred on them to mark their outstanding aviation achievements and preparation for Prestwick's Welcome Home Week helped to raise the spirits of a town still in thrall to rationing.

The balance of payments crisis in 1946 ensured that rationing would not only stay but expand and, while bread rationing began in Britain, the War Crimes Tribunal in Nuremburg put the Nazis on trial. In Prestwick, Councillor Crawford, the town's first woman Councillor, demanded twelve months of planning "for the living" and in a bout of serious debating about the structure of local government, amalgamation with Ayr was suggested. Conflict between the Council, the local community and the colliery erupted over pollution in the Pow Burn and a pit strike in Glenburn indicated the great unhappiness at services and conditions there.

The marriage of Princess Elizabeth and Phillip Mountbatten brought some sparkle to 1947, the year of the big freeze and the year in which signs proclaiming "This colliery is now under the ownership of the National Coal Board" went up outside collieries around Britain. The Reverend Donald Caskie was ordained minister of Prestwick St. Cuthberts's and a new Roman Catholic Hall at St. Quivox Church was opened. It was proposed that the Town Hall should be sold and the idea of a mini-railway on the Front provoked an outcry

from residents. Meanwhile, workers on the new Marchburn housing scheme were contributing to the wages spiral.

The NHS and the railways became national services in 1948. James Johnstone of 56 Glenburn Rows celebrated his Golden Wedding while recovering from the effects of a broken neck sustained in a pit accident. He had worked underground for 66 years since the age of eight! A meeting in Prestwick Town Hall attracted 700 people to protest at the allocation of a house to a cashier in the Burgh Chamberlain's office Down on the waterfront, the winner of the Prestwick Bathing Beauty contest received a free trip to Copenhagen, Stockholm, Oslo, Amsterdam or Paris with a cash prize of £80 to squander. Tragedy struck in October when 38 people died in the first civil air disaster at Prestwick Airport. A Constellation en route from Amsterdam to New York crashed outside Tarbolton.

The North Atlantic Treaty Organisation was founded and apartheid was introduced into South Africa in 1949. Stafford Cripps, The Labour Chancellor took a penny off a pint of beer! St. Cuthbert's Golf Club, formed by and for working men, celebrated its 50th anniversary and was proud of maintaining a tradition for democracy in golf. The Rotary Club took receipt of 350 11 lb food parcels from Queensland, Australia for distribution to people living alone and widows with children. Prestwick Bathing Lake housed 3,000 people during one summer heatwave. Baillie McNair called it a "seething mass". With the forties drawing to a close, The Scottish Chamber of Commerce was urging a long-term policy for Prestwick Airport, arguing that there was a need for the "primary facility" of air feeder services, that other airports were being heavily invested in and that Prestwick should be owned by a Scottish Public Utility Corporation. Roll on the Fifties!

The selection to follow is neither comprehensive nor definitive but it should be accessible in an immediate way. When John Still said that "the memories of men are too frail a thread to hang history from", it was a reminder to all of us that our lives and times live on in the records we leave. Continuing support for the study of local history is vital because of this.

Ian Welsh

20/12/91

1940

British merchant ships totalling 2,725,000 tonnes were sunk.

Food rationing began in Britain; Lord Woolton was made Minister of Food.

Germany invaded Norway and Denmark; then Holland, Luxembourg and Belgium.

Chamberlain resigned as Prime Minister, and Churchill formed a National Government.

British troops were evacuated from Dunkirk.

Ther German air force failed to defeat the R.A.F. in the Battle of Britain.

Large-scale bombing of Britain began.

12th January 1940

RIVER POLLUTION

Prestwick Council And The Pow Burn

At the monthly meeting of Prestwick Town Council on Tuesday Councillor Black drew attention to the condition of the Pow Burn. He knew that letters had been sent to Bairds and Dalmellington about the burn, but they had done no good. On the Prestwick and St. Cuthbert's golf courses there was a mark of black deposits right on to the banks ot the stream. There was also a thick black deposit at the bottom of the river bed. On several occasions he had seen dozens of small flounders lying dead in the burn. The burn used to be clean, and was a source of enjoyment to fishers and others. There was some way surely by which this pollution could be prevented.

The Provost—Where is the source of the trouble?

Mr Black—It seems to be coal dust from the pits.

The Provost—We could take the matter up with the coal-owners.

Mr Blunt — Or with the Department of Health.

Mr Steel—When you take up the matter of pollution with Messrs Baird and Dalmellington you should take up the question of the pit chimney from which the smoke blows into the houses.

Mr Blunt said that the matter had been taken up with Messrs Bairds but no satisfaction had been given.

Mr Govan said that this had been going on for over twenty years.

The Clerk — There was a committee appointed to deal with the matter.

Mr Blunt—The committee never met.

Mr Sawyers said that it simply required the chimney to be heightened.

It was agreed to get Mr Pritty to take up the matter with the coal company.

19th January 1940

DAILY FROM 2.30   PHONE 78272   CAR PARK

"THE BROADWAY" PRESTWICK

THE CINEMA WITH A CHARM ALL ITS OWN

To-day (Friday) and Saturday—
Gary Cooper in "BEAU GESTE" U 2.55, 5.45, 8.30

Monday, 22nd January—For Three Days—
Merle Oberon, Laurence Olivier, and David Niven in
"WUTHERING HEIGHTS" A 3. 5.45, 8.30
Laurel and Hardy in "BEAU CHUMPS" U 4.50, 7.35

Thursday, 25th January—For Three Days—
Warren William and Ida Lupino in
"THE LONE WOLF'S DAUGHTER" U 3.50, 6.35, 9.25
Barry K. Barnes in "SPIES OF THE AIR" A 2.20, 5.10, 7.55

19th January 1940

PRESTWICK PICTURE HOUSE

BRIDGE STREET   WEEK-DAYS from 5.30 p.m.   SATURDAYS from 2.30 p.m.

FRIDAY and SATURDAY—
LORETTA YOUNG, RICHARD GREENE in KENTUCKY U
PAUL KELLY in FORGED PASSPORT U

Monday, January 22—For Two Days—
JOHN GARFIELD
THE DEAD END KIDS in THEY MADE ME A CRIMINAL A
AND FULL SUPPORTING PROGRAMME

Wednesday, January 24—For Two Days—
HUMPHREY BOGART in KING OF THE UNDERWORLD A
THE THREE MESQUITEERS in SANTA FE STAMPEDE U

Friday, January 26—For Two Days—
SHIRLEY TEMPLE in REBECCA OF SUNNYBROOK FARM U
JUNE LANG in MEET THE GIRLS A

26th January 1940

COLD TRAINS

[To the Editor, *The Ayrshire Post*]

Sir,—We read the much vaunted "Travel in comfort by rail" posters; what are the actual facts? Being a daily traveller to Glasgow I have had four warm trains in four weeks to travel in. This morning the 7.7 from Prestwick starting at Ayr, my breath reaching my coat, turned to hoar even at Johnstone. On Monday, the 22nd, the same train was half an hour late in reaching Prestwick, starting at Ayr. We stood and shivered on the platform or in cold waiting rooms—we could not all get into the fire. A frozen journey with no steam heating and three-quarters of an hour late getting into Glasgow.

We all know there is a war on; the railways certainly are not letting us forget it. Their time running is hopeless, 15, 20, and 25 minutes, even up to an hour, late is the rule nowadays not the exception. Sunshine, fog, rain, any sort of weather gives an excuse for stopping 15 or 20 minutes sometimes 100 yards outside the station you want off at, with not a railway official or train anywhere on the landscape to stop us. To-night, the 23rd, we were half-an-hour late in leaving Glasgow and one hour five minutes late in reaching Prestwick. Any regular traveller, and there are many, can substantiate all that I have said.

16th February 1940

SIR HARRY LAUDER AT PRESTWICK

There was a capacity crowd at the Broadway Cinema, Prestwick, on Sunday when Sir Harry Lauder was the principal artist at a concert in aid of the Scottish Football Association's Fund for evacuated schoolboys. Sir Harry got a warm welcome, and his songs which were well received included "Keep Right on to the End of the Road." Sir Harry at the end of the programme auctioned several articles which realised a considerable sum. Other artists taking part were Ronald and Bert (acrobatics); The Elliott Sisters (dancers), Tommy Kenny (comedian), Herbert Cave (tenor), Telford and Connell (comedians), Ann Doel (personality girl), Arnold Crowther and Trixia (magician and conjuror), and Brunette (accordionist). The accompanist was Miss Betty Govan.

At the conclusion of the proceedings Mr Douglas Bowie, Ayr, president of the S.F.A., in moving a vote of thanks to Sir Harry, the artists, the directors, manager and staff of the Broadway, and all who had assisted to make the concert a success, stated that the fund had now reached the sum aimed at—£1500. The proceeds of the concert and the auctions was £125.

9th February 1940

A PLAUSIBLE ROGUE

Prestwick Woman Defrauded

A particularly mean fraud was disclosed in a case that came before Sheriff Scott at Ayr Sheriff Court on Wednesday, the accused being Andrew M. Scott, alias Stewart, alias Duncan (29), an unemployed gardener, of no fixed residence.

Accused admitted a board and lodging fraud on a Prestwick woman, Mrs McPherson, 3 Briarhill Road, and also having defrauded her of £14 5s., which he had received from her to pay for a load of wood.

It appeared from the statement made by the Fiscal (Mr W. R. D. Macmillan) that in October 18 last accused called at a garage in Prestwick and asked where he could get lodgings. He was recommended to Mrs McPherson who was told by accused that he was a native of Perth and had been in the R.A.F. for seven years. Mrs McPherson agreed to keep him until the following Saturday for the sum of £1. The accused left the house early but came back later wearing a boiler suit, and changed his story to the effect that he had found employment as a lorry driver.

Later, accused overheard a discussion between husband and wife concerning a load of wood which Mr McPherson, who was a cabinetmaker, had ordered from a Motherwell firm, and which he could not get delivery of owing to transport difficulties. Accused said he was going to Glasgow next day and he volunteered to go to Motherwell and get the wood. Next day, before accused left the house, Mrs McPherson gave him £14 5s. to pay for the wood as it was the first transaction her husband had had with the firm.

Accused was later observed in a teashop in Prestwick by two witnesses counting several pound notes and silver. He told several people that the money was a gratuity from the R.A.F. Police investigation revealed that there was no truth in accused's stories.

Accused, it was stated, had been sentenced to three months' imprisonment at Chester recently, and he was arrested, when he finished his term, for the Prestwick offence.

Sheriff Scott passed sentence of seven days' imprisonment on the first charge, and 60 days' imprisonment on the second, the sentences to run concurrently.

3rd May 1940

Prestwick A.R.P.

[To the Editor, *The Ayrshire Post*]

April 30, 1940.

Sir—It is with concern and wonder that I have watched the progress, and, I may add, the ultimate end, of A.R.P. as applied to the protection of those living in Prestwick.

Not long ago the Town Council, against the unanimous vote of the residents, purchased the Links Hotel in Links Road. £8000 to £12,000 will, I doubt not, be the ultimate cost, and I question if one would be far wrong in classing it as the most sumptuous suite of offices and chambers in Scotland.

Apparently their own personal comforts and ease-loving natures come before the needs of the ratepayers, who, if an air raid takes place (not improbable), will get a rude awakening. Originally the bathing lake was reconstructed internally as the principal, and I may say only, first aid post in the town. While not all that it might be still we got the place fitted out for the various duties, and offices necessary to A.R.P. work.

Five weeks ago we lost the tea room end. Apparently economy plays an important part in our Council's affairs when it does not affect themselves, £100 rental taking pre-eminence in their eyes to the needs, and rights, of the ratepayers. When the pool actually opens I am afraid A.R.P. services so far as it is concerned must close down.

The accommodation left us at present would be totally inadequate in time of need, A.R.P. equipment alone taking up a good deal of the space. The place itself is unheated, stone flooring throughout, and blankets covering holes for doors to keep the draught out. Can you imagine yourself lying either wounded or gassed in such a death trap? What could be worse or more likely to kill anyone seriously injured? When we contrast our civic lords in Links Hotel and our casualties at the bathing lake, Heaven and Hell are the only adequate comparison one can think of, and it fits.

3rd May 1940

REPORTED MISSING

Prestwick Man On H.M.S. Tarpon

Mrs Ferguson, 52 Marchburn Avenue, Prestwick, has received intimation from the Admiralty that her husband, Able Seaman John Ferguson, "is missing, believed killed on war service." Ferguson, who was 41 years of age and a time-expired reservist, was engaged as a postman, but re-joined the Navy on the outbreak of war, and was serving on H.M. submarine Tarpon, which the Admiralty on Tuesday intimated was "considerably over-due, and must be considered lost." He was for a time employed as a conductor on the Ayr Corporation Tramways, and afterwards became an auxiliary postman in Ayr. He was then taken on the establishment, and was appointed to Prestwick, where he was very popular and highly respected as a man of fine character and most engaging personality. He leaves a wife and five children.

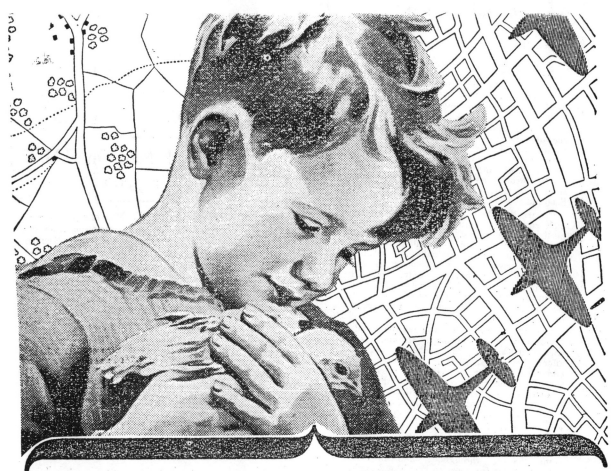

Who'll give a promise to keep this child safe?

This child's home is in the city. Up to the present his home has been safe. But let us face it : one of these days his home may be a ruin. There is no excuse for feeling falsely secure because nothing has happened yet. The danger of air-raids is as great now as it has ever been.

The Government is arranging to send this child, and some hundred thousands of others, to safety if raiders come. Each will need a home. Only one household in ten is caring for these children now. Volunteers are urgently needed. Plans must be made well ahead. There must be no hitch, no delay, in settling the children in safety. Here is *your* chance to help.

You can if you wish make an immediate contribution to this safety scheme. Many households have been looking after evacuated children for six months now. They will be grateful for a rest. If you can take over one of these children, you will be doing a very neighbourly deed and helping greatly in the nation's defence.

To enrol as a host of a child now or in the future, or to ask any questions about the scheme, please get in touch with your local Authority.

The Secretary of State, who has been entrusted by the Government with the conduct of evacuation, asks you urgently to join the Roll of those who are willing to receive children. Please apply to your local Council.

5th July 1940

SCOTTISH SABBATH

Stoutly Defended At Prestwick

SUNDAY GOLF

At the monthly meeting of the Prestwick Town Council on Tuesday—Provost Ferguson presiding—it was agreed, as an experiment, to open for a short time on Sundays during the next three months the Prestwick St. Nicholas Ladies (Municipal) Golf Course, and the Burgh putting greens.

The decision was not reached without strong protest from the veterans of the Council, one of whom asserted that as a result of the irreligious movement in Germany we were now waging war on young people who had grown up to be little more than savages.

Mr J. B. Black, who asked the Council to agree to the proposal for Sunday golf, said he desired to say little on the subject. He thought there would not be, in this year of grace, such hypocrites as would oppose his motion.

Mr William Shaw, the clerk, read a letter from the members of Prestwick St. Nicholas Ladies' Golf Club asking the Council to consider the matter of Sunday golf, adding that members of the club were only to play then owing to pressure of work.

Mr Sawyers, seconding Mr Black, said if it was the desire of the people to have the golf course open on Sunday it should be open. He also considered that the artisans who were working at other times should be considered.

Mr G. Blunt proposed as an amendment that no Sunday golf be allowed. He was, he said, a member of a religious body which did not think Sunday golf desirable. He believed that the people of the town did not want it. He regretted the matter being raised just now. He would rather see it as an election issue when the people of the town could show their approval or disapproval. He thought the Sunday should be a day of worship and rest.

Ex-Bailie Dunlop, seconding, pointed out that larger burghs did not have Sunday golf. There had never been any demand for it and those of them who believed in the Holy Bible and the Ten Commandments, on which Scotland was built, would be opposed to it, especially at a time like this when the enemy was at the gates. He referred to' the way in which the great evacuation of Dunkirk had been carried through, because, he thought, of God's providence. Unless we continued to respect and believe in the Bible, we would be faced with a long period of cruelty and hunger.

Bailie Allan said he was always opposed to Sunday golf. At the present time he saw no need to deviate from his former belief. The last time the matter was raised, there had been strong opposition from the churches in the town. He realised the necessity for golf courses and thought they were a good thing but he thought to open them on Sundays would be a very grave mistake. We ought to remember that the trouble in the world to-day was caused mainly through the fact that the German leaders had forbidden religious instruction to the young, and we were now waging war on young people who had grown up to be little more than savages. He hoped they would not forsake the old Scottish Sabbath day, because if that happened this country would drift into the very same position. No nation in history had forsaken God and survived. There were already three other private golf courses in the town where there was Sunday golf and it was up to the Council to set an example to the rest of the community in this matter of observance of the Sabbath day.

Bailie Brown recalled the fact that financial statements presented to the Town Council showed that they were experiencing a loss in running the courses. He had always been in his youth a strict Sabbatarian but he was not opposing the motion and one of the reasons for his giving support was the fact that Prestwick bathing lake was open on Sundays, and he did not feel they could oppose the one thing and sanction the other.

Provost Ferguson said he had no desire to restrict bona fide golfers from having golf on Sundays, and he had also no desire to attempt to dictate their spiritual welfare but he thought various factors had to be taken into consideration. There was the financial aspect, the Sabbatarian point of view and the third point, the suggestion that there was a genuine demand for such concessions. If there was such a demand he was not one who would stand in the way of it. He suggested as an amendment that the St. Nicholas Ladies' golf courses and the putting green should be opened from two o'clock each Sunday afternoon during the next three months as an experiment at the end of which time they could reconsider the whole matter.

Mr Dunsmore seconded him, adding that he was not satisfied that there was a genuine demand for Sunday golf at the present moment.

Mr Black, replying on the discussion, said it was no rest for the man who worked in an office or factory to sit in the house, or the church all day. He pointed out that there was a war on; killing went on on a Sunday as on any other day; men were working on Sunday to produce weapons of war, and so they should be able to relax on Sunday if that was the day which they were given to rest. He could not understand an intelligent being opposing his motion in this year of grace, 1940. He was agreeable to his motion being incorporated in what the Provost suggested, making it the motion.

On a vote, there voted for the amendment that there be no golf, 8; and for the motion, 8.

OFFICIAL INSTRUCTIONS ISSUED BY THE MINISTRY OF HOME SECURITY

GAS ATTACK

HOW TO PUT ON YOUR GAS MASK

Always keep your gas mask with you – day and night. Learn to put it on quickly. Practise wearing it.

1. Hold your breath.   2. Hold mask in front of face, with thumbs inside straps.
3. Thrust chin well forward into mask, pull straps over head as far as they will go.
4. Run finger round face-piece taking care head-straps are not twisted.

IF THE GAS RATTLES SOUND

1. Hold your breath. Put on mask wherever you are. Close window.

2. If out of doors, take off hat, put on your mask. Turn up collar.

3. Put on gloves or keep hands in pockets. Take cover in nearest building.

IF YOU GET GASSED

BY VAPOUR GAS Keep your gas mask on even if you feel discomfort
If discomfort continues go to First Aid Post

BY LIQUID or BLISTER GAS

1	2	3	4
Dab, but *don't rub* the splash with handkerchief. Then destroy handkerchief.	Rub No. 2 Ointment well into place. *(Buy a 6d. jar now from any chemist.)* In emergency chemists supply Bleach Cream free.	If you can't get Ointment or Cream within 5 minutes wash place with soap and warm water	Take off at once any garment splashed with gas.

16th August 1940

PRESTWICK EFFORT

Provost's Fund To Purchase A Spitfire

At a meeting held in the Provost's Room of the Town Buildings, Prestwick, on Wednesday evening it was decided to proceed with the raising of a fund with which to purchase a Spitfire fighter for presentation to the Government. The aircraft will bear the name and arms of the donating body as in similar presentation aeroplanes.

Provost Ferguson presided at the meeting, and it was decided to appoint an honorary secretary and treasurer to the fund and to forward to representative people in the burgh a letter asking them to attend a meeting on Wednesday to form a working committee, which will organise various entertainments and use other means to add to the private subscriptions which it is hoped will be speedily forthcoming in order that Prestwick may make a direct contribution to the gallant efforts of the Royal Air Force.

23rd August 1940

£150 ALREADY

Prestwick's Spitfire Fund

Since Prestwick inaugurated its Spitfire Fund over £150 has been subscribed. This was announced at a committee meeting held on Wednesday evening presided over by Provost Ferguson.

Provost Ferguson said that although the name of a Spitfire had been mentioned it had been suggested to him that a bomber should be purchased. But whether bomber or Spitfire the immediate business was to obtain the subscriptions and carry on with the prosecution of the scheme. Never had they been so united in a common cause, and never would they be able to reward the R.A.F. for their magnificent work and the rout of the Nazis. The Spitfire would be presented to the Minister of Aircraft Production who would hand it over for the destruction of the common enemy.

The question of forming avenues of revenue were discussed, and it was agreed to appoint someone to take charge of the entertainments, which would probably be held in the Broadway Cinema or Orangefield Hotel, someone to supervise the collection of shop boxes, and a liaison officer to keep in touch with the local authorities.

Mr Sawyers asked if there was to be a house to house collection.

MINISTRY OF INFORMATION

Western District Committee

WEEKLY
WAR COMMENTARY
"THE WAR IN THE AIR"

- BY -

R. B. HOUSE, Esq.

Film to be shown—Air Outposts

- IN -

THE BROADWAY CINEMA

PRESTWICK

- ON -

SUNDAY at 7.30 p.m.

Sir THOMAS MOORE, M.P., will take part.

ORDER OF THE EASTERN STAR WELFARE COMFORTS FUND.

PRESTWICK CHAPTER, No. 62.

WAR CHARITIES ACT, 1940.

NOTICE IS HEREBY GIVEN that it is proposed to apply to Prestwick Town Council for Registration under the above mentioned Act for Funds to supply Comforts to the boys belonging to the members of the O.E.S. The administrative centre is at O.E.S. Hall, Gardener Street, Prestwick.

Any objection to the proposed Registration should be sent in writing to the above mentioned Council within Fourteen Days from the date of this notice.

1st October, 1940.

(Signed) Mrs M. LEONARD, Secretary,
For and on behalf of above mentioned charity.

1941

The U.S. Congress approved the Lend-Lease Bill which gave dollar support to Britain's war effort.

Air-raids amd U-boat attacks continued.

Fighting continued in North Africa; German troops attacked Tobruk.

Germany invaded the Soviet Union; Britain and the Soviet Union agreed a mutual assistance pact.

Conscription stated for single women under 30.

Japanese aircraft bombed the U.S. naval base at Pearl Harbor; America declared war.

3rd January 1941

STORY OF A PRESTWICK VAN

After reporting a van, which he had been driving, as "stolen," a Prestwick man discovered that his father had taken the van which actually belonged to him. This was revealed in Ayr Sheriff Court on Monday when the son appeared before Hon. Sheriff W. H. McCosh and admitted having, on December 22, in Main Street, Prestwick, failed to immobilise the van.

It was stated by Mr W. B. Norwell, depute procurator fiscal, that the man went to Prestwick police station, and reported that his father's van had been stolen. The police made investigations and a description of the vehicle was circulated. About 1.30 that day, the van was intercepted in Prestwick Road, and it was found that the father was driving it. He explained that he had been passing the garage when he saw the van outside and had driven it away without telling his son. Owing to this false alarm, continued Mr Norwell, some expense had been incurred by the police which the father however, had paid for. The incident would not have happened if he had immobilised the vehicle as he should have done. A fine of five shillings was imposed.

Rails for War

A minute of the Lighting and Cleansing Committee bore that there was submitted a letter from the Ministry of Supply regarding the removal of railings belonging to the burgh for scrap. There was also submitted a report by the burgh surveyor recommending that the railings at the Cross be removed, and this was agreed to. It was also agreed that the burgh surveyor should report to the next meeting in regard to the removal of the railings round Bruce's Well at Kingcase.

On being asked by the Provost if anybody had given their railings to help in the national effort, Mr Pritty said that there had been a satisfactory response, but there were still others who were in a position to do so.

There was submitted at the meeting of the Coal Fund Committee replies received from the coal merchants in regard to the price of coal, and it was agreed that each person should get six tickets and that the price of coal should be 2s 4d, marked on the ticket.

Hopes of Victory

At the outset of the meeting, Provost Ferguson conveyed his wishes for a happy and prosperous new year to his colleagues. Unfortunately, he said, they were still living in an atmosphere shrouded with war clouds, but they could at the same time see the silver linings shining through, and there were many omens that could make them look forward to the new year, 1941, bringing with it victory for the democracies. He also conveyed to all branches of the voluntary services in the burgh his gratitude for their loyalty.

3rd January 1941

GOLDEN WEDDING

Prestwick Magistrate's Celebration

Bailie William Brown and Mrs Brown, 37 Midton Road, Prestwick, attained the fiftieth anniversary of their wedding on Tuesday. They were married in the Wilson Hall, Catrine, on December 31 by the late Rev. Henry Begg, the parish minister of Sorn.

Bailie Brown is a native of Auchinleck, and his wife is a native of Sorn. They have been 39 years in Prestwick, arriving there in the spring of 1902, and during that time both have taken an active part in the public life of the burgh. Mr Brown became a member of the Old School Board in 1913, and remained a member until such bodies were abolished under the Act of Parliament of 1918. He entered the Town Council in 1931 and is still a member, being now senior magistrate. Mrs Brown was a member of the Parish Council from 1925 till 1929, when it ceased to function under that name. In 1926 Mrs Brown was elected to the Unemployment Committee as a representative of employers, and is still a member.

Bailie Brown is at present in business at 60 Main Street, Prestwick, as a boot and shoe merchant, and with the exception of one other, is the oldest merchant in the burgh.

Of the union there was a family of eleven, seven girls and four boys, a son and daughter having died. The business is carried on by one of the sons, while one of them is serving with the R.A.F. Three of the daughters went abroad, two to America and one to Australia. The war (as did the last one at the silver wedding) will prevent them from returning for the coming celebration to be held on January 8. Bailie and Mrs Brown have six grandchildren. Mr Brown is 70 years of age, and Mrs Brown is 69, and both are highly respected in the town of their adoption.

3rd January 1941

MR. WM. HUNTER

Death Of Prestwick Veteran

The death has occurred at the age of 92 of Mr William Hunter, Maryville, Prestwick, one of the oldest residents of the sister burgh and a man who was well known to all. Until about a week before the end he was fairly active. He was a son of the late Mr Richard Hunter, who farmed Whitelees, and was educated at Ayr Academy, where he was dubbed "Secundus" from the fact that there were three other pupils of the same name in the class, and the name stuck to him through a long life.

In his youth Mr Hunter joined the firm of W. W. and J. Pollock, accountants, Ayr, which was associated with the Bank of Scotland. He served the firm for more than fifty years and was a well-known figure on the road between Ayr and Prestwick. When Mr William Pollock died about 1908, the firm was wound up and Mr Hunter went into the accountancy business on his own account. He retired about ten years ago.

In his younger days Mr Hunter was a keen golfer and was one of the "fathers" of Prestwick St Nicholas Golf Club. Another sport in which he took an active interest was curling, and he was secretary of the original Prestwick Curling Club.

10th January 1941

A HEAT QUESTION

Prestwick Bathing Lake Plant

The heating at the first aid post at Prestwick Bathing Lake was discussed at the monthly meeting of Prestwick Town Council, held in the Council Chambers on Tuesday, over which Provost Ferguson presided.

Mr Blunt raised the question, asking if the plant installed at the bathing lake was giving every satisfaction.

Mr Pritty, burgh engineer, said he understood that it was quite satisfactory, but added that the plant was not completed and required constant stoking.

Mr Blunt said he thought it a disgrace that they should ask young men to sacrifice their time to remain in the post while there was not proper heating accommodation for them.

The burgh engineer explained that the responsibility was the County Council's.

Replying, Mr Blunt said that if the Town Council was to purchase the plant after the cessation of hostilities, as they had in mind, he thought that they should see that it was kept in order meantime.

Bailie Dunsmore, as a member of the first aid party, said that the heat was not very great, but the contractors were unable to secure the necessary pump and until then the plant would not be completed.

The discussion then ended.

24th January 1941

MR JAMES HOWAT

Popular Prestwickian Passes

One of Prestwick's best known citizens and for many years a familiar figure in the sister burgh, Mr James Howat, died at his residence, Mooredge, on Friday at the age of 85. Until a few weeks before the end Mr Howat was able to ride his bicycle, his usual mode of conveyance when out and about in the district. His virility was apparent also in his feats as a golfer over his beloved St. Nicholas course. At the age of 72, it is stated, he went round the course in 72, and when 75 he attempted to emulate that feat by returning a 75, and just missed it by one stroke, his return being 76.

Mr Howat was the eldest of the family of the late Mr William Howat, head gardener at Adamton, remembered by many still alive, as he was an old man when he died. Mr Howat was brought to Adamton as a child, and resided with his father, who was succeeded by a son with whom the deceased stayed for a time.

For over forty years Mr Howat followed the profession of a teacher in Prestwick district. He was a pupil teacher under the late Mr Walter Beaton, and after completion of his training in Glasgow, became an assistant in Prestwick Public School, remaining there from 1880 until 1900, in which year he was appointed headmaster of Monkton Public School, a post he occupied for six years. In 1906 he was promoted headmaster of Prestwick Public School, and retired from that post in August, 1920. In his retirement he found much enjoyment from intercourse with his fellows, and it would be no exaggeration to say that he was the most popular of the older members of the St. Nicholas Golf Club. For over 60 years he was a member of St. Nicholas Club and at one time held the office of captain and he had the honour of being a life member. A brilliant raconteur, he took delight in spending an hour at the clubhouse after a game, recounting to his friends the historical highlights of the course for years past. In addition to being a notable golfer, Mr Howat was an enthusiastic bowler, and a life member of Prestwick Bowling Club. Another pastime which he enjoyed was angling, and for many years he spent part of his summer vacation, armed with rod and line, at the head of Loch Doon.

When Mr Howat concluded his life's work as a schoolmaster, the late Mr R. Bryden, Ayr, painted and presented to Prestwick Public School a striking portrait of Mr Howat, which was at that time hung in the hall of the school.

Mr Howat was unmarried. The funeral took place to Monkton Churchyard on Monday and was largely attended.

The Last Precentor

In St. Cuthbert's Church of Monkton and Prestwick on Sunday, the Rev. Luke M'Quitty, paid tribute to the deceased. He said it was with regret he had to intimate the death of their senior elder, Mr James Howat. He was ordained to office in 1905, and had thus served for more than 35 years. His chief interest was in the choir and he was convener of the choir committee for many years. Indeed, his last appearance in church, a few weeks ago, was in connection with the resignation of the organist. He had the distinction of being the last precentor in the church. It was his personality which made him so much esteemed and which would make him so much missed. Of a friendly and buoyant disposition, he had many friends among young and old. In spite of his advanced age he continued to take a deep interest in affairs, and did not laud the past at the expense of the present. In the best sense of the phrase, he "moved with the times." His place in church was seldom vacant, until failing health overtook him, and they would all miss his cordial greeting.

7th February 1941

COUNTY OF AYR.

PUBLIC ASSISTANCE DEPARTMENT.

EMERGENCY REST CENTRES.

INTIMATION IS HEREBY GIVEN that Rest Centres throughout the County have been earmarked for the temporary shelter of Persons rendered homeless by Enemy Attack.

"A" Centres must be first used.

"B" Centres will only be used if "A" Centres do not meet full requirements or are unfit for use.

The Centres for the Girvan, Maybole, Prestwick and Dalmellington County Districts are:—

LOCALITY	REST CENTRES	
Girvan	(A) High School	(B) South Church Hall
Dailly	(A) Public School	(B) Working Men's Club
Ballantrae	(A) Public School	(B) Village Hall
Maybole & Minishant	(A) Carrick Academy	(B) Old Parish Hall
		(B) Kincraig Church Hall
		(B) Minishant Public Hall
Monkton & Prestwick	(A) Prestwick High School	(B) St. Cuthbert's Hall, Monkton
		(B) Carvick Webster Hall, Monkton
Troon	(A) Public School	(B) Infant School
Dundonald	(A) Public School	(B) Montgomerie Hall
Tarbolton	(A) Public School	(B) Outbuildings, Manse
Annbank	(A) Public School	(B) Co-operative Hall
Symington	(A) Public School	(B) Village Hall
Dalmellington	(A) Higher Grade School	(B) Merrick Hall
Coylton	(A) Public School	(B) Claude Hamilton Memorial Hall
Dalrymple	(A) Public School	(B) Village Hall

Should an incident arise the necessary Rest Centres will be opened without delay, and the Police and Air Raid Wardens will direct enquirers to the nearest.

Food and Shelter will be provided at the Centres.

As the provision to be made is to be only of temporary nature it is advisable that Persons rendered homeless should, if possible, arrange for alternative accommodation for themselves with relatives or friends, to whom they can proceed should it be ascertained that damage to their homes is of such a nature as to preclude their immediate return thereto.

JAMES R. LOCKIE, County Clerk and A.R.P. Controller.
JAMES E. HOWIE, Public Assistance Officer.

County Buildings, Ayr, 7th February, 1941.

7th February 1941

"Settle Once And For All" Says Provost

PRESTWICK AFFAIRS

At the monthly meeting of Prestwick Town Council Mr Blunt raised objection to certain outlays of Mr Pritty, the burgh surveyor. Provost Ferguson presided.

It was pointed out by Provost Ferguson that the vouchers for all expenditure could be seen at the burgh treasurer's office.

Bailie Brown said he was in agreement with Mr Blunt. He thought there was some explanation required as well as some investigation in regard to the matter. He was not saying that these were not necessary, but there could be a little economy practised as was being done in other matters. He thought the council ought to know something about the hiring of cars for visits to the waterworks and to a farm in the district and sometimes to the council housing schemes.

Mr Blunt asked if it was necessary for Mr Pritty to go to the housing scheme in a car as it was only ten minutes' walk. He wanted to know if these expenses could be done without.

Provost Ferguson said he hoped that Bailie Brown and Mr Blunt would make a point of examining the vouchers in the burgh treasurer's office, and the matter was then dropped.

Close Voting.

A minute of the Housing committee stated that attention was drawn to the minute of meeting of the Town Council dated January 7, 1941, in which the question of appointment of an independent auditor was remitted to this committee for consideration. Mr Black moved that no further action be taken, and Bailie Brown seconded. Bailie Dunsmore moved that an independent auditor be appointed to advise the Town Council in regard to what rents should be charged, and Bailie Boylan Smith seconded. On a vote there voted for the amendment three, and for the motion five. Messrs Dougan and Steele did not vote.

Provost Ferguson moved disapproval of the minute. This question, he said, had been "see-sawing" for months. Always his absence or Mr Black's as well as other absences had hung the matter up from time to time. It was desirable that it should be settled now, once and for all. In addition to moving disapproval of the minute, he moved that an independent auditor be appointed to examine the housing accounts in conjunction with the burgh officials and report.

Bailie Boylan Smith, in seconding, added that as there was a full attendance of the council, they should have the matter finished.

Mr Black proposed approval of the minute. "I need hardly tell the council, and you, Mr Provost," he said, "that I am sick to death of this thing coming up month after month. It seems to be, according to your statement, a question of whether you or I am absent, and I think that state of affairs is definitely bad." He thought that when there was such a closeness in the voting the matter should go no further. He also drew the council's attention to a recent Court of Session decision which, he said, showed that the final decision lay with the council, and it was, he said, all the same if they employed all the auditors there were, they could do nothing but refer the council to that legal decision. They were only wasting time, he pointed out.

Mr Blunt seconded.

Mr Govan, supporting Mr Black's amendment, said he thought it unfair to the tenants to keep them in a disturbed state wondering what would be the outcome of these discussions. He did not think the present an opportune time for such alterations.

Provost Ferguson, replying on the debate, said there was a large percentage of poor ratepayers in the burgh who were being imposed upon by low rents. He was only considering the safeguarding of the ratepayers' interests.

Mr Blunt—You never considered the poor ratepayers when you put up the new Council Chambers.

After further discussion, a vote was taken. Provost Ferguson's motion was turned down by 5 votes to 4.

"Hopelessly Inadequate."

It was decided to write to Sir Thomas Moore, M.P. for Ayr Burghs, and to competent authority, to protest against the inadequacy of the payment to householders who have members of the forces billeted on them.

Mr Black stated that the money offered to householders might have been all right before the outbreak of war, but it was hopelessly inadequate now. The rise in the cost of living was out of all proportion. A householder, he said, was allowed threepence for a serving man's tea and fivepence for his supper. It was all very well, he said, for people with a certain regular income to pay something out of their own pockets to feed these boys and make them as happy as possible, but the council had to keep prominently before it the fact that many of these women were spinsters and widows who made their livelihood by using their houses as boarding houses, and it was absolutely impossible for them to carry on boarding these boys at threepence for a tea and fivepence for supper.

Provost Ferguson said he did not think it a matter for the council. It was entirely out of their province.

Mr Black said they would get nothing done unless they kicked up a dickens of a row.

After further discussion, it was agreed that the letters be sent.

Municipal Chambers.

A minute of the Finance committee stated that there was submitted a report by the burgh surveyor, giving in detail the cost of the various works in connection with the reconstruction of the municipal chambers, including the price of the building, as also the cost of the furnishings—making the total cost £8176 9s 8d—and this was approved. The question of remuneration to the burgh surveyor for his services was considered, when Bailie Dunlop moved that Mr Pritty be paid the sum of £100 for his professional services, and Bailie Dunsmore seconded, and this was agreed to. Bailie Brown desired his dissent to be entered.

7th March 1941

TOWN CLERKSHIP

Division Of Opinion At Prestwick

The townclerkship was again under discussion at the monthly meeting of Prestwick Town Council, held in the Council Chambers on Tuesday—Provost Ferguson presiding—a motion being submitted by the Provost that the town clerk's services be continued for a further year.

Provost Ferguson said there was a motion on the agenda by Bailie Boylan Smith that an interim town clerk be appointed, and he (Provost Ferguson) felt this was a most inopportune time to make any departure from the status quo. Mr Shaw (the clerk) had expressed his willingness to resign in terms of superannuation, and a special committee deemed it advisable that he should remain. It was imperative that the country should conserve man power, and it was not expedient to make any appointment of this nature when so many eligible men were serving their King and country. If an appointment were made it would be irregular without advertising.

Bailie Dunsmore, seconding, said that he did not think it an appropriate time to make any change. He pointed out that it would be very much cheaper for the town to keep the services of Mr Shaw if he were to be paid superannuation when he retired.

Bailie Boylan Smith suggested that Mr Shaw should not remain during the discussion and Mr Shaw said he thought he was justified in remaining.

It was eventually agreed that he should remain.

Bailie Brown asked if they were to assume that Mr Shaw had retired and that there was an extension not as town clerk but doing the services of the town clerk and that the extension continued until May of this year.

Mr Steele said he agreed with Bailie Brown that Mr Shaw had resigned. It did not strike him fully until Mr Shaw informed him that he had made arrangements to take up office in the new buildings. At any moment they might be bombed and it would take a young and active man to compete with all the difficulties when the trouble arose. He had proposed that Mr Black should take over the duties and he now proposed that Mr Shaw retire and they appoint a young man.

Bailie Boylan Smith said that in his opinion Mr Shaw was showing signs of age as everyone else did through time, and they had signs of a lack of attention on his part. He moved as an amendment that they advertise for an interim town clerk and Mr Shaw could apply if he liked.

Bailie Blunt pointed out that Prestwick had now a population of over 10,000 and he did not think that a man of Mr Shaw's age could attend to all the necessary duties. He moved that a full-time clerk be appointed and Bailie Brown seconded.

Bailie Boylan Smith moved that they advertise for a part-time clerk and Mr Sawyers seconded.

Seven voted in favour of Mr Blunt as against two for Bailie Smith.

Mr Blunt's amendment was put against the Provost's motion and four voted for the amendment and live for the motion and accordingly Mr Shaw was continued in office for another year.

28th March 1941

VAIN SEARCH

Noble Gesture By Glenburn Miners

As a result of the recent blitz on Clydeside, 28 miners at Glenburn Pit, offered to search for the relatives of Mr John Thom, mining contractor, 89 Glenburn, Prestwick, one of their workmates. Since the raid, nothing has been heard of Mr Thom's aged mother, Mrs Margaret Thom; his sister, Mrs Kelly; and her two children. All four were in the thick of the raid, being in a shelter which received a direct hit. Though the shelter has been cleared, the bodies of Mr Thom's relatives have not been discovered.

Mr Thom himself visited Clydeside on Saturday, calling at several hospitals, rest centres and mortuaries in an unsuccessful attempt to trace the missing people.

It was when Mr Thom expressed the belief that they might be buried in the bombed shelter, that a party of his workmates volunteered to make the journey to Clydeside and further Mr Thom's search. Accordingly the party of miners went by 'bus to Clydeside, when they came off the shift on Monday, the men insisting on paying their own fares. When they arrived at Clydeside, dinner had been prepared for them at a hall. The miners, however, refused to eat until they had cleared away the shelter. They went about the work in a systematic manner, and were highly praised by the chief A.F.S. officer in the district.

No trace of the missing family, however, resulted from the excavations, although articles were discovered which proved helpful in identifying other victims.

Mr Thom said he still cherished some hope for his sister, whose husband was in a Glasgow infirmary with two broken arms which he sustained in protecting his son whom he managed to save. He feared, however, for the safety of his mother who was up in years.

7th March 1941

ALLEGED LEAKAGE

Prestwick Town Council Criticism

MR GOVAN'S PROTEST

At the outset, as a protest against an alleged leakage of information from a committee meeting regarding a Government contract which had been put before Prestwick, and also in the matter of appointing Miss Jean Baird as housing factor, Mr Govan left the meeting of Prestwick Town Council on Tuesday—Provost Ferguson in the chair. He pointed out that the burgh of Prestwick was severely left in the matter of housing affairs, as a result of information leaking out. If there was going to be no admission of this he was going to leave the meeting.

A minute of special meeting of the Town Council bore that the appointment of housing factor was considered, and after discussion, Mr Duncan moved that the matter be remitted to next committee meeting and that counsel's opinion be taken and Provost Ferguson seconded. Mr Govan moved that no opinion be taken and Mr Sawyers seconded. On a vote there supported the amendment 6, and for the motion 3, and accordingly the amendment was declared carried. Thereafter Provost Ferguson moved that Miss Baird's services be retained as factor until the end of the war and that she be paid a salary of £150 per annum, plus £30 for rent of office, and Bailie Dunsmore seconded. Mr Govan moved that Miss Baird's appointment be terminated at the end of April and that the burgh treasurer and burgh surveyor be appointed to carry through the work, at salaries of £100 and £60 per annum respectively, and that Mr Hoy be appointed collector of rents, at £10 per annum, and Mr Sawyers seconded. On a vote there voted for the amendment 4—Messrs Govan, Sawyers, Black and Blunt—and for the motion 4—Provost Ferguson, Bailies Dunsmore, Dunlop and Mr Duncan. The Provost gave his casting vote in favour of the motion. Messrs Dougan and Steele, being tenants of Corporation houses, did not vote.

Bailie Dunsmore admitted that he had spoken to Miss Baird because the last meeting was a statutory one and as nothing was to be decided afterwards, he thought he was doing no harm to the Council. He spoke to her after the meeting, and if it had been a committee meeting he would not have said anything, but as the matter had been fixed, his speaking could not have altered it.

Mr Govan said that Miss Baird was approached and she decided to accept the terms.

Provost Ferguson said there were no terms before the meeting and anything he heard previous to the meeting was through Mr Shaw, and all he heard was that Miss Baird was prepared to take assistance and he made mention of it at the meeting.

Mr Govan—You must admit that she was approached.

Mr Blunt considered it a breach of trust, and any councillor who did that should be severely reprimanded. There was far too much of that anyway, he added.

Mr Govan said they were let down in regard to the housing matter. At the committee meeting, at which they were sworn to secrecy, it appeared that someone had divulged information to an Ayr firm, and Prestwick got nothing out of it. He added that he felt that it was not worth staying.

Bailie Brown said he thought Mr Govan was making a mistake. Mr Dunsmore had explained the position and he thought it all was rather foolish.

Mr Govan replied that he knew what he was talking about, and as a protest he was leaving, which he did.

Bailie Brown said he was protesting against holding a meeting previous to a motion being put forward. He thought it ridiculous that a man should be able to come forward and try to influence one's mind as to his vote.

Provost Ferguson thought it impossible that Miss Baird could have been approached and asked to agree to terms before the meeting as they were not adjusted until then, when he had proposed them.

Bailie Boylan Smith declared that Mr Dunsmore's action was mistaken for something it was not, and any person was entitled to anything which took place at a public meeting.

Provost Ferguson pointed out that it was a special council meeting and while Mr Dunsmore did reveal the information he did not know how long afterwards. He thought it should not be revealed until after the minutes were printed.

4th April 1941

Prestwick

Youth Group. — The activities of the winter session of the Youth Group were terminated on Friday, when a dance was held in the Higher Grade School. Close on one hundred attended and the success of previous meetings was well maintained. Dr. Meiklejohn, assistant to the director of education, was present. During an interval in the proceedings Mr J. Murdoch, superintendent of the Continuation Classes, read a letter from Mr Boyd, depute director of education, congratulating the Youth Group on its successful session. Mr Jack McVey, a member of the Group, expressing good wishes to Mr Robert Steele, who is being married, voiced the gratitude of the Group to Mr R. Steele and Mr S. Steele for the instructive and enjoyable evenings they had arranged. Miss Anderson handed over to Mr R. Steele a log-box, an umbrella stand, and a hall mirror in brass, as a token of their good wishes for his future happiness. In reply, Mr Steele said he felt rewarded by the enthusiasm of the members, and that he was safe in saying he spoke for Mr S. Steele when he stated that it was a pleasure to provide enjoyment for such an eager and agreeable company of girls and youths.

7th March 1941

AIR TRAINING CORPS

A minute of the Finance Committee stated that Provost Ferguson indicated that he had gone carefully into this matter and it was incumbent on the town council to lend their support to this scheme, the primary purpose of which was to provide boys over the age of 16 with the opportunity of acquiring spare-time preliminary instruction in subjects which would be of value to them at the age of 18, when they attested for the Royal Air Force.

Provost Ferguson said they were going to co-opt a local committee to create a flight of boys in Prestwick.

7th March 1941

ALLOTMENTS

From a minute of the Golf Course, Shores and Public Parks committee it appeared that it was indicated that authority had been granted by the L.M. and S. Railway Company, allowing the Council to utilise the area of ground at Mansewell Road for allotments. There was submitted a list of applications for these and it was left to the Provost to allocate the same. After consideration, it was agreed that these allotments should be given free. It was also agreed that the town clerk should write the representatives of the late Mr King, enquiring if they would allow the piece of ground at Bridge Street to be let to plotholders. The town clerk was also instructed to write the proprietors of any other vacant ground in the burgh asking their authority to use the same for allotments.

Provost Ferguson said that while they were on the matter of allotments, he had learned that they had over 100 now and all were doing well.

Your own vegetables all the year round . . .

if you

DIG FOR VICTORY NOW

11th April 1941

PRESTWICK PREPARES

Discussions At Town Council

BILLETING ALLOWANCES

The enthusiam of allotment holders was made known at the monthly meeting of Prestwick Town Council, held in the Council Chambers on Tuesday, Provost Ferguson presiding.

At the outset of the meeting, Bailie Dunlop said he would like to see more care being taken in the burgh with regard to the salvage waste paper. A considerable quantity came in loose, and ashes and other extraneous matter were, in many cases, mixed up with the paper. Considerable cost was involved in salvaging the paper, and he wished to appeal to householders to exercise greater care in the collecting of it. People who were careless with the paper were often exposed, as envelopes bearing their names and addresses were discovered among the refuse.

Chalets

Referring to a clause in the burgh engineer's report which stated that thirty-one chalets had been booked following an advertisement in the press, Mr Steele asked if they had decided where they were going to place these shelters. He moved that they do not put them in the same places as last year, and that, instead, they be placed along the foothills where they should remain permanently, thus saving the cost of conveying the chalets.

Bailie Dunsmore said he thought that so many should be put on the shore and so many on top, those on top being let at a cheaper rate.

The matter was finally remitted to the committee.

Emergency Tins

Mr Blunt referred to the burgh surveyor's report which stated that a number of four-gallon tins which had been secured for temporary provision of water to householders in an emergency, were available to the public on application and could be obtained at a price of 2½d each. These were extremely useful as vessels for containing water for the use of the stirrup pump.

Mr Blunt said that if the tins could be had for 2½d each there would be a big demand for them, and he thought a good idea would be to have them advertised.

Bailie Brown asked if suitable bags were supplied for the purpose.

Mr Blunt added that he understood Mr Pritty was in possession of these bags and that anyone desirous of saving paper was at liberty to make application for them.

Mr Pritty replied stating that this was the case.

Services of Mr Henderson

The Provost made reference to the fact that Mr Henderson, the bathing lake superintendent, who is a marine engineer, had been recalled for service by the Ministry of Labour. The Provost said that Mr Henderson had been most conscientious in the execution of his duties and had proved a very trustworthy servant.

Bailie Dunsmore endorsed the Provost's tribute.

Billeting Allowances

The clerk read a letter from Sir Thomas Moore, M.P. for Ayr Burghs (U.), with regard to billeting allowances for airmen. In his letter, Sir Thomas said that further to his correspondence regarding allowances he had taken the matter up as promised with the Minister for Air, and he had just recently received a considered reply from Sir Hugh Seely, his parlimentary secretary. In his reply, Sir Hugh stated that the billeting rates —whether for lodging and attendance or for meals—were statutory rates of the Army and Air Force Acts and precluded any variations of the scales of payments in individual cases. He regretted, therefore, that all their information on the question led them to the conclusion that the existing rates were adequate and that there was no course by which they could be justifiably increased.

War Advances

A minute of the Finance Committee stated that there were submitted letters from the Joint Industrial Councils for local authority services in Scotland in regard to war service allowances and further war advance to manual workers, together with letter from the National Union of General and Municipal Workers thereanent. It was indicated that they recommended an increase of 3s per week to all able-bodied male employees, making the total war advance up to 8s per week, and that female and part-time employees be granted a proportion of this amount; that this further war advance would come into operation as from April 1, 1941, and would not operate so as to increase any wage beyond £6 15s per week. Mr Govan moved adoption of the report, and this was agreed to.

No Dogs

From the burgh factor's report it appeared that with regard to the keeping of dogs in corporation houses, it was agreed that owing to complaints by tenants who were cultivating their gardens, of the destruction caused to same by dogs, intimation should be sent to tenants in the scheme that no dogs were to be kept and that owners of dogs must put them away, otherwise action would be taken against them.

Salvage of Waste Food

In regard to the scheme for the salvage of waste food material, a minute bore that there was submitted a letter from the burgh surveyor suggesting that, as there were approximately 3000 houses in the burgh and it would be necessary to have one bin for every twelve houses, the total number of bins required would be 250, and submitting offers for the same. It was agreed to continue the matter until the next meeting of committee for further consideration.

2nd May 1941

A MAD WORLD

Points From Prestwick War Commentary

A WOMAN'S APPEAL

The view that the present conflict of nations was a phase of the battle of Armageddon, predicted in the Book of Revelation, was expressed by Major Burn Callander at the Broadway Cinema, Prestwick, on Sunday evening where, with Miss Walker of the Ministry of Labour, Edinburgh, he spoke under the auspices of the Ministry of Information. Provost Ferguson presided.

How disconcerting it was to the mind to look around on Easter day, the day which symbolised for them resurrection and regeneration, and view the ghastly chaotic state of affairs in the world, he said. To the young people who had been taught along truly ethical and spiritual lines this planet must appear a mad world completely out of joint with the teachings they had been given. Evil had become incarnate. Christianity nevertheless was the greatest revelation of divine wisdom, which had ever been given to the world. Why, after two thousand years, were they placed in the present position? In his opinion, the answer was that this was really a war of spiritual things. Ages ago, long before historical times, an event, a cataclysm had occurred, which had affected this planet ever since. That even was recorded in the book of Genesis, and it was the foundation of all the trouble in the world to-day. Some people believed, he said, that it was human nature to grab and fight; he did not think so, for God had made man in his own image. The fact of the matter was that the whole history of the world had been coloured by that event in Genesis. The present war was a phase of the battle of Armageddon, and after it was over the evil which had desecrated the world would gradually disappear.

WORKERS WANTED

Mr Churchill's words, "Give us the tools and we will finish the job," were quoted by Miss Jean Walker, when she spoke as guest speaker. Miss Walker said that she had toured the munition factories in England, and what had impressed her most was the really urgent need for women workers. She had found machine shops, some of them as big as the Broadway cinema, standing half empty because there was no local labour available. In other factories she found machines standing idle on account of the fact that there were no women workers. It was a truism to say that they were in the front line; it was equally true to say that the women of the country had endured much, and would endure more before the war was finished. Women could retaliate in the only language that Hitler understood, by going into the munitions factories and turning out more guns, more shells, and more bombs. She would like to see as many girls as possible from the Prestwick area taking up this essential work. If a girl went down to England from Prestwick she would have an opportunity of going along with other girls from the same district, and it would be possible for them to be working in the same factory and to stay in the same billets.

The welfare arrangements were very good. The firms as a rule found billets for the girls. Up to the present the general rule was that the firm found the girls private lodgings. When the girls went to England from Scotland they were met at the station of the town where they were going to work by a representative of the firm, given a good meal and taken to their lodgings. Inside the factories the firms provided excellent recreational facilities. Some of the new factories, she said, were absolutely beautiful. Concerts were given at the dinner and other intervals, and radiograms were installed in all the factories. The work was not difficult, and it could be done by women

GENEROUS PRESTWICK

Notable Gifts For Blitzed City Areas

When Lord Provost Sir P. J. Dollan, Glasgow, was at the Broadway Cinema, Prestwick on Sunday night giving an address (reported elsewhere in this issue) Provost Ferguson introduced to him a Prestwick septuagenarian, Mrs David Brown, Briarhill Road, Prestwick, and announced that she had been doing wonderful work by baking scones and pancakes, from the sale of which she had gathered a sum of money, £3, which she wished to be sent to the unfortunate victims of the Clydeside blitz.

Accepting the donation, Sir Patrick laughingly remarked, "I thought there was no other woman who could bake scones so well as my mother." He warmly shook Mrs Brown by the hand, and said he hoped that when she attained her next birthday she would send him a sample of her baking. Sir Patrick assisted 'Mrs Brown to get down from the platform, and later he went over to where she sat and chatted with her.

"One of the Best."

A further donation to the fund for the Clydeside victims was made by Mr J. S. Morrison, chief warden of Prestwick, who handed over a draft for £61 4s 6d which had been collected by the civil defence and auxiliary services in Prestwick.

Sir Patrick expressed his grateful thanks, and announced that earlier in the day he had received £325 for the same purpose from the workers of the Scottish Aviation Ltd.

Mr Morrison has since received a letter from Sir Patrick Dollan, expressing his appreciation of the gift from the civil defence workers, and describing it as one of the best donations received from any civil defence organisation in the West of Scotland.

2nd May 1941

GOLF CLUBMASTER

Death Of Mr Ernest Deeley, Prestwick

The death took place in a nursing home at Prestwick on Tuesday of Mr Ernest Deeley, clubmaster of Prestwick Golf Club for the past 20 years. Mr Deeley met with an accident during the blackout in February when alighting from a 'bus, and since then he had been laid aside from the effects of his injuries. Before going to the Prestwick Golf Club, Mr Deeley was a butler with the late Mr John Strain, Cassillis House, for twelve years. Mr Deeley possessed in rare measure those qualities that fitted him for such a post as clubmaster, and his death is regretted by the members of the Club and by all who knew him.

Outside his duties at the club, Mr Deeley took an active interest in bowling, and was a prominent member of the Prestwick Club. He is survived by his wife, two daughters and a son.

WINNING THE WAR

Lord Provost Dollan At Prestwick

A DIG AT CUMNOCK

When Sir Patrick J. Dollan, Lord Provost of Glasgow, spoke at the Broadway cinema, Prestwick, on Sunday evening under the auspices of the Ministry of Information, it was his third meeting that day. He told the large audience, presided over by Provost Ferguson, that he had addressed the miners of Muirkirk, the middle classes of Cumnock, and was finishing up with the Prestwick millionaires.

War Weapons Week, he said, had met with some opposition in Cumnock.. The Town Council was so anxious to finish the war quickly, that they had declined to support War Weapons Week; they believed that the Government should conscript all wealth, nationalise the banks, and make some other changes to get the job done as quickly as possible. (Laughter). When he got to Cumnock he found that was not their real reason. The cause of the opposition was that the Council were a bit hesitant about supporting the war. If he thought that they were in earnest about demanding conscription of wealth he would support that demand wholeheartedly provided there was any chance of getting that conscription into operation without causing confusion. It was an easy thing to demand conscription of wealth, but it was a more difficult thing to put it into operation. If it meant the conscription of the rich man's funds then it must also mean the conscription of the funds of the poor man as well. He had been telling some people in Cumnock that Keir Hardie would have been ashamed of them for the stand they had taken with regard to War Weapons Week.

The rich people, said Sir Patrick, were compelled to invest their money in 2½ per cent. bonds in which they received a lower rate of interest than people of humbler means, and after they had paid income tax the 2½ per cent. was reduced to 1½ or 1¼ per cent. At the beginning of the war he had written an article advocating a standard rate of interest of 2½ per cent. He did not expect that it would be adopted by the Government. It had now been adopted by a Government which was led by a prime minister whom he was proud to follow. "I am theoretically a republican," declared Sir Patrick, "but I know that a constitutional monarchy works." He would be worse than a fool, who would throw away a constitutional monarchy, which worked well in practice, for a republic which did not. A constitutional monarchy was the most democratic form of government that he knew, because the king and queen were not the dictators of the country but the willing servants of their people, and none surpassed them in devotion to duty. (Applause). They could have absented themselves from London, but they elected, and wisely so, to remain with their people, and share whatever sorrows might be imposed on their comrades.

2nd May 1941

A UNITED COUNTRY

Referring to the present position of Britain, Sir Patrick said that he would go so far as to say that in his 27 years of political life he had never known this country to be so well united as it was at the present time, and he referred not merely to the widespread expressions of support for the war, but also to the unity of good will towards one another. Prestwick had made that goodwill manifest in the way in which they had received the blitzed people who had to leave their homes. If the Germans thought they could beat them by bombing residential places instead of military targets then they had made a big mistake.

It was too much to expect victory in the course of this year, he said. This war was going to be won by the side that had the stiffest endurance, by the side that had the best morale and the best equipment. If the war had to go on for two or three years so that victory might be won it was because they had neglected the preparation for peace that they should have made. Even in the past year they had seen an unwillingness to build up the strength required for victory. If they were defeated on land it was not because their men were lacking in bravery, it would be because they did not have the mechanical equipment and power. There was only one thing which counted with the other side. It was not a copy of the Sermon on the Mount; the only thing the dictators understood was superior force. "We are not going to discuss terms of peace," he declared, "until we are sure we are able to defend ourselves." How many in this audience knew that in 1939 the number of fighting aeroplanes they had in this country was 400! Why did they have 400 fighting planes? Because they were not prepared. They thought that air service might not be needed, but they saw now it would have been much better to spend several million pounds on the Royal Air Force then than it was to spend the untold millions now trying to obtain parity in the air with Germany. "We are winning the war," he went on, "because the invasion promised for last year is as far away as ever." He concluded: "Sooner or later we must contemplate the invasion of Germany. I am going to harden your morale by asking for greater effort and I am doing so in the full knowledge that all of us have not done as much as we ought to have done."

16th May 1941

BOY KILLED

Chimney Collapse Near Glenburn

An accident resulting in the death of a boy messenger, 14 years of age, George Kedans, 36 Marchburn Avenue, Prestwick, occurred on Friday evening at a disused burgh coup near his home. In connection with what was the incinerator is a chimney-stalk some 17 feet in height, and along with other companions Kedans had been at the place.

It appeared they were picking at the bricks near the base of the chimney when it began to topple, and the boys ran off. Kedans apparently was too late in getting clear for much of the mass of material fell upon him, pinning him to the ground. Death was instantaneous.

23rd May 1941

Opened For The Season
By The Provost

Prestwick Bathing Lake was opened for the season on Saturday by Provost Ferguson. Following the opening ceremony a gala was held.

Bailie Dunsmore, convener of the Attractions Committee, said he was glad to see the great interest being taken in the lake, which was the more remarkable on account of the circumstances prevailing at the present time. It was really only a year since the war had started for them in this country. The clouds of war were still hanging over them and there might be dark days before we came to final victory. Health was very important to all those who were engaged in Civil Defence work, and he commended to them the splendid recreative facilities of the municipal bowling and putting greens, golf courses, and last but not least, the swimming pool. Swimming was beneficial to adults, in that it equipped them for the arduous duties which they were called upon to perform. It was also good for the children as it helped to build their bodies and develop habits of cleanliness. Mr Dunsmore then referred to the appointment of the new bathmaster, Mr James Beaty, R.L.S.S., who, he said, had a life-long connection with swimming. He concluded by calling on Provost Ferguson to open the lake.

On this auspicious occasion, said the Provost, he was glad to extend a cordial welcome to those present. It was more imperative than ever that they participate in outdoor sport, and as they had all national commitments during the week, he therefore made the invitation doubly welcome. He extended a special welcome to the members of H.M. Forces, for whom the Town Council had reduced the tariff feets to half price. The popularity of the Lake was increasing year by year, and it was gratifying to observe that the number of swimmers in Prestwick constituted a record in relation to the population. They were proud of the fact that many of the young men who had learned swimming at the Lake were now in the services. The "Learn to Swim" slogan, was one of the foremost in the keep-fit movement at the moment, and it was encouraging to note that the education authority were taking full advantage of the sport. Along with the Town Council, he wished to couple the name of their energetic convener, Bailie Dunsmore, who had given consideration to the welfare of the bathers. Behind the scenes there was also a great mass of machinery which merited attention and which comprised the necessary filtration plant which kept the water clean. The dressing accommodation at the lake was somewhat restricted as part of it had been requisitioned owing to war conditions. There were, however, excellent facilities for teaching children to swim and he hoped these would be taken advantage of. They had a very attractive programme before them which was to have been conducted by their late bathmaster, Mr David Crabb, but who was unfortunately indisposed, and unable to be present. His place would be taken by his deputy, Mr Tom Williamson. The Provost concluded by complimenting the burgh surveyor, Mr Francis Pritty, and the staff of the Council, who had helped to bring the lake to its present state of perfection.

Mr Williamson said he was sure that, like himself, those present would regret very much the unavoidable absence of their good friend, Mr David Crabb, bathmaster at Motherwell. Ever since the opening of Prestwick Bathing Lake in 1931, Mr Crabb had been present at each opening gala, either as bathmaster, performer or compere, and had contributed in no small measure to the success of these events by his careful tuition. His inability to be with them that day was doubly regretted, but he had been assured that Mr Crabb's pupils were at the top of their form.

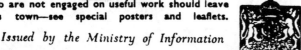

Beating the INVADER

A MESSAGE FROM THE PRIME MINISTER

IF invasion comes, everyone—young or old, men and women—will be eager to play their part worthily. By far the greater part of the country will not be immediately involved. Even along our coasts, the greater part will remain unaffected. But where the enemy lands, or tries to land, there will be most violent fighting. Not only will there be the battles when the enemy tries to come ashore, but afterwards there will fall upon his lodgments very heavy British counter-attacks, and all the time the lodgments will be under the heaviest attack by British bombers. The fewer civilians or non-combatants in these areas, the better—apart from essential workers who must remain. So if you are advised by the authorities to leave the place where you live, it is your duty to go elsewhere when you are told to leave When the attack begins, it will be too late to go ; and, unless you receive definite instructions to move, your duty then will be to stay where you are. You will have to get into the safest place you can find, and stay there until the battle is over. For all of you then the order and the duty will be : "STAND FIRM ".

This also applies to people inland if any considerable number of parachutists or air-borne troops are landed in their neighbourhood. Above all, they must not cumber the roads. Like their fellow-countrymen on the coasts, they must " STAND FIRM ". The Home Guard, supported by strong mobile columns wherever the enemy's numbers require it, will immediately come to grips with the invaders, and there is little doubt will soon destroy them.

Throughout the rest of the country where there is no fighting going on and no close cannon fire or rifle fire can be heard, everyone will govern his conduct by the second great order and duty, namely, " CARRY ON ". It may easily be some weeks before the invader has been totally destroyed, that is to say, killed or captured to the last man who has landed on our shores. Meanwhile, all work must be continued to the utmost, and no time lost.

The following notes have been prepared to tell everyone in rather more detail what to do, and they should be carefully studied. Each man and woman should think out a clear plan of personal action in accordance with the general scheme

Winston S. Churchill

STAND FIRM

I. What do I do if fighting breaks out in my neighbourhood?

Keep indoors or in your shelter until the battle is over. If you can have a trench ready in your garden or field, so much the better. You may want to use it for protection if your house is damaged. But if you are at work, or if you have special orders, carry on as long as possible and only take cover when danger approaches. If you are on your way to work, finish your journey if you can.

If you see an enemy tank, or a few enemy soldiers, do not assume that the enemy are in control of the area. What you have seen may be a party sent on in advance, or stragglers from the main body who can easily be rounded up

CARRY ON

2. What do I do in areas which are some way from the fighting?

Stay in your district and carry on. Go to work whether in shop, field, factory or office. Do your shopping, send your children to school until you are told not to. Do not try to go and live somewhere else. Do not use the roads for any unnecessary journey; they must be left free for troop movements even a long way from the district where actual fighting is taking place.

3. Will certain roads and railways be reserved for the use of the Military, even in areas far from the scene of action?

Yes, certain roads will have to be reserved for important troop movements; but such reservations should be only temporary. As far as possible, bus companies and railways will try to maintain essential public services, though it may be necessary to cut these down. Bicyclists and pedestrians may use the roads for journeys to work, unless instructed not to do so.

ADVICE AND ORDERS

4. Whom shall I ask for advice?

The police and A.R.P. wardens.

5. From whom shall I take orders?

In most cases from the police and A.R.P. wardens. But there may be times when you will have to take orders from the military and the Home Guard in uniform.

6. Is there any means by which I can tell that an order is a true order and not faked?

You will generally know your policeman and your A.R.P. wardens by sight, and can trust them. With a bit of common sense you can tell if a soldier is really British or only pretending to be so. If in doubt ask a policeman, or ask a soldier whom you know personally.

INSTRUCTIONS

7. What does it mean when the church bells are rung?

It is a warning to the local garrison that troops have been seen landing from the air in the neighbourhood of the church in question. Church bells will *not* be rung all over the country as a general warning that invasion has taken place. The ringing of church bells in one place will not be taken up in neighbouring churches.

8. Will instructions be given over the wireless?

Yes; so far as possible. But remember that the enemy can overhear any wireless message, so that the wireless cannot be used for instructions which might give him valuable information.

9. In what other ways will instructions be given?

Through the Press; by loudspeaker vans; and perhaps by leaflets and posters. But remember that genuine Government leaflets will be given to you only by the policeman, your A.R.P. warden or your postman; while genuine posters and instructions will be put up only on Ministry of Information notice boards and official sites, such as police stations, post offices, A.R.P. posts, town halls and schools.

FOOD

10. Should I try to lay in extra food?

No. If you have already laid in a stock of food, keep it for a real emergency; but do not add to it. The Government has made arrangements for food supplies.

NEWS

II. Will normal news services continue?

Yes. Careful plans have been made to enable newspapers and wireless broadcasts to carry on, and in case of need there are emergency measures which will bring you the news. But if there should be some temporary breakdown in news supply, it is very important that you should not listen to rumours nor pass them on, but should wait till real news comes through again. Do not use the telephones or send telegrams if you can possibly avoid it.

MOTOR-CARS

12. Should I put my car, lorry or motor-bicycle out of action?

Yes, when you are told to do so by the police, A.R.P. wardens or military; or when it is obvious that there is an immediate risk of its being seized by the enemy—then disable and hide your bicycle and destroy your maps.

13. How should it be put out of action?

Remove distributor head and leads and either empty the tank or remove the carburettor. If you don't know how to do this, find out now from your nearest garage. In the case of diesel engines remove the injection pump and connection. The parts removed must be hidden well away from the vehicle.

THE ENEMY

14. Should I defend myself against the enemy?

The enemy is not likely to turn aside to attack separate houses. If small parties are going about threatening persons and property in an area not under enemy control and come your way, you have the right of every man and woman to do what you can to protect yourself, your family and your home.

GIVE ALL THE HELP YOU CAN TO OUR TROOPS

Do not tell the enemy anything

Do not give him anything

Do not help him in any way

(1649) 9997? Wt. 46391/P1009 250M 5/41 W.P. Ltd. Gp. 8

15th August 1941

PRESTWICK PREPARED

Fire Fighting During A Blitz

GOOD ADVICE

That Prestwick's liking for open spaces might prove helpful in the event of showers of incendiaries raining upon the town, was mentioned by Mr J. S. Morrison, chief air raid warden of that burgh, when he gave a lecture in the Broadway Cinema, Prestwick, on Sunday evening under the auspices of the Ministry of Information. Provost Ferguson presided.

Mr Morrison said they had to be thankful for Prestwick's geographical position, but since Northern Ireland had been blitzed everyone had to admit that no place was immune from attack, so that they had no cause to be complacent in Prestwick. They had in the fire bomb one of the most vicious forms of attack, and one of the most destructive weapons. They had the oil bomb which could only be tackled by the heaviest firefighting services, and they had the ordinary coal fire in the grate which could be scattered all over the place by the blast of a high explosive bomb. He warned his audience never to leave a fire burning through the night, but always to put it out before going to bed. Explaining about the incendiary bomb, Mr Morrison stated that one aircraft could carry about 2000 of them, but there were two consoling features about them—they were not made to go off very easily, and probably only one in ten would start a fire. Prestwick had a Town Council which was keen on open spaces, and to-day they had to be thankful for this. If a shoal of incendiary bombs were dropped on Prestwick, most of them would fall on gardens, roads, and golf courses, where they would burn themselves out without doing any damage.

Faith In Fire Fighters

To combat fires, they had a very efficient and enthusiastic auxiliary fire service with four trailer pumps, and he had every reason to believe it was equal to anything of equivalent size anywhere. They had the fire fighters and, said Mr Morrison, he had abounding faith in them. Time was the greatest handicap with regard to fires, for when the fire brigade arrived on the scene of a fire usually all they could do was to keep it from spreading, but with fire-watchers on the scene they would be cutting down the danger of fire breaking out. The best method of dealing with incendiary bombs was with the stirrup pump. The other way was with sand, but very few housewives liked to keep sand in the house; and it was

not so good as the stirrup pump. In Prestwick they had about 650 stirrup pumps recorded all over the burgh, an average of about one to every five houses, and it was a question if any other town was so well equipped. Any man who took the attitude that the pump was only to be used by himself, was no use, they were all interdependant on each other, and each person should make his pump the property of the community. One important thing was that an adequate supply of water had to be kept. Prestwick's main water supplies were carried in two pipes which ran close to each other, and if one was damaged the other would probably be damaged also, but Prestwick had three emergency water supplies, and they were not likely to be troubled in this way. Mr Morrison warned his audience not to use the stirrup pump in the garden to spray roses with, as it became corroded with the spray.

Stay Indoors

When the siren went, continued Mr Morrison, the wardens would give a short blast on their whistles, warning everyone to be on the full alert. The best thing they could do when they heard the whistles was to stay indoors, as the quickest way to detect fires in their house was from indoors. If the fire became too big for them to handle they could go out to the street and shout to the fire fighters who would be patrolling the street, that there was a fire in the house, and there would be a better chance of putting it out with the minimum of damage. Another danger of going out to the street was the danger of flying shrapnel. They never knew the day when an anti-aircraft unit would be stationed outside the town, and during the battle shrapnel would be flying all over the place.

Every able-bodied person should be fire-watching. Some people thought that because they fire watched at their employer's business that that was enough and they did not need to

fire-watch in their own district. It was their homes that were at stake, and they had only to look at the homeless people from the recent blitzes to see the state they would be in. In combating fire the people were doing a great service to the country as well as to themselves. When they talked of the wealth of a country they meant the natural resources and the houses, factories, and other buildings in it, and by helping to safeguard them the fire-watchers were doing a service to the country. Prestwick had six wardens' posts which were manned day and night, and any fire party who required information regarding fire fighting should go along to any of those posts and the wardens would be glad to help them. Mr Morrison said he had behind him a splendid body of men, and leading them was the most interesting thing he had done in his life.

On the call of the Provost, a hearty vote of thanks was accorded the speaker.

5th September 1941

PUBS AND CLOSING

Prestwick Told To Follow Ayr

From a minute submitted to Prestwick Town Council on Tuesday evening it appeared that there was submitted a letter from the agent of the Prestwick licence-holders desiring to have a weekly holiday in respect of the shortage of whisky and beer.

There was also submitted a report from the chief constable in regard to the matter, indicating that in his view it would be better to restrict the daily hours of sale rather than have one day in the week, and that a number of the licensed premises in Ayr were closing before the expiry of the official permitted hours, but the customers already on the premises were permitted to remain until normal closing time, though they may not get further supplies.

Mr Dale having been heard on behalf of the license-holders, it was decided that the business hours should remain as at present, but that no objection would be taken if the license-holders followed the course adopted in Ayr.

Prestwick Services' First Supper

Prestwick Civil Defence Services held their first supper in the Bathing Lake Tea Room on Thursday of last week. Mr J. S. Morrison, head warden of Prestwick, acted as chairman.

It was needless to say anything in support of the civil services, said the chairman, for in the cities which had been blitzed, examples of the useful work being done by them were well known.

In proposing the toast "The Civil Defence Services of Prestwick," Mr John W. Robertson, chief air raid warden for Ayr, said, that the Civil Defence Services of Prestwick were very thorough. When A.R.P. was introduced it was the subject of merriment but now they had covered themselves with fame and proved that they were indispensable. The Civil Services had had a great burden placed upon them in helping to maintain the morale of the people, for there were many people who raised their voices in a terrible wail and shouted defeat. This band of people in the country were Goebbel's fifth columnists, bleak, unworthy, and a disgrace to the country of their birth. It was the duty of the Civil Defence Services to put this band of people in their places.

Replies were made by Mr F. Pritty, Commandant A.F.S., the Rev. G. N. Christie (First-Aid), Mr H. F. Munro, county chief constable, and Mr Morrison, head warden.

Mr Brand, who is a member of the casualty service in Glasgow, proposed the toast "County of Ayr,"

GETTING TOGETHER

In replying to the toast Mr J. R. Lockie, county clerk and A.R.P. controller, said that the social side of A.R.P. should not be neglected, and although they had more serious jobs to do they required a respite to get together to cement the friendship necessary to make A.R.P. the success it must be. He readily believed that the staff of the Ayr County Council all pulled their weight before the war and it was a tribute to them to have been able to take the additional work which the war had brought, and he wished to pay tribute to his own staff and also to those who had made A.R.P. possible. The established strength of A.R.P. workers in the county had been fixed two years ago and totalled 4000, but the volunteers before the war totalled 7000 and he had to send a special application to train the extra 3000. This, he thought, was a tremendous achievement. Ayr County Council decided to buy three mobile canteens and in doing so had the distinctintion of being the first County Council to realise the necessity for mobile canteens. Ayr had pulled its weight and would pull its weight to an even greater extent. This was a time when technical boundaries didn't matter, concluded Mr Lockie, it was the country and the Empire that mattered.

Mr Neilson proposed "Our Guests," and Mr Davidson, A.R.P. organiser, replied, in the course of which he, on behalf of the Troon head warden, challenged Ayr and Prestwick to an inter-area golf tournament and the challenge was accepted.

"The Burgh of Prestwick" was proposed by Deputy Chief Constable Lobban, who said that his earliest association with the burgh was in 1910 and since then he had seen and heard of Prestwick growing from a population of 2,700 in 1910 to the present day total of 11,600 exclusive of evacuees and others. If he were a native of Prestwick, he continued, he would be very proud of it.

28th November 1941

EMERGENCY POWERS (DEFENCE)

REGISTRATION FOR CIVIL DEFENCE DUTIES.

NOTICE TO MEN BORN BETWEEN 7th SEPTEMBER, 1881, AND 6th SEPTEMBER, 1923.

REQUIREMENT TO REGISTER ON SUNDAY, 14th SEPTEMBER, SATURDAY, 20th SEPT., and SUNDAY, 21st SEPT., 1941.

NOTICE IS HEREBY GIVEN by the Council of the Royal Burgh of Ayr that all male British subjects who, on the 6th day of September, 1941, are resident in the Royal Burgh of Ayr, and are not less than eighteen but under sixty years of age, are, unless they are exempted persons as specified in the Schedule hereto, required to apply in the manner hereinafter mentioned to be registered under the Civil Defence Duties (Compulsory Enrolment) Order, 1941.

The application for registration is required to be made in writing on a form which will be provided, and the applicant is required to state his names in full, his home address, his age, the date of his birth, his National Registration Identity Number, and his occupation or profession.

The application is required to be made in person on the appropriate day as specified below according to the applicant's age, at any one of the following places, namely:—
CARRICK STREET HALL, AYR,
TOWN HALL, PRESTWICK.

The form on which the application is to be made will be supplied to the applicant when he attends for the purpose of making his application for registration. APPLICANTS WILL BE ASKED TO PRODUCE THEIR NATIONAL REGISTRATION IDENTITY CARDS WHEN REGISTERING.

28th November 1941

NOTED ORGANIST

Death Of Mr A. T. Hart Prestwick

Prestwick has lost a notable citizen by the death of Mr Alfred Thomas Hart at the age of 82. Mr Hart died at the home of his nephew (Mr Thomas Rumbold, Briarhill Road), on Tuesday, and had been confined to bed little more than a week before the end.

His record as a church organist must be well nigh unique, as for the long period of 56 years he held that

position in St. Cuthbert's Church of Monkton and Prestwick. On the occasion of his jubilee in March, 1934, Mr Hart received tangible token of esteem from the congregation and the choir. On that occasion he recalled that Prestwick, when he entered it in December, 1884, was little bigger than a village, and he had almost to grope his way about as there was not a lamp in the streets. Curious that he should have lived to see another blackout nearly sixty years later but for another reason! One of the men Mr Hart met at that time was the late Mr James Howat, schoolmaster, with whom he struck up a friendship which was only dissolved by death. In these far off days too, a Mr Andrew who later became an elder, blew the organ in the church. On this matter of elders he stated that when he came to the church there were 8 or 10 elders, and nowadays the number was around 30, showing the enormous growth of the church.

A native of Marlborough, Wiltshire, Mr Hart was in Scotland as assistant to his uncle, a music master and organist in Coatbridge, before going to Prestwick, where he became the first organist of the St. Cuthbert's church, the temporary precentor of which pending the installation of the Kist O' Whustles was Mr Howat. The Rev. John Patrick, D.D., afterwards Professor Patrick, was then minister of the congregation, and he was followed by the Rev. D. A. Reid (1888-1923), and the

present minister, the Rev. Luke McQuitty, with all three of whom he was on the best terms, and doubtless by reason of his position as organist he had to listen to more sermons than the average individual member of the congregation. Mr Hart retired from active duty as organist last year, having completed 56 years of loyal and devoted service. Loyally the successive choirs of the church supported Mr Hart, and at one time and another the choir had more than a local reputation. A strict disciplinarian Mr Hart was nevertheless looked up to and respected by all the members, and the practice nights have been described as "sacred hours" not to be intruded upon by anyone. For at least 40 years Mr Hart was the principal music teacher in Prestwick, and many of his pianoforte pupils throughout the years became prominent in musical circles.

Mr Hart took a great deal of his leisure in the open air, and indulged in long walks, for many years pursuing the hobby of amateur photography. He was a member of Prestwick St. Nicholas Golf Club and the Prestwick bowling club, and had a great fund of reminiscence of the town and its worthies. Mr Hart was unmarried, and came of a family noted for its longevity. Two brothers and two sisters survive him.

PRESTWICK COUNCILLOR'S PROTEST

Too Few Discussions In Public Alleged

Several items of business were remitted back at the monthly meeting of Prestwick Town Council on Tuesday, Provost Ferguson presiding, and objection was taken to this course by Mr Steele.

"There is far too much of this remitting back," said Mr Steele, "and if we are going to hold a public meeting, we may as well tranact some of the business in public."

A motion by Provost Ferguson had just been carried, by 6 votes to 5, that a motion by Bailie Boylan Smith be deferred to the end of the public business. Bailie Smith's motion was to the effect that the council proceed to the appointment of a deputy Town Clerk.

STIRRUP PUMPS

Reference was made to a minute of the A.R.P. committee, which stated that there was submitted a statement by the burgh treasurer in regard to the purchase and sale of stirrup pumps to date, and it was agreed that the town clerk should write to the various parties whose payments were outstanding, indicating that unless the sums due were paid at once, the stirrup pumps would be uplifted.

The clerk (Mr Shaw), said he had written to the various parties, but there were still some payments outstanding, and it was agreed to leave the matter to the end of the meeting.

LAY-OUT OF PLOTS

Bailie Brown stated that a meeting of the Golf Course Shores and Public Parks commitee had been held, and a report drawn up on the layout of plots, and Provost Ferguson read the report.

Mr Adamson stated that the Provost had said that the plants were to be sold to the public of Prestwick, and he (Mr Adamson) wanted to know if they were going to stipulate that none of the plants grown were going to be sold to shops for resale.

Raising the question of tomatoes, which had been grown last year, Mr Adamson asked "Who got the tomatoes?" He wanted to know what value had been derived from them. He had raised the question before, but it had never been answered. He moved that they should not sell any of the produce to shopkeepers.

Provost Ferguson said he rather thought that that was out of their province.

When he had last raised the matter, said Mr Adamson, he had been told that the plants were to be sold wholesale, and he would like to know if it had been made known that such a sale would take place. How were the shopkeepers to know of such a sale?

Provost Ferguson interrupted to say that he knew that several of the shopkeepers got the tomatoes.

Mr Adamson went on to say that he understood the revenue which they had received to be £19. Girvan had stated in the press that their's was £60 and if Girvan could do that surely they could do better.

Provost Ferguson said he would have a record prepared for the next meeting.

Mr Blunt said they had been discussing this matter for a long time.

Mr Blunt said they had been discussing this matter for a long time, and they had never got any information about it. How many shopkeepers purchased the tomatoes?

The Provost replied that three or four firms purchased them at market price.

Asked by Mr Adamson what loss they were going to make, Bailie Brown said that they were going to grow them at a profit. He would prepare a report on the matter to put before the next meeting of the council.

WAR RELIEF FUND

Provost Ferguson intimated that there had been a letter from the honorary secretary of the Ayrshire War Relief Fund. The position was that Prestwick had contributed something like £450 and a contribution of 10/- per household or £1,500, had been expected.

Mr Sawyers said he thought the County Council was asking a little too much although he had full sympathy for the scheme.

The Provost said he was instrumental in getting £450 and he could assure them it was a very difficult job.

It was agreed that the same committee, as before, should be continued in order to make further appeals.

MEMBERS WALK OUT

Incident At Prestwick Meeting

All the magistrates, including Provost Ferguson, and the conveners and sub-conveners, were re-appointed en bloc at the statutory and monthly meeting of Prestwick Town Council held in the Council Chambers on Friday.

Mr Govan moved that the Provost, magistrates and conveners be re-appointed en bloc, and was seconded by Bailie Boylan Smith.

Mr Steele, moving that they go on and appoint a Provost and magistrates in the normal way, said that the government who were conducting the most terrible war in history thought that changes should be made, and he thought changes should be made in the council.

Mr Dougan seconded.

On a vote being taken, 10 voted for the motion, and 2 for the amendment.

Mr Steele thought it very unfair. Last year various councillors expressed the view that the honours should go round, and he was of the opinion that the same should hold good for this year.

As a protest, he and Mr Dougan left the meeting.

CLOSING OF SHOPS

A letter was submitted from the Scottish Home Department with reference to the early closing of shops during the winter months and Bailie Brown reported that the hours suggested by the Department, 6 p.m. during the week, and 7 p.m. on a Saturday, had been generally adhered to.

1942

Clement Attlee became Deputy Prime Minister.
American forces arrived in Britain to establish military bases.
The German air force began its "Baedeker" raids directed against Britain's architectural heritage.
The British army halted Germany's advance across North Africa at the Battle of el Alamein.
The Beveridge report on Social Security in Britain was published.
Britain began to suffer acute shortages of goods and food; white bread was banned and there was only a limited supply of utility goods.

23rd January 1942

Prestwick's Municipal Expenditure

[To the Editor, *The Ayrshire Post*]

Prestwick, 15/1/42.

Sir,—The poplation of Prestwick before the present war was 10,000, and this can fairly be taken as the normal one. According to the auditor's report the total expenditure legally authorised was, for the year ended May 15, 1941, £100,241, or £10 per head of the population. This is a wild increase since 1936 when it was £80,125. Loans outstanding at May, 1941, amounted to £176,130, or nearly £18 per head of the population. These figures are exclusive of loans for housing.

The total expenditure for wages for year ended May 15, 1941, was £6702, equal to 1s 4d in the £ of the rates. Salaries for the same period amounted to £2936, or 7d in the £.

Although Prestwick is a burgh fully equipped with officials we are dependent on our neighbours for vital essentials. We paid the burgh of Ayr £356 for fire brigade, £430 for cleansing, £136 for sewer charges —a total of £922 or 2¼d in the £ of the rates. We paid Troon for water £1432, equal to 3¼d in the £. We get supplies of gas from outside the burgh and we have very elementary cleansing and salvage arrangements. What have we or what do we get for the very high rates we have to pay, the highest in the county, in comparison with other burghs? We have a full assortment of officials and seem to be well set out to run a fully equipped burgh, but from a report published we don't appear to be able to grow tomatoes as profitably as other burghs.

Last year hire of horses cost the burgh £1583, compared with £841 in 1936. The removing of sea wrack cost in 1937 £81, 1938 £39, 1939 £61, 1940 £65, 1941 £54. What becomes of the sea wrack after it has been removed from the shore? Is there nothing got for it? It is a valuable manure and is surely worth the cost of carting seeing there is such a scarcity of animal manure. Ayr burgh does not allow the wrack they gather to disappear into oblivion. They make something out of it.

Hires to reservoir is a costly item, varying in different years from £9 8s to £23 last year. At the February public meeting of the Town Council when the question of an official's expenses was raised the chairman is reported in the Press to have said, "I appeal to you to raise these matters elsewhere." He said that vouchers for all expenditure could be seen in the treasurer's office. This is much like locking the stable door after the horse has disappeared.

Telephones cost the burgh a tidy sum per annum all over, but as the charges are hidden away among other items it is difficult to get at the actual cost. I have no doubt that there will be receipts in the treasurer's office but that will not keep down unnecessary expense. However, telephone charges in the water account last year amounted to £17 8s 11d, double what they were the previous year. Are employers of the burgh allowed to use the telephones for private purposes free of charge? Telephones and hires to the reservoir cost the ratepayers over 15s per week. Is this necessary for actual burgh requirements?

What about a Ratepayers' Association to keep an eye on our municipal expenditure?

RATEPAYER.

23rd January 1942

Railings For Scrap

[To the Editor, *The Ayrshire Post*]

Sir,—I am surprised at the remarks about railings under "Postscripts." I take it that this correspondent has no railings of his own, therefore he wants every person to part with theirs. There is a widespread feeling against this spoiling of property, although only a few has objected as yet. There will be plenty whenever this vandalism begins. I myself have parted with all the scrap, and assisted the cause in many other ways. I object to my railings being taken away as it will spoil the look of the property. If they have to go I expect the government will be good enough to replace them with a brick wall, and that might be a fair deal. There is still hundreds of tons of scrap about if people would only give it up. Surely this will be seen to before it comes to spoiling property and the look of the town.

ONE WHO DOES NOT WANT PROPERTY SPOILED.

6th February 1942

MERCAT CROSS

Suggestion Removal At Prestwick

There was little business requiring the attention of Prestwick Town Council at its monthly meeting held in the Council chambers on Tuesday. Bailie Brown presided in the absence of Provost Ferguson.

Mr Sawyers again drew attention to the rather poor gas supply in the Glenburn district.

Mr Blunt said that the gas supply was low all over the burgh, and there had been several complaints to that effect.

The clerk (Mr Wm. Shaw) pointed out that the gas supply had to be conserved at the present time, and the matter was again allowed to drop.

WARSHIP WEEK

The clerk intimated that he had attended a meeting in Ayr in connection with the forthcoming Warship Week. The campaign would be run on similar lines to that of War Weapons Week held some time ago. It was suggested, said Mr Shaw, that each area should fix its own target, and it was agreed that a meeting should be held to discuss the arrangements to be made.

QUEUE BARRIERS

A minute of the Roads and Footpaths committee stated that there was submitted a report by the burgh surveyor in regard to the proposed erection of queue barriers at the Cross and town hall and indicating that it would be necessary to obtain the sanction of the County Council, who act as agents of the Ministry of War Transport, before any alteration could be made.

MERCAT CROSS

A minute of the Roads and Footpaths committee bore that there was submitted a report by the burgh surveyor, with plan showing the proposed new site of the Mercat Cross 10 feet from the front of the burgh chambers, which would allow pavement room of 9 feet in width from the Cross to the kerb. It was indicated that the sanction of the Ministry of Works and Buildings would be required under the new Defence General Regulations 1939, Regulation 56a, which prohibits expenditure on any building during the war, without authority. On the motion of Mr Govan, seconded by Mr Sawyers, it was agreed that the Mercat Cross should not be removed at the present time.

REMOVAL OF RAILINGS

A minute of the Lighting and Cleansing committee stated that a report was submitted by the burgh surveyor with reference to the removal of railings in the burgh, together with a list of the various appeals lodged to date, giving the recommendations of the town clerk and burgh surveyor in regard to same. Mr Dougan moved that these recommendations be accepted and Mr Steele seconded. Mr Govan moved that the recommendations be accepted, subject to the gates remaining, and Provost Ferguson seconded. On a vote there supported the amendment 6, and the motion, 4, and accordingly the amendment was declared carried.

6th March 1942

PRESTWICK ENVIES TROON

Suggestion For British Restaurant Favoured

THE PARKS DEPARTMENT

When the clerk (Mr Wm. Shaw) submitted a circular letter from the Ministry of Food regarding the requisitioning powers of local authorities to take possession of buildings for British restaurants, Mr Steele said he would like very much if the Council pushed on with such a project. As a representative who attended the opening of the restaurant at Troon he was very much impressed with it. There were undoubtedly certain arrangements made for feeding people in the event of a blitz in Prestwick, but he did not think these would be as adequate as a British restaurant could provide. When one considered the serious position they were in at the present time due to the attack in the Pacific he thought that in the near future they would have to be tightening the belts, and he thought they should consider the provision of such a restaurant to make sure that proper meals would be provided for the workers. These restaurants were essential for the morale and the strength of the workers. The whole cry to-day was for production, and they must be sure that they could carry on. The venture had been highly successful at Troon since the opening.

The Provost said he heard of the great success that was attending the restaurant in Troon, and speaking for himself, he favoured the idea.

Bailie Brown said he could endorse what Mr Steele had said as to Troon. He had been much impressed with the whole outlook of the British restaurant. The equipment there was most adequate, and the only drawback at Troon seemed to be that they were going to have too many to feed. He thought there was just the possibility that Prestwick could do with a British restaurant too.

On the suggestion of the clerk, the matter was remitted to the Public Health Committee for consideration.

PARKS DEPARTMENT.

A minute of sub-committee regarding the administration of the Parks department bore that they went into in detail the expenditure in the Parks department and certain explanations were given in regard to same. It was thought that the labour employed in connection with the department was excessive in war time and it was agreed to recommend that . . . public works the wages should be reduced to £600 per annum and that materials and repairs should not exceed £350. The general administration of the department was also gone into and considered, when it was agreed, on the motion of Mr Govan, seconded by Bailie Boylan-Smith, that the whole administration of the Parks department should be put under the supervision of the burgh engineer's department.

From the minute of the Public Parks, &c., full committee it appeared that a general discussion took place on the sub-committee's proposal. Provost Ferguson moved that the first paragraph regarding the reduction in wages, etc., should be approved as in the minute and Mr Govan seconded, and this was agreed to. With regard to the administration of the department, Mr Govan moved the adoption of the second part of the minute and Bailie Boylan-Smith seconded. Provost Ferguson moved that the administration of the Parks department remain as at present and Mr Steele seconded. On a vote, there voted for the amendment, six, and for the motion five, and accordingly the amendment was declared carried.

Ex-Provost Govan moved the disapproval of the parent committee and that the finding of the sub-committee should stand.

Bailie Boylan Smith seconded.

The Provost moved the approval of the minute, which was seconded by Mr Steele.

There was no discussion on the matter beyond that Mr Steele suggested that he would have liked to see the minute dealt with in two parts, and contended that they would be saddling their burgh engineer with a vast amount of work.

On a division, the minute of the parent committee was approved by 7 votes to 4.

REMOVAL OF RAILINGS.

A minute of meeting of the Lighting and Cleansing committee bore that there was submitted a letter from the Ministry of Works and Buildings regarding further particulars desired by them of the length and height of each railing in the burgh; also pointing out that local authorities are only excluding gates and balusters where the parapet wall is of sufficient height to afford some protection to the property — i.e., where the wall is 2 feet 6 inches or over—and this was agreed to.

Mr G. Blunt raised the matter of railings at the housing schemes at Glenburn which had been erected only two years ago.

Mr F. Pritty, the burgh engineer, said he agreed with the speaker's point of view, but he could not see they could do much about it as they were scheduled for removal.

Mr Blunt said there was any amount of old iron to be seen at pitheads and that should be removed before private railings were taken.

Bailie Boylan Smith said it could be represented that in order to preserve the gardens these railings should be the last to be removed

Agreed to.

A PROTEST.

The clerk submitted a protest from residents in Broompark Avenue, Broompark Crescent and Tronmore Crescent against proposals to make allotments on vacant ground in these roads.

Bailie Brown said it was considered that the people resident in that area would want the ground cultivated, but it was apparent they did not want it.

It was agreed to take no action.

CHALETS POPULAR.

Mr Sawyers asked how it came about that out of all the bathing chalets there were only eight available.

Mr Pritty—It means that 42 are already let. (Laughter.)

Mr Steele said that last year when he wished the site of the chalets altered he was told he was too late, and apparently he was too late again.

Mr Adamson asked if it had not been customary to advertise.

The Provost— Yes. But they are so popular they have been taken up quickly.

Mr Steele said he would like to give notice for next year that we alter the position of them. He would then get a chance to propose it. (Laughter.)

TELEPHONE ACCOUNTS.

"Quite staggering" was how the Provost described the amount of money the Council was spending on telephone calls, and he moved that enquiry be made at once.

Bailie Dunsmore seconded.

In reply to a member, the Provost said the total amount was £47 7s 8d for the quarter.

The motion was agreed to.

27th March 1942

PRESTWICK AMBULANCE PRESENTED

At Prestwick Burgh Buildings on Saturday afternoon the 25 h.p. Armstrong Siddeley ambulance bought by funds raised by public subscription, was handed over to the County Council for the duration of the war. Provost Ferguson on behalf of the subscribers asked Lieut.-Commander G. Hughes-Onslow, vice-convener of the county, to accept custody.

The ambulance, apart from some few details, was ready for use, and it was greatly admired when opened to public inspection. It has accommodation for the transport of three stretcher cases. The pre-selective gears makes the engine particularly suited for emergency driving.

17th April 1942

PRESTWICK RESIGNATIONS

Provost And Bailie Boylan Smith

The resignation of Provost Ferguson as Provost and as a member of Prestwick Town Council gave rise to a lively discussion at a meeting of that body in the Council Chambers on Tuesday evening — Baillie Brown in the chair.

Mr Steele asked if it was true that Bailie Boylan Smith had also retired.

Bailie Brown replied that it was true as he had received a letter to that effect the previous morning.

Mr Steele said that he should like to take that opportunity of expressing regret that two of the leading members of the council had seen fit to resign. It was no wonder, he added, because of the way the council had been run for the past two or three years. The members of the council, he was afraid, were getting old and amused him with the acrobatics they came out with. They had not made a decision at the council for a long time.

Mr Dunsmore intervened here and asked if this was in order.

Mr Steele voiced his objection to the interruption and ended by expressing the view that something should be done in the matter about which he had spoken.

Bailie Brown said that they all regretted and no one more than he did the action which Provost Ferguson had taken at a time like the present.

Mr Blunt said it would be unfortunate if they were to allow this opportunity to pass without at least saying to Provost Ferguson, "Thank you," for the services he had rendered to the community, especially in these trying and anxious moments. There had been many calls made upon him and he had given these ungrudgingly and always taken the load when there was any work to be done. During the "blitz" at Clydebank and Greenock he had worked "like a Trojan" trying to find accommodation for the evacuees. During the inauguration of the various war weapons week, and appeals which had been made by the services in the town, he had always taken the lead and given every support. He never tired of doing what he thought was right whether his colleagues thought him right or wrong. He was sure that the members of the council _____ him well in his retirement _____ municipal work. On behalf _____ electors of the fourth _____ he ward committee he tendered sincere thanks to Provost and Mrs Ferguson.

Mr Blunt also expressed regret at the resignation of Bailie Boylan-Smith and said he was a hearty worker and an able councillor.

Bailie Brown and Mr Duncan expressed their desire to be associated with Mr Blunt's remarks.

Mr Adamson said that he did not wish to be associated with the remarks made by Mr Blunt, alleging that Provost Ferguson had sent a letter to those councillors who had supported a recent motion but not to others. He (Mr Adamson) had not received a copy of that letter.

Mr Steele asked that Provost Ferguson's letter of resignation be read out in public.

Mr Govan stated that he would in that case read out the letter from Bailie Boylan-Smith.

Bailie Brown thought it would be inadvisable to do this, and it was finally agreed to discuss the matter in private.

FREE GIFT SALE.

A letter was read from the secretary of the Ayr and South Ayrshire Free Gift Sale desiring Prestwick to participate in their efforts in October next and after a short discussion it was agreed to leave the matter over in the meantime.

HOUSE PLANNING CONFERENCE.

It was agreed to send the convener and sub-convener of the housing committee and the burgh surveyor to the annual conference of the Scottish National Housing Council in Aberdeen on May 22 and 23.

CONVENTION DUES.

A minute of the Finance committee bore that there was submitted a letter from the clerk to the Burghs Convention, indicating that a new scale of dues had now been recommended, fixing the dues on a fairer basis. It was indicated that the sum payable by the burgh of Prestwick would now be £10 10s, and it was agreed that this should be authorised for payment.

THE KING'S FUND.

A minute of a meeting of the A.R.P. committee bore that there was submitted a circular from the Ministry of Home Security, indicating the benefits which would be supplied by the "King's Fund (1940)" for the assistance of disabled members of the services, or widows and dependants of those who have lost their lives in the defence of this country; and that the fund was maintained entirely by donations, bequests and contributions from private funds, and it is hoped it will be made known as widely as possible. This was noted.

QUESTION OF DISSENT.

From a minute of the Attractions committee it appeared that there was again considered the letter from the Autoway Company offering a discount of 83½ per cent. on all the machines installed at the bathing lake, but it was agreed to insist on 50 per cent. from the ordinary weighing machines similar to last year.

8th May 1942

PRESTWICK'S NEW COUNCILLORS

There was little business of public importance transacted at the monthly meeting of Prestwick Town Council on Monday — Bailie Brown presiding.

At a special meeting before the public meeting the new councillor for the Fourth Ward, Mr Matthew Flanigan, was introduced, took the usual oath, and was welcomed by Bailie Brown. The clerk read a letter from the First Ward committee stating that it had been unanimously decided to recommend that Mr James Brock be nominated to fill the vacancy caused by the resignation of Bailie Boylan-Smith.

MINISTRY [MF] OF FOOD

SOAP RATIONING

FROM MONDAY, FEBRUARY 9TH, soap may be bought only against a coupon or buying permit. The oils and fats used in soap manufacture occupy much shipping space, and some of this must be saved for food. You will have 4 coupons in each 4-weekly period, and will be able to use these how and when you like within the period. There will be no registration, and you may buy from any shop stocking the kind you require.

Each of the four coupons which make up a four-weeks' ration will entitle you to any one of the following :—

either
4 ozs. Hard Soap (common Household Soap in bars or pieces)
or **3 ozs.** Toilet Soap
or **3 ozs.** Soap Flakes or Chips
or **6 ozs.** Soap Powder No. 1
or **12 ozs.** Soap Powder No. 2
or **6 ozs.** Soft Soap.

Rationing will not apply to shaving soaps or dental soaps, shampoo powders, liquid soap, or scourers.

The coupons to be used are those in the frame at the top of Page 15 of the YELLOW BOOK (RB 9)—the book you use for jam. Coupon numbers and periods will be the same as for sugar and tea, *so that you will start with coupons 29 to 32 for the first period*—February 9th to March 8th. Coupons 1-28 are of no value.

Coupons will not be cut out, but must be cancelled by the shopkeeper in ink or indelible pencil.

¶ **MEMBERS OF THE SERVICES, ETC.**
Holders of the Services Registration Card (RB 8 X) will use the frame of coupons at the bottom of page 4. Holders of Leave or Duty Ration Cards (RB 8) will use the coupons marked "Y" on page 2. Special coupons will be issued to other members of the services. Weekly Seamen holding Ration Book RB 6 will use the coupons marked "A" on the last green page (leaf 11).

¶ **TRAVELLERS**
Persons who have been granted travellers' facilities will use the frame of coupons at the top of Form RT 2 inserted in their ration books.

¶ **ESTABLISHMENTS AND BUSINESS USERS**
Residential establishments will use the Yellow Ration Books of their residents, as they do for rationed foods. Public Authorities and Business users must ask the local Food Office for a Permit application Form. This covers institutions, catering establishments, shops, offices, and factories which buy soap for washrooms and cleaning, textile manufacturers, and also such concerns as laundries and those who regularly take in washing.

TO WHOLESALERS AND RETAILERS OF SOAP

No further sales of soap must be made to consumers except against a coupon or buying permit. Ask your Food Office for a copy of Soap Instructions No. 1 and No. 2 (for retailers only) which contain full trade instructions.

Shopkeepers are reminded that they must cancel coupons in ink or indelible pencil, starting with No. 29.

15th May 1942

INVASION!

Advice At A Prestwick Meeting

That invasion might well materialise as Hitler's last desperate throw was a point stressed by the Rev. Langland Seath, Eaglesham, when he spoke at the Broadway Cinema, Prestwick, on Sunday on the subject of "Invasion."

Mr Seath, referring to Sir Archibald Sinclair's recent speech in which he visualised the hammering of the Luftwaffe by the R.A.F., and afterwards, invasion, not of Britain by the Hun, but of the Continent by ourselves, told how the Air Minister said that they must be careful of invasion of this country right to the end, as it might well materialise as Hitler's last desperate throw. There was a constant threat of invasion, said the speaker, and although it was not imminent or inevitable, it was an eventuality which they must provide for to the best of their ability.

The formation of Invasion Committees in the towns of the West of Scotland was one of the answers to the threat of German invasion, and their formation had inspired a question in the House of Commons, Mr Herbert Morrison being asked if the composition of these committees would be decided by ability, not social status. Mr Seath could not visualise anyone, not likely to be of use, being a member of the committee, especially when it was remembered that if the Germans came and overran Prestwick, the committee would not be treated politely, they would merely be put against the wall—1, 2, 3, 4, 5, 6, 7, 8—and that would be the end of the Invasion Committee! The purpose of the committee was to have a definite scheme worked out, whereby, whenever the bells were rung, every able-bodied person in Prestwick should know exactly what to do for the defence of their town.

Mr Seath elaborated the duties of the defenders of the invaded town and showed how, with prior organisation, a town would have a far greater chance of withstanding invasion. Concluding, Mr Seath said that it was up to the people of Prestwick to give the Invasion Committee every possible assistance, to co-operate whole-heartedly, so that should the hour come, and the bells ring out, they would know absolutely what they had to do and would be able to do it.

10th July 1942

DEAF AND DUMB

Prestwick Council's Donation

COUNTY DEMAND

At the monthly meeting of the Prestwick Town Council on Tuesday evening—Provost Dunsmore presiding—a letter was submitted by the clerk (Mr Wm. Shaw) from the Department of Health suggesting that local authorities could make contributions to the Deaf and Dumb societies which were seriously hampered by lack of funds.

It was stated that assistance given in this way might enable the societies to extend the work, particularly in placing in industry people who might otherwise become a charge upon the public funds.

In the short discussion which followed mention was made of the society known as the Ayrshire Mission to the Deaf and Dumb.

Mr Steele said it would be better if the Ministry of Health asked the Government to support these people rather than the local authorities.

The Provost said that meantime they could give a donation as they did to some other bodies.

Mr Sawyers, seconded by Mr Dougan, moved that they give £5, the mover suggesting that they had been asked to be as generous as possible.

Bailie Dunlop, seconded by the Provost, moved two guineas as a donation.

On a division, the £5 was carried by 6 votes to 4.

British Restaurant

Plans and estimates for the British restaurant at Prestwick are at present under consideration, and a decision is expected at an early date.

Bailie Brown reported on the Kilmarnock restaurant, the opening of which he attended on Saturday last. It was well equipped and had accommodation for serving 212 persons. The building had been opened 59 days after it had been secured for the purpose, and he hoped once they started they would get through as expeditiously. He had no doubt that at Kilmarnock such a restaurant would be a great success.

It was agreed that a representative be sent to the opening of a similar restaurant at Ardrossan on July 11.

COUNTY REQUISITION

The clerk intimated that the amount requisitioned by the County Council from the burgh was £44,158 19s. 9d. as against £42,920 12s. 2d., an increase of £1238 7s. 7d. The first instalment was due on December 1, 1942.

Burgh Cleansing

From a minute of the sub-committee on burgh cleansing, it appeared that there was submitted a report by the burgh engineer re burgh cleansing, copies of which had been sent to the members of the sub-committee. It was agreed, after consideration, to recommend the Council that it would be injudicious to do anything meantime in regard to alterations in the cleansing, until after the war.

Bailie Dunlop, as convener of the committee, mentioned that while the saving effected since they left the Ayr scheme was £500, they had £433 for new vehicles, paid for at the time instead of being spread over ten years. The burgh surveyor and his staff, he said, deserved to be complimented on the manner in which salvage had been disposed of not only from an economic point of view but in regard to public improvements that might be carried out in the future. Some of the men had worked like Trojans, and they were fortunate that they had remained with the Council at a time when they might have gone elsewhere and got higher wages. He suggested that they should not be forgotten later on.

The minute was approved.

Gardener's Department

From a minute of the Parks Committee it appeared that Bailie Brown gave his views generally in regard to the working of the gardener's department, and it was agreed that the town clerk should write the gardener indicating that he should keep the plots tidy and assist in the work himself. Bailie Govan moved, seconded by Provost Dunsmore, that the burgh gardener should be supplied with a bicycle to enable him to get more quickly over the distances between the plots, and Mr Blunt moved the previous question and Mr Adamson seconded. On a vote, there supported the amendment 4, and the motion 6. The convener indicated that he had taken one of the workmen from the St. Nicholas golf course to assist the gardener, and that extra work had fallen on the present greenkeeper at the golf course. It was agreed that he should be paid an extra 5s per week to cover the longer hours he was employed. It was agreed also to draw the attention of the police to the malicious damage being done in the public park, and to ask them to give this matter their attention.

Broadway, Prestwick, on Sunday evening one of the most moving heard there under the auspices of the M.O.I.

Ex-Provost Ferguson, who presided, told the audience that Mr Honig, although born in Poland, is a naturalised British subject.

At the outset his subject, "Europe In Chains," led him o speak of the chaining of prisoners, which had shocked people everywhere, and he gave an imaginary dialogue between Dr. Goebbels and Hitler which was punctuated with laughter. He showed that Hitler's patience was at an end, and he added, "his patience from time to time comes to an end." Hitler told Goebbels that he could stand it no longer, and the latter exhorts him to chain the prisoners taken in the raids. Hitler says, "Oh no! it is too terrible. Are we Germans or are we Englishmen or Scotsmen, or what are we?" It was, said the speaker, a most diabolical and devilish type of propaganda that was put over by Goebbels. But he (the speaker) could assure them that there were to-day hundreds of thousands of people literally in chains under the Nazis — good and true men and women, languishing and dying in concentration camps. Because of the inherent kindness of the British people it was difficult for them to realise what was meant by a massacre of 53,000 people in one town alone, mentioned the other day by Mr Churchill. They simply could not realise it. People seemed to forget that since 1924, the youth of Germany had been schooled in murder and crime. When he heard people saing that they were fighting Hitler it made his blood boil; they were not fighting Hitler; they could "get" Hitler, and they would "get" him, but the Poles, the Russians and the Jews would get him first. (Applause.) What he wanted to impress upon them was that it was not Hitler they were fighting and whom they must destroy, but four million and more little Hitlers. Hitler was merely a figurehead, and the German army general staff really despised him. He must warn them against wishful thinking; he would be an enemy of the Allies, their mortal enemy, if he told them that the task ahead was going to be an easy one. It was not going to be easy because the Germans were beginning now, slowly, to realise that they were not liked in the world; indeed, very much disliked, and it was up to them to transform that feeling into action. Having described how thousands of children were dying of starvation in many towns and cities of occupied countries, the speaker drew a terrible picture of the fate that befel people whom he had known in happier days, and having done so, exclaimed in agony—"How can I explain such horrors to the people of Scotland? I can only speak your language indifferently. How can I explain the agony and the suffering that these people are going through?" He concluded by an exhortation to the people of Britain to see to it that such horrors could not happen here, and that they would strive on to help the enslaved peoples of Europe to regain their freedom.

10th July 1942

JOTTINGS

Monkton and Prestwick Nursing Association has been granted permission to hold Forget-Me-Not Day at the Cross, Prestwick, on Saturday, July 25.

An application by Mr Robert Horne, desiring permission to run a carnival in the public park at Prestwick during the Glasgow Fair has been refused by the Town Council.

Prestwick has now completed 239 air raid shelters which will provide accommodation for 3002 persons, and Morrison table shelters to accommodate 138 persons have been distributed.

Bailie Dougan, Prestwick, having directed attention to the restriction placed on the numbers allowed into the dances in the Town Hall, it has been explained that the police desired the restriction imposed.

At the request of the director of education children at present attending a holiday camp in the High School, Prestwick, are to have swimming instruction at the bathing pool on the same terms as the local school pupils.

Ayr Kiddies' Concert Party are to give a show in the Picture House, High Street, on Sunday evening, July 26, in aid of Jock's Box. It is hoped to introduce a popular guest artist. The concert is under the patronage of Colonel C. L. C. Hamilton of Rozelle, aund Bailie Willison is to preside.

As a result of collections taken at musical recitals given on June 19 and 30 by the pupils of Miss Abernethy, L.R.A.M., A.R.C.M., £4 14/- in aid of the Seamen's Canteen and £10 by the pupils of Cambusdoon preparatory school in aid of comforts for the merchant seamen have been handed over.

24th July 1942

BURGH OF PRESTWICK — BATHING LAKE

OPEN GALA

(Under S.A.S.A. and W.C.A.S.A. Rules)
by the
PRESTWICK AMATEUR SWIMMING CLUB

On SATURDAY, 1st AUGUST

At 3 15 p.m. Doors open at 2.30 p.m.
Chairman—Councillor STEELE
(Convener, Attractions Committee)

Events:
100 Yards Free Style, Open, Gents.
(H.M. Forces)
50 Yards Handicap, Open, Ladies
50 Yards Handicap, Open, Gents.
35 Yards Blindfold Race, Open, Ladies
Under-Water Swimming, Open, Gents.
Display by Members of H.M. Forces
Four-a-Side Relay Race (Gents.), Cumnock Kilmarnock, Troon Prestwick
Mixed Relay Race (3 Ladies, 3 Gents.) Cumnock, Kilmarnock, Troon, Prestwick
Exhibition of Diving by Messrs F. MORT and R. HUNTER.

COMEDY ITEMS
POLO MATCH—PRESTWICK v. TROON

Entries (FREE) to Lake Superintendent
Entries (FREE) for Open Handicap Races to Mr E. MURRAY, 115 Elderpark Street, Glasgow, S.W.1, by 30th July.

ADMISSION (including Tax):
ADULTS, 9d; JUVENILES, 6d;
H.M. FORCES (in uniform) 6d
Season and Period Tickets do not permit to this Gala
Gala Covener, Mr F. S. BERKLEY

17th July 1942

LONG SERVICE

Medal For Prestwick Postman

The name of Mr William Lambie, postman, Prestwick, appeared at the week-end in a list of officers of the Home Civil Service awarded the Imperial Service Medal.

Mr Lambie has been a well-known and popular figure in the sister burgh for many years, indeed, since his youthful days, as his period of service with the Post Office in Prestwick extends to over 47 years, and he is still on part-time owing to the demands of the war. A certificate from the Postmaster-General re-received by Mr Lambie expresses appreciation of the faithful service rendered to the State during a period of more than 47 years. Mr Lambie belongs to Mauchline, but went to Prestwick as a schoolboy, and on leaving school entered the postal service at Prestwick as a telegraph messenger, the post office in those days being at Bute Place (61 Main Street), a small place compared with the modern premises of to-day, rendered necessary by the expansion of the burgh. Later, Mr Lambie was associated with the office at the Kettledrum (49 Main Street), and then for long was at the other building in Main Street before the change over to the premises at The Cross. Mr Lambie was appointed postman at the age of 18, and has been continuously engaged since then, with the exception of the last Great War, when he served as a combatant in the 3rd Scottish Rifles, the 17th H.L.I., and the 9th Royal Scots, and he was later with the Royal Engineers (postal section) in France with the army of occupation after the war.

He has served under five sub-postmasters — Messrs MacPherson, Arthur, Sim, Kirk and Halliday—and served under each with much acceptance. Mr Lambie recalls a time when thatched houses were quite common both in Main Street and Church Street, but it was now changed days as he explained, and one could almost detect a lurking regret that much which was picturesque in the town of the former Freemen had passed to the limbo of forgotten things.

17th July 1942

HERO'S DEATH

Prestwick Fusilier's Deed

The story of the heroic death of Private Edwin Bunyan, R.S.F. (aged 28), in the invasion of Madagascar, is told in a letter received by his mother from the commander of her son's platoon.

In the letter it is stated that, "He was one of the finest soldiers in the regiment, and gallantly gave his life to save his comrades. It was by that gallant self sacrifice that the remainder of his section remain alive. He saw death hurtling towards them in the form of a high explosive bomb and, realising instantly the danger to his comrades, he threw himself forward and smothered the bomb with his own body as it exploded."

"Edwin's name," continued the letter, "will live for ever in the history of the R.S.F. as a man who, by unequalled heroism, died so that his comrades could live and triumph during the British invasion of Madagascar on May 6, 1942."

The letter was signed by the platoon commander, Peter M. Welsh.

Private Bunyan, who is the only son of Mr and Mrs A. Bunyan, 25 Boydfield Avenue, Prestwick, was called to the forces in 1940, and prior to that was employed as a porter with the L.M.S. Railway Company at Prestwick Station. He was for a time previous to that assistant greenkeeper on Prestwick Bowling Green. In his youth Private Bunyan was an enthusiastic member of the 11th Prestwick Company of the Boys' Brigade, and held the rank of staff-sergeant in that organisation.

31st July 1942

ALLOTMENTS

Prestwick Council And Produce

DAMAGE TO TREES

At the outset of the monthly meeting of Prestwick Town Council held in the Burgh Chambers on Tuesday evening, Provost Dunsmore, who presided, moved that the council send a letter of condolence to the Rev. Luke McQuitty on the great loss sustained in the death of Mrs McQuitty.

This was unanimously agreed to.

It was reported that a letter had been received from the Department of Agriculture regarding the disposal of surplus produce from allotments. The Department suggested that they get in touch with the local food officer.

Bailie Brown said he thought the council should take a greater interest in the allotments in the burgh. In Ayr the allotments had been a great success, and it could be so in Prestwick but the council did not take enough interest in them. He thought there was a good deal of food being produced on them and a good deal of surplus for which a market would have to be found.

Provost Dunsmore said the allotments at St. Ninian's golf course were sadly handicapped by the lack of water. There was no water laid on there, and it was most disheartening for the allotment holders to see their crops wither away before their eyes. He suggested that before next season something be done about the matter.

Mr Steele remarked that there had been no time during the season when he had noticed the need for watering.

Mr Sawyers agreed with Bailie Brown, and suggested that they should send the surplus to hospitals or some other charitable institutions.

Bailie Brown said that he wanted the council to give all the help possible. He had no doubt that if they assisted and co-operated with the Allotments Committee in the disposal of the surplus it would eliminate the waste.

Mr Adamson said the allotment holders had done very well; the allotments along Mansewell Road were some of the finest in the place.

The Provost referred to the allotments they had at St. Ninian's golf course, and to the trouble they were having with children stealing the beans and peas. He suggested that they might put up a notice in the hope that it might deter the children.

Bailie Govan suggested that they might put up a notice, "Please do not steal the beans and peas." (Laughter.)

This led to a discussion on the damage being done by children to the trees at the roadsides in various parts of the burgh.

Mr Kinghorn instanced the trees in Monkton Road, and said that many of these had been broken down by children.

Mr Sawyers also referred to trees in another part of the town which were receiving rough treatment at the hands of the children.

The Provost, returning to the original question, said he thought that the solution of the question regarding the disposal of the surplus allotments produce lay with the food officer.

The council agreed.

HOUSING SCHEMES.

A minute of meeting of the Housing Committee bore that there was submitted a report by Mr Mair, architect, in regard to the progress that was being made with the building at the housing scheme in view of the present circumstances, and the same was noted. It was also indicated that a letter had been received from the Department of Health indicating that they were not in a position to release further timber immediately, and asking for further details in regard to the stage of advancement of the houses involved.

COURAGEOUS CO-OPERATION

THE men who first taught the Home Guard how to be 'tough' were firm believers in Co-operation. They knew that modern war calls for initiative; especially in the lower ranks. They knew that the days of " Ours not to reason why . . ." were ended. They knew that initiative arises from confidence in Co-operation.

To-day, the whole of the British Isles is garrisoned by trained, disciplined bodies of Men-With-Initiative; men who, because of close-knit Co-operation, are able and ready to take on all comers—at any time, anywhere, anyhow!

The Home Guard is still in being. Should the day ever come when it will have to be disbanded, then some believer in Co-operation will eulogise the Force in terms similar to those used by Tom Wintringham when speaking of his comrades of the 16th Battalion of the International Brigade: "They were known by the men who commanded them and by the men they commanded to be equals in courage and in comradeship to the fighting men of the past whose names wake pride in the Scottish, Irish, and English peoples."

4th September 1942

PRESTWICK WORK

Progress Of British Restaurant

It was reported at a meeting of the Prestwick Town Council held in the Council Chambers there on Tuesday—Bailie Brown presiding in the absence of Provost Dunsmore—that the foundation of Prestwick's British Restaurant had been laid and work was proceeding well.

This information was given in answer to a question put by Mr Duncan as to when the restaurant would be functioning. The council were also informed that the restaurant would probably be in working order in about six months' time.

Mr F. Pritty, burgh engineer, was asked to try and hurry on the work as much as possible.

BILLETING.

Mr Blunt said that there was another case of a local war-worker not being able to find rooms in Prestwick, and he had to cycle from Maybole to his work in the pit every morning.

Mr W. Shaw, town clerk, explained that the order for billeting applied only to aerodrome workers and not to miners.

Bailie Brown said that it had been brought to the notice of the council that some of the ladies in the burgh were not intimating to the billeting officer when lodgers were leaving, and he thought the matter should be given publicity, because if they did not report to the billeting officer as soon as such persons left their house, they would find themselves in serious trouble.

VITAL STATISTICS.

Dr. Bignold, the medical officer of health, reported that during the month ended August 25 there were 10 births, 7 males and 3 females, equal to a rate of 12.1 per 1000 per annum of the population. There were 7 marriages, equal to a rate of 8.4 per 1000 per annum.. Of the 13 deaths registered, equal to a rate of 15.7 per 1000, 6 were of 65 years or upwards. Four cases of infectious disease were notified and removed to hospital.

WATER.

The water engineer (Mr F. Pritty) reported that the depth of water in the reservoir on August 25 last was 26 feet 3 inches, being 31,745,390 gallons in storage. The rainfall for the month to August 25 was 4.41 inches as compared with 4.71 inches for the corresponding month last year. The Loch Bradan meter indicated a total consumpt for the month to date of 10,000,000 gallons, being an average daily consumpt of 400,000 gallons. The Venturi meter indicated a total consumpt for the month to date of 17,533,000 gallons, being an average daily consumpt of 701,320 gallons.

WASTE PAPER DRIVE.

Mr Pritty's report contained figures realised for waste materials, which showed that for June the amount received for paper was £138 16s 6d and for July £141 15s 1d. There was an increase of £255 6s 4d on the amount received for waste materials to the end of July as compared with the same period of last year. The total amount of paper collected in May, June and July in connection with the National contest was 54 tons 3¾ cwts.

Shelters providing accommodation for 3242 persons have been provided, it was reported, and Morrison table shelters have also been distributed.

OTHER MATTERS.

Mr Duncan put a suggestion to the council that the cemetery gates should be opened at 11 a.m. instead of 2 p.m., and the suggestion was noted.

It was agreed to send the burgh surveyor (Mr F. Pritty) to the annual conference of the Town and County Planning Association at Bridge of Allan on September 12 and 13.

28th August 1942

WOMAN C.O.

Former Prestwick War Worker's Appeal

At a sitting of the Conscientious Objectors' Appeal Tribunal in Edinburgh on Wednesday the cases heard—for the first time—were those concerned with applications by women to have their names restored to the roll of conscientious objectors. Lord Elphinstone presided.

Miss Jeanette B. Wright, 70 St. Quivox Road, Prestwick, admitted that during the period of the present war she had worked for 14 months in a large engineering establishment very much concerned with war work. Her explanation was that she had done that to please her mother, but on the latter's death she had given that work up in favour of her present vocation. She was at present engaged in teaching children with the object of bringing out and developing culture, and she added, "There is nothing more important to me."

The decision in her case was that her work in that direction would be continued in a children's hospital or war-time nursery.

Please Mummy!

Keep those Sunlight Flakes for my *bonnet* and *gloves*

Go gently with those Sunlight Flakes! Keep them for washing Baby's things —and see how gently *they* deal with the wash. And here are two worth-while hints: Measure out with a spoon just enough flakes to give a satisfactory lather. Use just sufficient water to cover the clothes. These hints will make your ration go further.

Sold loose at 7½d per lb.

3 oz.—ONE COUPON

Not obtainable in Eire

BF105-836-65

LEVER BROTHERS, PORT SUNLIGHT, LIMITED

PRESTWICK M.C.

Saved Men And Tank

A letter has been received by Captain and Mrs Randal Findlay, Queen's Hotel, Prestwick, and at present of Kirkton Inn, Dalrymple, from their elder son Captain John C. Balharrie, Royal Tank Regiment, which gives them the news that he has received the Military Cross for services rendered in Libya. The honour has since been gazetted.

The citation concerning Captain Balharrie is as follows: "On July 22, 1942, while heavily engaged with strong enemy forces, the tank troop

led by Captain John Charles Balharrie became involved in an enemy minefield. This officer at once dismounted in full view of the enemy and under fire cleared a path by lifting wires. He then led his tanks on foot out of the mines. This gallant action undoubtedly saved his tanks from total destruction."

The letter received by his mother tells how during an enemy attack at the end of May he was taken prisoner by a German column which worked round to their rear and cut them off. While the British artillery were shelling the enemy column the British prisoners were making a nuisance of themselves in an endeavour to delay the Germans as much as possible. The letter goes on to say: "up to this time I had been with my men, as I had taken down my badges of rank, because all captured officers are flown immediately to Italy. All this time I had been keeping my eyes open with a view to escaping, but the opportunity had not occurred. Suddenly there was a lot of commotion, and the Germans started loading us back into the lorries again and started to move off. It seemed some of our tanks were attacking. I managed to hide behind a burnt out lorry with some of my men and when the Germans moved off crept to one of our lorries which had been abandoned. All this time the German tanks were firing on our men and I was between them.

Anyhow, I got into the lorry with 20 men and drove off at a high speed. We were fired on but managed to get away. I drove for about 40 miles, and luckily I managed to conceal my compass. Unfortunately we ran on to one of our own minefields and were blown up; but somehow only one man was wounded and we were soon back in our own lines. By a piece of luck I met up with my unit next morning."

Capt. Balharrie, who is 22 years of age, was a Glasgow Academical and while at the Academy took an active part in the O.T.C. and won the prize for the best platoon officer three years in succession. On leaving school he commenced his studies preparatory to entering Sandhurst but at the outbreak of war enlisted and received his commission. At the age of 21 he was promoted captain. He has been in Libya for a year. His younger brother is serving with the R.A.F. and is stationed in Karachi.

18th December 1942

BIRTHDAY MESSAGE

Prestwick Flier's Clever Feat

Using a rocky island to screen his approach the Scottish pilot of a Coastal Command Hampden aircraft surprised a heavily escorted convoy off the Norwegian coast on Wednesday of last week and hit a medium-sized supply ship with a torpedo, states the Air Ministry News Service.

"I first sighted the convoy in a narrow channel between steep cliffs and a number of small islands," said the pilot, Flight Sergeant John Strain, of 21 Grangemuir Road, Prestwick. "There was an escort vessel with each supply ship, but not one of them spotted us.

"I went down low, came round the back of an island and let go my torpedo before they knew we were there.

"The ships were taken completely by surprise, and it was only when we were well away that my rear-gunner saw the ships open fire with a few bursts of machine-gun fire which did not come anywhere near us.

"Before we got round the far side of the island I saw the torpedo run straight towards the largest ship, and less than a minute later there was a cloud of brown smoke coming from forward of the bridge where the torpedo struck home."

Flight Sergeant Strain is the youngest son of Mr S. Strain, and the late Mrs Strain, 21 Grangemuir Road, Prestwick. He is a native of Glasgow, where he was educated at Shawlands Academy and the Royal Technical College. He was training for an accountancy career but in 1937 gave up that idea and joined the Glasgow Squadron of the R.A.F. After serving there for a period of about four years he volunteered for the R.A.F.V.R., but was rejected on medical grounds. He was for some time a commercial traveller with Messrs. Walter Gregory and Company, selling animal medicines. He then went before a medical board again, and was accepted. Flight Sergeant Strain is 30 years of age, and his thrilling encounter with the enemy took place on his birthday.

An older brother, Sam, is in the Royal Corps of Signals and holds the rank of sergeant. Sam, who came through Dunkirk and had exciting experiences in France, served throughout the Great War.

STOP THAT TAP DRIPPING!

Do you know that a hot tap can drip away 3 gallons of water a day wasting the heating power of 1½ lbs. of coal?

Multiply this by the millions of wasteful taps in the Country. Think how thousands of tons of coal can be saved to make more Guns, Planes, Ships and Tanks.

If we all cut down the use of hot water for baths and other purposes, the saving will be greater still.

Never waste any water, hot or cold. Turn all taps right off. Start now.

LESS WATER— MORE PLANES

ISSUED BY THE MINISTRY OF FUEL AND POWER

1943

Russian troops defeated the German attack at Stalingrad.

The R.A.F. raided Berlin.

Churchill broadcast on post-war reconstruction.

Mussolini fell from power in Italy, which was invaded by the Allies.

Soviet troops took back territory captured by the Germans.

Churchill, Roosevelt and Stalin met to plan the final overthrow of Germany.

Italy surrendered unconditionally to the Allies and declared war on Germany.

8th January 1943

CLUNE ROAD

Prestwick Town Council Decision

NEW MEMBER

At the monthly meeting of Prestwick Town Council held in the Burgh Chambers there on Tuesday evening, Mr Robt. L. MacDonald, 30 Broompark Avenue, Prestwick, took his seat as a councillor of the burgh. Mr MacDonald was co-opted to the vacancy caused by the resignation of ex-Bailie Brown in the Third Ward.

Provost Dunsmore, on behalf of the magistrates and councillors welcomed Mr MacDonald, and said that he had come to them with experience on practical and commercial lines. He hoped the work on the council would be congenial, and that he would have a pleasant time amongst them.

After the War

Before proceeding with the meeting Provost Dunsmore said that he would like to extend to them heartiest wishes for a prosperous New Year. During the past year they had had many troubles and tribulations, but they could now see the silver lining in the clouds. He hoped they would work not only for the victory which would certainly be theirs, but for the peace which would follow. There would be plenty of work before the council to consider and carry out ideas of what they were going to make Prestwick after the war.

A Protest

Bailie Dougan protested to the council that the minutes of the meeting of the Housing Committee were not correct. There had, he said, been questions and answers at the meeting which had not been put into the minutes. People who had access to the minutes were asking why they did not make any decisions, and he wanted this matter put right.

It was agreed that the items mentioned should be included in the minutes.

Mr Steele drew attention to the motion to increase the rents which Mr Duncan had placed before the council at the last meeting, and said that he considered the council should take a broader view of that matter and should allow every councillor to vote. There were three councillors living in municipally-owned houses and they had not been allowed to vote. They represented a large proportion of the people in the burgh.

It was explained by the Provost that they depended on Mr Shaw to instruct them on matters of law, and it was illegal for any person with any interest in a matter to vote. That was the law and they could not go against it.

Cadet Dance.—Prestwick Company, Army Cadet Force, held on Monday in the Town Hall a Christmas dance. Among those present were: Provost Dunsmore, Major Leitch and C/Major and Mrs Kennedy Smith, Ayr. During the evening C/Capt. MacBean spoke of the success of this movement in Prestwick and C/Major Kennedy Smith presented the badge of Certificate A to C.S.M. Dunn, Corpl. Tnom, and L/Corpl. Kinghorn, and congratulated the company on its progress. Corpl. Anderson and Drummer Buxton (pipe and drums), Cadet Anderson (mouth organ), Miss Kirby (songs), and potted pantomime, written and produced by Lieuts. Milligan and McEwan, added to th eevening's entertainment. All the parts were taken by the officers and sergeants, and the local allusions were much appreciated. Posters adorning the walls embodied training precepts but applied to the evening's fun.

Red Cross. — During the school term, from September to December, 1942, the children of Glenburn Public School have subscribed £4 15s to the funds of the Red Cross. In September £1 was sent to the British Red Cross; in November, collections at the school film shows brought in £1 5s which was sent to Mrs Churchill's "Aid to Russia" Fund, and at a children's concert of Christmas carols held in the school on Tuesday of last week, the children subscribed £2 10s, which has been sent to the "United Aid to China" Fund.

FOOD FACTS

GOOD RESOLUTIONS

Rations. Vegetables. Grain Foods

Remember the balanced diet!

1943

—a New Year on the Kitchen Front. Another chance for making and *keeping* those good resolutions of yours.

You've always planned to take up all your allowance of Household Milk and Dried Egg. You've always meant to make use of your full cheese ration. You've always intended to eat potatoes instead of bread. You've often thought of serving more vegetables.

Well, here again is your opportunity to do all those things you've always meant to do on the food front. You make the resolutions, follow the method given here, and you'll keep them in 1943.

POET'S CORNER

Auntie threw her rinds away.
To the lock-up she was taken.
There she is and there she'll stay
Till she learns to save her bacon.

•

When in winter Nature limits what the *cows* hold
Your trusty grocer helps you out with ' Household '.

•

Don't waste fuel
On a vegetabuel;
It's more to your credit
To shred it.

LISTEN TO THE KITCHEN FRONT EVERY MORNING AT 8.15

1943 IN THE KITCHEN :—

1 See that each one of the family has his own full rations, and remember this includes Dried Egg and Household Milk. Make the most of your cheese ration.

2 Eat at least 1 lb. of potatoes every day. Don't peel them. Cook them in their skins. They are better for you and tastier, too.

3 Eat plenty of green vegetables and salads, and when you can't get greens eat root vegetables, especially swedes and carrots.

4 Cook your vegetables the modern way. Use very little boiling water. Shred or slice your vegetables first. Cook very quickly with the lid on. Eat as soon as cooked.

1943 IN THE SHOPS :—

5 Do your shopping in as few bits as possible. It will save the shopkeeper's time and paper. Try and buy a week's supply of goods at one time. This isn't easy for you, but your shopkeeper, who is very short-handed, will be *very* grateful.

6 Take paper or piece of cloth to wrap your shopping in. Especially save paper at the butcher's whenever possible.

7 Always return milk bottles well rinsed and don't forget to save the milk bottle caps for the milkman.

1943 IN THE LARDER :—

8 Don't throw away a scrap of food. Bits of leftover fish or vegetables make splendid sandwich fillings. Odds and ends of bread can be used in puddings. Use cheese rind for flavouring sauces. Shred the outside leaves of cabbages and use them in soups and stews.

9 Don't hoard your Dried Egg. It is meant to be used now. Keep it in a dry cool place.

10 Don't forget to ask for your Household Milk at the grocers. And read the instructions on the tin before you use it.

THE MINISTRY OF FOOD. LONDON. W.1.   FOOD FACTS No. 130

Clune Road

Mr Steele, before speaking to his motion "that the name of Glenburn Road be changed to Clune Road," asked the town clerk if the changing of the name would entail any expense for the householders in altering title deeds or any other matter.

Mr Shaw said that there would be no such difficulty. When a person wished to sell a house all that was necessary was to say — sometime known as Glenburn Road and now as Clune Road.

Mr Steele then told the council that there had been a great deal of confusion between Glenburn Road and Glenburn Rows. There was a new part of the road near completion which would run past what they called the Clune wood and he moved that the name ben altered to Clune Road.

Bailie Blunt seconded, and it was agreed that the name should be changed.

Vegetables v. Flowers

Bailie Dunlop, speaking to this motion "that vegetables should be grown instead of flowers on corporation ground," said that in the national emergency they had to grow as much food as possible. They had to get vegetables for their British Restaurant and the cheapest way was to grow them themselves.

Mr Flanigan seconded.

Mr Brock said that as convener of the Parks Committee it behoved him to say a word. He did not think the plots they had in which flowers were grown would be suitable for growing vegetables. He quite agreed that it would be a good thing to grow these but the cost would be great and they would not be able to get the necessary manure. The burgh gardener considered that only the plot in Marchburn Road was suitable. He therefore moved an amendment "that they carry on as in previous years."

After further discussion, Bailie Dunlop agreed to drop the motion and have consultation later with the parks convener.

Town Planning

It was agreed that the burgh engineer and the convener of the Housing Committee, Mr Sawyers, should represent the council at the Town Planning Council.

Cleansing Grouse

Bailie Blunt, with regard to cleansing arrangements in the burgh, said that ash-buckets in the fourth ward had, at times, not been emptied for eight or nine days. Some people were even taking them and dumping them in fields. As far as cleansing went the burgh was in a terrible state. They had been remitting the matter for two or three months, and if they did not do something they would have an epidemic in the town.

The Casting Vote

A minute of a special meeting of the Town Council bore that there was submitted a letter from the secretary of the Third Ward committee recommending Mr Robert Lamb MacDonald, 30 Broompark Avenue, Prestwick, commercial manager, for co-option as a member of the Council in room of ex-Bailie Brown. After consideration Mr Steele moved that Mr Peter Pierce Power, Dunleary, 81 St. Quivox Road, Prestwick, should be appointed councillor and Bailie Dougan seconded. Mr Adamson moved that Mr Robert Lamb MacDonald, being the recommendation of the Ward committee, be appointed and Provost Dunsmore seconded. On a vote four voted for the amendment, and four for the motion, and the Provost gave his casting vote in favour of Mr MacDonald.

No Widening Of Pavement

A minute of the Roads and Footpaths committee bore that the burgh surveyor reported that the limited crossfall on the pavement on the east side of the Main Street necessitated considerable expense in regrading the roadway, and it was questionable whether materials would be released for this during the present emergency, and as the cost of the work would be nearly £350, he was of opinion that the widening should not be proceeded with at the present time. This was agreed to.

New Fire Station

A minute of the meeting of the Golf Course Shores and Public Parks committee bore that there was submitted a letter from the Fire Force Commander, Paisley, indicating that the accommodation at present available at the Fire Station was inadequate, and it was his intention to have five pumps with additional whole-time personnel stationed in Prestwick, and it would be necessary to erect two prefabricated huts and a brick built garage to house same. He also indicated that he had viewed a site at the access road on the Ladies' Golf Course, which he considered would be suitable for the purpose, and asked the authority of the Town Council for the use of this site for the duration of the war. After consideration, it was agreed to continue the matter until the next meeting of committee in order to give the committee a further opportunity of going into the matter.

Fire Guards

A minute of the meeting of the A.R.P. committee bore that there was submitted a circular letter from the Scottish Home Department regarding the procedure where a local authority posts a fire guard from its pool to business premises that are deficient in personnel, and indicating that the local authority will be relieved of responsibility for payment to the fire guard so posted, this to be paid by the occupiers.

5th February 1943

PRESTWICK
TOWN COUNCIL

That there would be no alteration in the frequency of the 'bus service from Glenburn as a result of alterations in the local services was the reply received from the S.M.T. Bus Company to a letter sent by Prestwick Town Council to ascertain the position in that respect, and which was read at the monthly meeting of the Town Council on Tuesday— Provost Dunsmore presiding.

A motion by Mr Sawyers "that the house factor be granted a bonus of £10," was remitted to the Finance committee with powers.

Mr Brock's motion "that an increase be made in the recreational facilities in the burgh," was remitted to the Golf course, shores, and public parks committee.

It was agreed to remit the letter from the burgh surveyor re obtaining a new refuse collector to the Cleansing committee.

BRITISH RESTAURANT.

A minute of the meeting of the British Restaurant committee bore that there was submitted a letter from the burgh surveyor indicating that he hoped to have everything completed by February 27, and that arrangements might now be made for the opening on that date. It was agreed to leave it to the convener, sub-convener, and town clerk to make the necessary arrangements in regard to sending out of invitations. It was also indicated that some applications had been received for the position of cook-supervisor and manageress. It was also agreed to leave this matter in the hands of the convener, sub-convener, and town clerk to make the appointment. The report submitted to the council by the burgh surveyor bore that the construction of the British Restaurant was well advanced. The first-coat painting of the inside walls and roof had been completed, all cooking equipment set in position, and this was at present being connected up with various services. The installation of central heating apparatus was proceeding.

Ten plain facts about

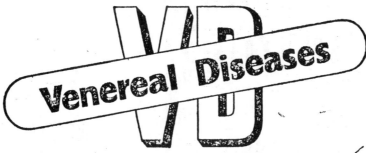

Venereal Diseases are alarmingly on the increase. Their spread should be prevented by every possible means.

Thomas Johnston

SECRETARY OF STATE FOR SCOTLAND.

1. Venereal Diseases have increased since the war and are still increasing; 70,000 new cases are now occurring yearly among civilians alone. Venereal diseases cause much misery. They bring tragedy into many homes, and considerably damage our war effort by causing reduced efficiency and wasted hours.

2. Ignorance and secrecy are highly dangerous. Only from a plain and frank statement of the facts can we all know what these diseases are, how they are spread, how they can be avoided and how and where they can be cured.

3. The two principal venereal diseases are syphilis and gonorrhœa. They are caused by quite different living organisms or germs.

4. Syphilis is a dangerous, a killing disease. If not treated early and thoroughly by a doctor it can cause serious mutilation, heart disease, paralysis, and insanity, any of which may be fatal. Syphilis can be passed on to an unborn child from its mother and (unless skilled treatment is given early in pregnancy) is one of the causes of blindness, deafness, and mental defects.

5. Gonorrhœa, though not so dangerous to life, is more serious than is generally believed, and is one of the causes of arthritis, sterility, and chronic ill-health.

6. Syphilis and gonorrhœa are almost always contracted through intercourse with an infected person. The germs of these diseases quickly die outside the human body. In practice, therefore, there is no need to fear their spread by accidental infection.

7. Clean living is the only way to avoid infection : abstinence is not harmful. Free and easy sex behaviour must mean a risk of infection and cannot be made safe. An infected person may convey the infection to an innocent partner.

8. Venereal diseases can be cured if treated *early* by a specialist doctor. Advice and treatment are available at all local authorities' clinics set up for the purpose. Treatment is free, confidential and *effective*. Any family doctor or Medical Officer of Health will give the address of the nearest clinic. Quack treatment or self-treatment is absolutely useless and may even be disastrous.

9. Disappearance of the early symptoms does not necessarily mean that the patient has been cured. It is essential to continue the treatment until the doctor says it may be stopped.

10. Anyone who has the slightest reason to suspect infection should seek medical treatment AT ONCE. A doctor or clinic should be consulted immediately about any suspicious sore or unusual discharge. It may not be venereal disease, but it is best to be sure.

Further information can be obtained IN CONFIDENCE from the Medical Officer of Health.

ISSUED BY THE DEPARTMENT OF HEALTH FOR SCOTLAND
(V.D.1 SCOTLAND)

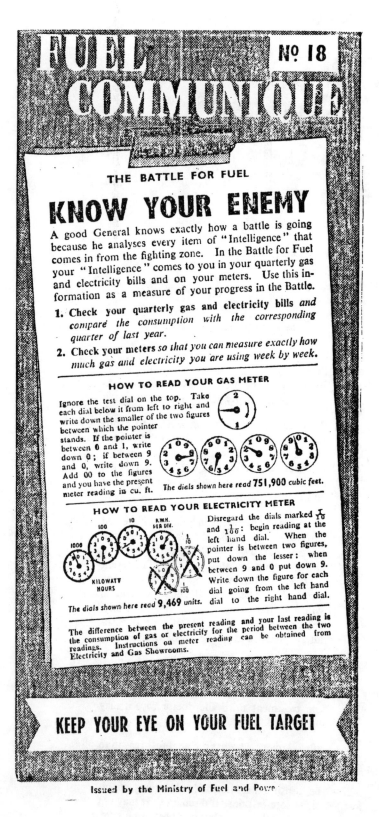

FUEL COMMUNIQUE

No. 18

THE BATTLE FOR FUEL

KNOW YOUR ENEMY

A good General knows exactly how a battle is going because he analyses every item of "Intelligence" that comes in from the fighting zone. In the Battle for Fuel your "Intelligence" comes to you in your quarterly gas and electricity bills and on your meters. Use this information as a measure of your progress in the Battle.

1. **Check your quarterly gas and electricity bills** and compare the consumption with the corresponding quarter of last year.

2. **Check your meters** so that you can measure exactly how much gas and electricity you are using week by week.

HOW TO READ YOUR GAS METER

Ignore the test dial on the top. Take each dial below it from left to right and write down the smaller of the two figures between which the pointer stands. If the pointer is between 0 and 1, write down 0; if between 9 and 0, write down 9. Add 00 to the figures and you have the present meter reading in cu. ft.

The dials shown here read 751,900 cubic feet.

HOW TO READ YOUR ELECTRICITY METER

Disregard the dials marked ⅟₁₀ and ⅟₁₀₀: begin reading at the left hand dial. When the pointer is between two figures, put down the lesser; when between 9 and 0 put down 9. Write down the figure for each dial going from the left hand dial to the right hand dial.

The dials shown here read 9,469 units.

The difference between the present reading and your last reading is the consumption of gas or electricity for the period between the two readings. Instructions on meter reading can be obtained from Electricity and Gas Showrooms.

KEEP YOUR EYE ON YOUR FUEL TARGET

Issued by the Ministry of Fuel and Power

26th February 1943

SALUTE TO THE RED ARMY

Sir Patrick Dollan At Prestwick Meeting

'Had there been an alliance between Britain, Russia and America round about 1920 the rise of Fascism in Italy and Nazism in Germany, and the present conflict might have been avoided was one of the views advanced by Sir Patrick Dollan, Glasgow, when he addressed a large meeting in the Broadway picture house, Prestwick, on Sunday evening, under the aegis of the Ministry of Information. Mr G. Macindoe presided.

The speaker's subject, "Mutual Aid for Britain and Russia" gave him ample scope for wandering over a wide field, and this he did, touching on many phases of the war and the peace that will follow. An understanding between Russia and Britain, he said, was necessary not only for the winning of the war but for the making of the peace which would be more difficult, in his opinion, than the winning of the war. An effective peace would only be possible if all, irrespective of class, party, nationality and creed were willing to make whatever sacrifices were necessary to give that peace basic foundations at home and abroad. (Applause.) Incidentally, he might say to those who were planning a new world and a new heaven that he could not see that this country or any country would be flowing with milk and honey when the war was over. Great Britain that day was celebrating with their allies the 25th anniversary of the formation of the Red Army, and that afternoon he had attended a meeting in Glasgow representative of all parties, and at which speeches were made by Mr Duff Cooper and Mr Tom Johnston. He was reminded at that meeting that it was exactly 26 years ago since he presided in the same hall to welcome the Russian Revolution in 1917, or almost a year before the Red Army came into being. He had felt then that the overthrow of Czardom in Russia was the beginning of a new democracy, and that the time would come when it would be of great assistance not only culturally but in trade, commerce and in many directions, and had an alliance between Britain, America, and Russia been brought about in 1920 he was sure there would have been no rise of Fascism in Italy or Nazism in Germany, and that this war would have been prevented. It took a long time for new ideas to take root in the minds of peoples, and the pioneers, of whom he thought he was one in this connection, must get some grain of second-hand satisfaction, as he had done that day, in seeing the platform party that assembled in Glasgow for the celebration of the Red Army, because he could recall that not one of them was there 26 years ago. Examining what had been done by Russia in the past 25 years, the speaker said it was a mistake for the perfervid admirers of Russia in Great Britain to assume that because some workers had been improved in some parts of Russia that the whole level of the workers there was comparable with the social level of workers in Great Britain, because such was not the case, and it would be foolish to expect that it would be so because a nation in 25 years could not expect to establish a standard that had taken Britain almost two centuries to establish.

A BRAVE PEOPLE.

Pointing out that nationhood above everything else had brought out the best that was in Russia and in Britain, Sir Patrick said that an international basis could only be erected upon the foundations of nationhood, giving to each country its own place, its own culture, and at the same time allowing it to make its own contribution to the advancement of the whole. When they celebrated the formation of the Red Army they did so particularly out of a spirit of gratitude because many of them felt that had it not been for the strong stand taken by Russia in the last 18 months the course of the war might have turned in a different direction. When they saluted the Red Army they could not but respect the fortitude and the sacrifice of the Russian people. In Leningrad there had been no household coal for two winters—all the services which meant so much to people living in cities had been cut off or disorganised—but the people had fought on, and they had been asked in this country to conserve fuel, the idea being that some of it so saved could be sent to Leningrad and other relieved cities of Russia. The Red Army could not have accomplished the great deeds they had achieved had the people behind the army not been as brave as those in uniform. (Applause.) Commenting on the many houses that would be necessary to replace those in the ruined cities and towns of Russia, the speaker commended the policy adopted in Russia to-day of completing the building of houses that had been started before the war in many parts, remarking that there was nothing so demoralising as to see civilians without homes. "I feel," he said, "that a good deal of American help for Russia and the bravery of the men of the convoys to Murmansk and elsewhere, Sir Patrick condemned the clamour of those who wanted a second front, remarking that they had many fronts at the present time, and an invasion of Europe should not be undertaken until all the equipment was available in order to give their forces a chance of following up with success. He mentioned that it had taken 825 ships to carry the men and materials for Egypt and North Africa, and this represented the output of shipyard workers in this country working seven days a week for three years, which gave some idea of the marine transport required to land and maintain a modern army. There was still much to do before the mortal blow was administered to the enemy, and while they celebrated the accomplishment of the Red Army they in this country should not lag behind in making all the sacrifices they could to enable us to deliver a telling blow at the enemies of mankind. Alluding briefly to the recent debate in the House of Commons on the Beveridge Report, he suggested that people should not get too heated about something that might not concern them for several years. Concluding and making reference to the treaty with Russia which was to last for 20 years after the war, the speaker expressed the hope that it would last for all time, because these were two nations that were concerned with the standard of living of their own people; and in the scheme of things he wanted to see a France, resurrected and strong, Poland and other countries making their contribution.

There were numerous questions at the close, which Sir Patrick answered with evident zest, so much so that he suggested that at a future date there might be a meeting for questions only.

Answering one as to why Hess was not shot, Sir Patrick said it was unfortunate that he was not shot when sailing over Ayrshire, but to have shot him since his capture would have resulted in reprisals on some of our prisoners. In replying to another question he said he could not help thinking that Sir William Beveridge had got far more fun out of the recent discussion than anyone else. He declared that the Report was not new as a man called Robert Burns wrote the basic principles of it in "Man was made to mourn." (Laughter.) Sir Patrick, mentioning the sacrifices that would have to be made, said one of the greatest authorities in the world had informed him that there would be a seven years' scarcity in Europe after the war.

A hearty vote of thanks was accorded at the close.

5th March 1943

PRESTWICK'S BRITISH RESTAURANT

Sir Thos. Moore M.P. On Their Advantages

A new rivalry amongst Ayrshire seaboard towns was mentioned on Saturday at the opening of the bright, attractive and well-equipped British restaurant at Prestwick, opened on Saturday afternoon, in presence of a representative gathering, by Sir Thomas Moore, C.B.E., M.P. for Ayr Burghs.

Prior to the luncheon on Saturday which took the form of the usual substantial meal to be obtained by the workers there, the company inspected the premises and were high in their praise of the accommodation provided for 250 diners and the modern equipment for cooking and preparing the food behind the scenes. The restaurant is situated at the United Services Club in Templerigg Street, and the dining hall is an entirely new building.

The Rev. Luke M'Quitty, Monkton and Prestwick, asked a blessing on the restaurant and the food

Provost Dunsmore, who presided, characterised the opening of the restaurant as "a unique and historic event and a milestone in the municipal life of Prestwick." As an additional social service, it created, he said, a new relationship between the municipality and the citizens of the town. Mr Pritty, their burgh engineer, who acted as the architect for the buildings, had supervised the contractors in the construction and had certainly made the most of the site and the buildings thereon. He thought he was right in saying that Prestwick's British Restaurant was second to none of the whole of Ayrshire, if not in Scotland. They had been fortunate in securing the services of Miss Margaret Hutton, Troon, as supervisor, who had had a great deal of experience on the staff of the County Kitchen at Seafield, Ayr, and from what he had seen of her she would "fill the bill" and give customers every satisfaction. Having remarked that there seemed to be some misconception as to the type of person to be served in the restaurant, the Provost stated that meals would be served to men and women who were workers, to the general public, and to visitors.

At the outset Sir Thomas Moore stated that but for a recent bereavement, Lady Moore would have been present. A few months ago, he proceeded, when he had the privilege of opening Ayr's restaurant he had remarked that he had never seen a more compact, a more efficient or a better equipped eating house in his life. He somewhat jocularly remarked to the town clerk of Prestwick, Mr Wm. Shaw, that Prestwick had something pretty good to live up to and something pretty difficult to compete with. Mr Shaw, like another distinguished man, said: "You wait and see." (Laughter.) That remark, said Sir Thomas, had been well worth while, for he could

say with the utmost sincerity that Prestwick had lived up to its high reputation. As with its golf courses and its swimming pool, Prestwick must always have the best, and so it was with the British restaurant. (Laughter and applause.) Having referred to the origin of the British restaurant, which he hoped would play a useful and increasing part in their national life, Sir Thomas said the original purpose was to serve the working population — a term which about covered them all these days — but fundamentally it was for those engaged in the great industrial enterprise without which victory could never be achieved. Having paid tribute to Lord Woolton and to the part played by "that magnificent, courageous, self-sacrificing body known as the Merchant Navy," a remark greeted with loud applause, Sir Thomas said they had to admit that it would be quite impossible to set up, conduct, or make successful such restaurants were it not for the public spirit and sense of civic responsibility shown by local authorities.

The Catering Bill

In an allusion to the Catering Bill, recently before Parliament, Sir Thomas said the principle underneath Mr Bevin's idea was sound because, after the war, we would have visitors coming to this country, and when they did arrive we did not want merely to show them the blitzed buildings; we wanted to feed them well, and if Mr Bevin had his way, not only would we welcome the visitors but retain them. It would be hard enough to pay our way after this war without some new sources of revenue, and visitors who left us good money would be amongst our major industries. (Laughter and applause). Paraphrasing the prayer used in the Royal Navy when a new ship is launched, Sir Thomas concluded: God bless this restaurant and all who serve in it."

Provost Brown, Troon, said that at the present time Troon was making an extension of their restaurant in order that it could accommodate 60 to 80 more people. Troon, the pioneer in Ayrshire, was more or less being left behind, so it was not too much of an advantage to be first in the field. (Laughter.)

The 2001st

Alluding to the tremendous strides that had been made, Mr Ninian S. Pattman, divisional food officer, said they had now in the West of Scotland 44 British restaurants; in Ayrshire they had six and there were three others about completed which, he thought, was a very good record. Prestwick's was the 2001st restaurant in the country. (Applause.) The purpose of the British restaurant, he emphasised, was to feed everyone.

Mr J. R. Lockie, county clerk and

head of the Civil Defence services of the county area, told of the great work done in the feeding of school children, to whom 15,000 meals were served daily, and he stated that if it came to emergency feeding that figure could be doubled. Those meals would require to be transported from the central kitchen to the various areas in which they were needed, and transport would always be more difficult under blitz conditions. On behalf of the County Council he might say how much they welcomed the local facilities for feeding such as they had in several of the burghs. He congratulated Prestwick Town Council on what had been done and wished the restaurant all success. (Applause.)

Mr R. L. Angus, D.L., of Ladykirk, Monkton, who was present along with Mrs Angus, expressed satisfaction at the lunch served, remarking that it was his misfortune to travel a good deal recently and he could say that many hotels in London and Glasgow had not such good meals these days as had been supplied to them that day. He congratulated all concerned on the result of their efforts, and, as a member of the public, wished the restaurant every success in the future.

Councillor Steele, sub-convener of the Restaurant Committee, proposed an inclusive vote of thanks.

26th March 1943

War Production at Home

(To the Editor, *The Ayrshire Post*).
24 Seabank Road,
Prestwick, March 1, 1943.

Sir,—In view of the urgency for the production of arms and equipment for our armed forces, and the limited man power now available in this country, you may be able to deal with this subject in your columns.

In some of the peace-time industries of this country it is possible for certain of the operations to be carried out at home, or in a building where a number of people can be engaged at a time. It has been found that the same idea can operate successfully with certain classes of war equipment, and this is now in operation on a small scale, but can be expanded very considerably.

The technical press recently reported such a scheme, where the head-quarters were in a large room of a private house. This group have paid £500 income tax, and the remainder of the first £1500 received for work done, was given to charity.

In another district the local factory farmed out some of the work, and eventually found that they had as many man hours outside as inside the factory.

These schemes are made to suit the limited number of hours and persons available, and the work is usually of the simple repetition type, which can be learned quickly with the minimum amount of instructions.

There is no doubt that such a scheme would suit this area, but the following conditions would require to be satisfied :—

1. Work of a suitable type would be available from some factory in the neighbourhood, or in Glasgow.

2. Transport of the parts would be provided by the factory concerned, and also tools.

3. A building would be available in which to carry out the work.

4. The instructors and workers would all be volunteers, and would receive no pay, as all earnings would go to charity, but they must agree to work for a certain period each week, probably after 6 p.m. or Saturday afternoon, at the commencement of the scheme.

This scheme would undoubtedly give many persons the opportunity of engaging in some useful work for short periods each week, and thereby tend to shorten the war and aid charity.

D. P. MUIRHEAD,
A.M.I.Mech E., M.I.A.E., M.I.E I.

'*Fry's is the stuff for chaps like me*'

SAYS THE A.T.C. CADET

AT seventeen he's doing a man-size job — at work during the day, and training to be an airman too. His mother sees that he gets plenty of Fry's Cocoa all the year round. She knows it's a real food, filled with nourishment and energy, and that it's a useful source of *natural* iron, so essential to young people.

FRY'S COCOA
Real CHOCOLATE FLAVOUR
and food value

5D QTR LB · 9½D HALF LB

C565.14443

Something to look forward to

when Victory is won — VIMTO the popular non-alcoholic Bracing Beverage. With Victory VIMTO will be back again — unchanged and for your enjoyment.

VIMTO

J. N. NICHOLS & CO. LTD., MANCHESTER 16.

your new
RATION BOOKS

This year you will get, at one visit, your food ration book and clothing book (bound together but detachable) and, if you're over 16, a new identity card. **Do not post your application.**

The new books and cards are being prepared and issued in alphabetical order of holders' surnames. This and other advertisements will tell you when and where your book will be ready. It is no good going to any other place or at any other time. Take your identity card and present food ration book with you. A friend can go for you, *but only* at the time and place advertised for *your* surname.

NAMES BEGINNING:	WHEN TO GO:	WHERE TO GO:

Residents in Postal Area of
MONKTON AND PRESTWICK

A to C	TUESDAY, 18th May.	Prestwick Public School
D to H	WEDNESDAY, 19th May.	„ „ „
I to M	THURSDAY, 20th May.	„ „ „
Mc to R	FRIDAY, 21st May.	„ „ „
S to Z	SATURDAY, 22nd May.	„ „ „

Hours of Business: 10 - 1 and 2.30 - 8

If the first letter of your surname does not appear in the left-hand column above and has not been printed in an earlier announcement, you should wait until an advertisement is published later which does contain your initial. You will also find posters in your local cinema, Post Office and elsewhere. Do not apply for your new books until your initial is called.

you must do this
before you apply

Fill in page 3 (the Reference Leaf) of your present ration book exactly as directed on that page.

Disregard the printing on the other side of the Reference Leaf (page 4) in both the General (buff) Book and the Child's (green) Book. In the General (buff) Book, write at the top of page 4 the name and address of the MILK retailer with whom you are *now* registered, that is your *present* milk supplier. (see left-hand diagram).

On page 4 of the Child's (green) Book write the name and address of the MILK retailer and also the names and addresses of the MEAT and EGGS retailers (see right-hand diagram).

General (BUFF) Book Write in name and address of your present Milk retailer.

Child's (GREEN) Book Write in names and addresses of child's present Milk, Meat and Eggs retailers.

DO NOT REMOVE THIS LEAF FROM THE BOOK

Issued by the Ministry of Food, London, W.1.

7th May 1943

PRESTWICK'S AIM

A £76,000 target for "Wings for Victory" Week in Prestwick was announced by Provost Dunsmore who presided at the meeting of Prestwick Town Council in the Council Chambers there on Tuesday evening.

They had had, said Provost Dunsmore, a meeting of the "Wings for Victory" committee and it had been decided to hold a drum-head service in Boydfield gardens at three o'clock on Sunday, May 23. In the evening of that day there would be two speakers at the War Commentary in the Broadway cinema; one, a Flight-Lieutenant, would speak on aviation matters, while the other would take as his subject the object of the "Wings for Victory" week. The following Wednesday there would be a procession of all Civil Defence services in the town and local military. On this occasion the salute would be taken by the Provost, magistrates and councillors and certain officers. To raise funds it was proposed to hold a whist drive and a dance on convenient nights. A five hundred pound bomb would be placed in Boydfield Gardens, when it was hoped that the public would stick stamps upon it to ensure its safe arrival in Germany.

It was pointed out that stamps bought during the "Wings for Victory" week can be placed in the ordinary National savings book. It is proposed to get the aid of the banks in the town so that at W.V.S. shop for the sale of stamps one can get stamps converted into savings certificates without going to a post office.

The target figure, announced by the Provost, is estimated to cover the cost of 15 Spitfires.

'TOUGH' FRAME

DEVELOPING MUSCLES

STRONG CONSTITUTION

STURDY LEGS

THANKS TO Weetabix

Prestwick

Army Cadets. — General Walker, Cadet Colonel Commandant, paid a visit of inspection to Prestwick Town Hall on Tuesday evening when he saw the boys of the Army Cadet Force on parade. Platoon 11 gave a display of squad drill, and Platoon 12 of rifle drill. The signals section staged a demonstration of W/T, and C.Q.M.S. May and Sergt. Anderson gave a lesson on the Bren gun. Gen. Walker congratulated Capt. MacBean on the excellent turnout, splendid appearance and high efficiency of the company, and afterwards gave the boys a lantern tale on Gen. Allenby's campaign in Palestine. Although well up to strength, the Army Cadet Force in Prestwick can take a few recruits for a new class now forming.

Charity Golf Match

(To the Editor, *The Ayrshire Post*)
County Buildings, Ayr,
May 17, 1943.

Sir,—We should like to draw the attention of your readers to the charity exhibition golf match which has been arranged to take place at Prestwick St. Nicholas Golf Course, Prestwick, on Saturday, May 29, 1943, commencing at 2.30 p.m.

The proceeds of the match will be divided equally between the Red Cross Sportsmen's Fund and the Ayrshire War Relief Fund.

The players taking part will be Henry Cotton, Harry Bentley, Gordon Lockhart and William Campbell. All players have agreed to give their services gratuitously and will meet their own expenses.

The committee in charge of the Ayrshire War Relief Fund are grateful for the opportunity of participating in the proceeds of this match and feel confident that the people of Ayrshire will be glad once again to support these charities and will, at the same time, appreciate the excellence of the standard of golf which the match is bound to provide.

The charge for admission to the course for the match will be 2/6d per person, but the committee will welcome any additional sums which may be donated in aid of these worthy causes.

At the conclusion of the match the golf balls used in play will be auctioned, together with a number of other articles donated for the purpose.

We are all aware of the substantial sums already raised for war charities throughout Great Britain by the efforts of sportsmen. Let us ensure that in this famed golfing county the efforts of these players will meet with outstanding success.

CHARLES FERGUSSON,
Lord Lieutenant of the County
of Ayr.

GLASGOW,
Convener of the County of Ayr.

4th June 1943

"WINGS FOR VICTORY" WEEK

South Ayrshire Raises A Total Of £926,061

Once again South Ayrshire has shot through its target in a special savings campaign, the total of £926,061, being £171,061 beyond the target figure.

In this amount are included a number of free gifts to the Chancellor of the Exchequer which were received by Mr P. A. Thomson, hon. secretary of the South Ayrshire Savings Committee, among them being: from the people of Kilkerran village per Miss Mary R. Hopson, Drumgirnan, Kilkerran, £21; staff of Messrs. D. and J. Dunlop, solicitors, Ayr, £4 4s.; "Widow's Mite," £2; proceeds of public presentation to Mr R. Milne, schoolmaster, Patna, per Mr C. Knox, 6 Institute Row, Patna, £19; pupils of Heathfield school, Ayr, £2 2s.; Mrs Guthrie, 15 Montgomerie Street, Tarbolton, £5 5s.; share of proceeds of fete held by Ayr Brownie Packs, £56; Miss Margaret Hopkins, proceeds of dancing display, £12 10s.; Straiton school, £200.

The Ayr Centre W.V.S. War Savings Group collected £14,556, compared with just over £5000 during Warships Week.

The figures from day to day for the week which started on Saturday, May 22, are: Saturday, £118,808; Monday, £106,614; Tuesday, £72,610; Wednesday, £90,123; Thursday, £119,487; Friday, £212,915, and Saturday £187,101, which shows that although the total was still far off by the middle of the week a decided burst in the last few days brought the desired sum, and more.

In War Weapons week in 1941 the area total was £862,811, and in Warship Week last year it was £822,553. The following table gives the comparison between each of the three special savings weeks, targets for the various districts for "Wings" week being given in parenthesis:

Ayr Grammar School, setting themselves a target of £2000, a sum greater than ever they had collected before, raised £2815.

PRESTWICK'S EFFORT

Great satisfaction with the result of Prestwick's "Wings for Victory" effort was expressed in the report submitted at the monthly meeting of Prestwick Town Council on Tuesday evening — Provost Dunsmore presiding.

The Provost said the target was £76,000 which was to buy fifteen Spitfires, and anyone who had seen the thermometer at The Cross would have seen that they had drawn £84,760. (Applause). He thought it was a most excellent result, and it confounded those people who thought that they had fixed far too high a target. It was proof that the higher the target the greater the effort. He moved that they minute notice of their thanks to all concerned, who had organised, or helped in any way during the week to bring about that result.

The draw for the football, autographed by numerous players which had been presented for raffle was carried out by Provost Dunsmore who intimated that the amount drawn from the sale of tickets was £25. The ball was won by Mr D. Findlay, 145 Glenburn, Prestwick.

	Wings for Victory.		Warships.	War Weapons.
Ayr	£326,669	(£300,000)	£378,490	£349,949
Cumnock	£195,792	(£150,000)	£152,356	£233,044
Troon	£126,558	(£125,000)	£121,484	£74,294
Prestwick	£84,751	(£76,000)	£77,761	£53,605
Girvan	£78,195	(£18,000)	£70,537	£55,977
Maybole	£40,769	(£40,000)	£41,767	£34,839
Dalmellington	£37,325	(£20,000)	£19,226	£20,844

27th August 1943

Old Age Pensions.

(To the Editor, *The Ayrshire Post*)
Prestwick,
August 23, 1943.

Sir,—Much has been written and much has been said regarding the rise in the Old Age Pensions, only as yet nothing has been done in the matter. Now take the great number of old age pensioners who have given from two to four sons to the army, and hundreds of those old pensioners will never see their brave sons again. They reared them, fed them and clothed them, and just when they had come to the age of being help to the old folk they were told to join the army and the old folk are left to live on the paltry sum of £1 a week between them. How in the name of heaven can they be expected to pay for food, clothes, fire, rent and taxes and keep out of debt? Let those who have the power to get the pension up use their power to some purpose and without delay so that those old age pensioners may have a little more comfort in their remaining days.

A Son of the Soil.

8th October 1943

PRESTWICK GAS

Inspector To Be Appointed

Dissatisfaction with the gas supply to the town was expressed at the monthly meeting of the Prestwick Town Council held on Tuesday evening—Provost Dunsmore presiding.

Before the matter could be raised the standing orders were suspended.

Mr Duncan said that since the matter was last brought up he had asked quite a number of people what their experience had been. He did not like to repeat the answer he got in some cases, but it meant that the supply was very bad. It seemed to him that the Council had a duty to discharge and that duty was to see that the ratepayers got a fair supply of gas. He had been told of people who had to put sticks on their gas to boil some water. If the answer to this complaint was to appoint an inspector then they should not shirk from this. He thought, however, that in the first instance it would be advisable to appoint a small committee to meet representatives of Newton Gas Company to see what they were going to do about it. He moved that a committee be appointed.

Bailie Govan seconded.

Mr Adamson said they were promised better gas when the pipe was laid in Briarhill Road, and it was still as bad as ever in that area. The company now intended installing a new plant and promised that the gas would be better in three months. He contended that an inspector should be appointed on behalf of the ratepayers, and moved accordingly.

Mr Macdonald seconded.

Provost Dunsmore thought it would be more desirable to appoint a small committee first to meet with the Gas Company, before taking action. He mentioned several of the war calls which were being made on the company and said he felt they had a good case if it had to go before the Sheriff.

Mr Dougan favoured Mr Adamson's motion. The Gas Company had failed to comply with the standards laid down in the Act, he said.

Mr Flanigan said he did not think the company had any right to say that the war was the cause of the bad gas. Long before the war the gas was bad.

Mr Blunt said at certain periods of the day the householders could not get enough gas to boil an egg.

On the suggestion of Mr Brock, Mr Duncan amended his motion to include the attendance of an expert, and Bailie Govan seconded.

Mr Adamson held to his original motion that an inspector be appointed immediately.

On a vote, Mr Adamson's amendment was carried by six votes to five.

HOUSING SITES

The matter of post-war housing sites was discussed at a meeting of the Housing committee, following a letter read from the Department of Health for Scotland. It stated that the housing sites belonging to or earmarked by the council at Adamton Road (4), Heathfield, Pleasantfield Road and Carrick View had been inspected by one of the Department's planning officers in consultation with the council's technical officers. After considering the planning officer's report, the Department suggested that the Council should utilise the site extending to 30 acres at Adamton Road for their first housing development after the war. This site would accommodate 142 houses.

The minute bore that it was agreed to inform the Department that the lay-out plans of the sites had already been prepared, and it was remitted to the burgh surveyor to prepare plans for the extension of water, drainage, gas and electricity services.

29th October 1943

Prestwick

Brains Trust. — The Discussion Group had a most successful and entertaining evening on Friday last, when a crowded and enthusiastic audience in the High School welcomed a "Brains Trust" of our American allies on the subject of the U.S.A. Mr MacBean was in the chair and the team comprised Sergt. Dargin, Mass.; Sergts. Schwartz and Arnzen, Kentucky; and Cpl. Barron, Texas. The visitors dealt ably with a barrage of questions and answered fully, tactfully and wittily. It was the unanimous desire of all that such a treat should be repeated, and it is hoped to arrange this. To-night the Group discusses "Current Events," and all interested are welcome.

22nd October 1943

PRESTWICK GIRL'S ESCAPE FROM NAZI-OCCUPIED DENMARK

Among a number of British girls who have recently escaped from Nazi-occupied Denmark is Miss Margaret Dunlop, youngest daughter of Bailie and Mrs Dunlop, Midland, Mansewell Road, Prestwick, who obtained her diploma in physical education at the International Gymnastic Institute in Jutland a few days before the outbreak of war.

A telegram received by her parents on Saturday gives the news that Miss Dunlop arrived at Trelleborg in Sweden with other two Scottish girls, but states that some of the girls stayed in Denmark. It is not known how Miss Dunlop made her escape, but it has been previously reported that a number of the girls swam the four miles from Denmark to Sweden.

The students, it is understood, were residing with families through-

ou Denmark, and Miss Dunlop had a variety of experiences, having spent the summer on various farms and the winters with two families in the suburbs of Copenhagen. Red Cross messages and personal letters have arrived from time to time giving comforting news of Miss Dunlop's welfare.

Prior to the outbreak of war Miss Dunlop had spent three years in Denmark, and when war broke out students were allowed to complete their training before the college was taken over by military authorities and the students scattered.

Miss Dunlop was educated at Prestwick High School and Ayr Academy, and while attending the latter took a prominent place in sport. She was a playing member of the hockey first eleven for a number of years and captained the side. An all-round sportswoman, she had outstanding success in athletics winning the girl's sports championship on three successive occasions.

Two brothers, Robert and David, are on service, holding commissions in the R.A.F and R.N. respectively.

REPATRIATED

Prestwick Soldier's Birthdays

Four years ago a Prestwick soldier went abroad on service on his birthday, and on Monday he celebrated another milestone in life's journey when he landed on these shores from a prison camp in Germany.

On Monday his mother, Mrs Cowan, 33 Marchburn Avenue, Prestwick, received the following telegram:—"Arrived in England. Hope see you soon. Writing. Andy." The news did not come as a surprise altogether for on October 20 Mr and Mrs Cowan were apprised of the fact officially that their son, Driver Andrew Cowan, R.A.S.C., attached to the R.A.M.C. was to be repatriated.

Andrew is the eldest son, and is 26 years of age. He was captured in the attack on Crete on June 2, 1941, and since then has been a prisoner of war in Stalag 8B camp, Germany, from which he had always written cheery letters. Cowan was unwounded, his mother states, and she thinks that possibly he is one of the hospital orderlies. Prior to enlistment in 1939 Cowan was employed as gardener and chauffeur with the Misses Paul, Flatfield House, Symington.

29th October 1943

Prestwick Man's Prize

At the graduation ceremony in Glasgow University on Saturday the Frances Melville Medal and Prize for the most distinguished candidate in the honours group of mental philosophy was presented to David C. Hicks, M.A.

He is the son of Mrs F. A. Hicks, 32 Ayr Road, Prestwick, and went up to the university from Ayr Academy in 1939.

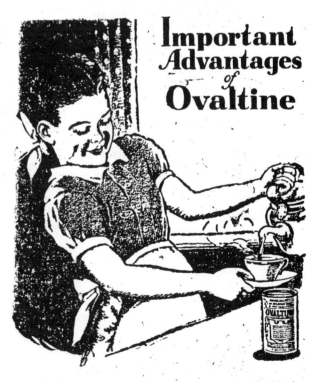

12th November 1943

PRESTWICK PERTURBED

Publicity And Possibility Of Bombing

"Prestwick may have been put on the aeronautical map of the world, but I am afraid that it has also been put on the bombing map of Germany," said Provost Dunsmore in a strong protest against the wide publicity recently given to Prestwick aerodrome, when he presided at the statutory and monthly meeting of Prestwick Town Council held in the Council Chambers there on Friday.

Before beginning the regular business Provost Dunsmore said he would like to refer to an article published in "The Glasgow Herald" of October 29, which gave a very full account of the Allied Supply Routes. In this account the aerodrome at Prestwick had certainly received a great deal of publicity. The article, he believed, had also been published extensively by other British and American papers, thereby giving it world-wide publicity.

As the location of the aerodrome had always been regarded as a military secret, they had all been under the impression that to divulge its position and activities to any of their friends abroad, would have immediately laid them open to be tried and probably shot for traitorous conduct.

While they all welcomed the knowledge of the great developments at the aerodrome and the great prospects of the aerodrome becoming one of the principal aeronautical ports of the world, and as a council, they were prepared to the utmost of their ability to further the objects for it, yet he most strongly deplored the unnecessary publicity given in the articles.

He would agree that Prestwick might have been put on the aeronautical map of the world, but he was afraid that it had also been put on the bombing map of Germany, and it was the latter aspect which was disturbing the peace of mind of the citizens of Prestwick. To reassure the people he hoped the Civil Defence forces would keep themselves on their tiptoes and be ready for any possible emergency.

In answer to discussion, Provost Dunsmore said there was no doubt that Prestwick aerodrome had been put forward as one of the busiest in the world, and the Germans might try to strike at it. The Government still kept Civil Defence forces in being, and that meant they still felt there was a possibility of bombing in this area.

Bailie Blunt asked if the Provost had had any complaints from the public.

The Provost replied that he had had a number of complaints.

Mr J. Sawyers said that the sanction for publication of the article had been given by H.M. Stationery Office, and when the sanction came from there they could do nothing about it.

Provost Dunsmore said he was speaking on behalf of the people of Prestwick. They all supported the developments at the aerodrome but they deplored the danger brought to the people of the town.

The Silver Lining.

At the outset of the meeting Provost Dunsmore said the war was still with us, but we were happily beginning to see the silver lining in the clouds and he hoped that before next November we would have attained a resounding victory and peace, goodwill and happiness for the whole world.

It was unfortunate that the war had practically extinguished almost all municipal and social progress in the town, but he took the opportunity of thanking all the officials and the various staffs under their jurisdiction, along with the Civil Defence services and all other voluntary organisations for the excellent service they had rendered during the past year, often under very great difficulties.

Provost Dunsmore also issued a welcome on behalf of the magistrates and councillors to Driver Andrew Cowan, R.A.M.C., 83 Marchburn Avenue, one of the repatriated prisoners of war who recently returned to this country, and offered congratulations to Bailie and Mrs Dunlop, Prestwick, whose daughter Miss Margaret Dunlop, had escaped from enemy-occupied Denmark to Sweden.

The town clerk (Mr W. Shaw) indicated that a letter had been received by the council from the session of Kingcase Church, Prestwick, requesting their attendance at the ninth anniversary service to be held on November 28, and that it had been decided at the informal meeting that the council should attend.

Gas Examiner Appointed.

A minute of the Lighting and Cleansing committee meeting bore that it was agreed to appoint Mr A. R. Campbell, of Messrs R. R. Tatlock and Thomson, as gas inspector and to indicate that meantime he could report when six tests had been made. It was also agreed to pay him the fee of £3 3s per test, with travelling expenses in addition, and after his report had been received the matter could again be gone into.

NEW ROAD OPENED
AT PRESTWICK

Lord Sherwood And Air Expansion

ATLANTIC TERMINAL

"Until the war is won the future cannot be unfolded as we wish it to be," was remarked by Lord Sherwood, Parliamentary Under Secretary of State for Air when on Friday he opened the Glenburn Road extension in presence of a large company of members of the County Council and Prestwick Town Council, officials and members of the public.

The Earl of Glasgow, convener of the county, presided, and on the platform with him were Lord Sherwood, his Parliamentary private secretary, Lord Wimborne; Sir Charles Mac-Andrew, M.P. for North Ayrshire; Sir Thomas Moore, M.P. for Ayr Burghs; Commander Hughes-Onslow, vice-convener of Ayrshire; Provost Dunsmore, Prestwick; and Colonel W. T. R. Houldsworth, convener of the Highways Committee of the County Council.

Opposite the platform which held the principals was a white tape stretched across the roadway, on either side of which the crowd had assembled, some coming by bus and motor from the eastern end along the new roadway.

Introducing Lord Sherwood, the convener said that before he took on his present duties he had served the Government well in other capacities. He was also a squadron-leader in the R.A.F.; in fact, he was squadron-leader of the Nottingham bombing squadron. The road they saw that day was near the old one which many knew so well, and over which they who lived on the north side used to travel to the Ayr races with zest, and sometimes with hope. (Laughter.) This new road was no ordinary road but a symbol of the expansion of what, he thought, was going to be one of the greatest air ports in the country. (Hear, hear.) The mere fact of Lord Sherwood coming there that day showed that the Government was interested in this part of Ayrshire. Many people from the county had gone forth to fight for freedom as they had done in days gone by, and when they returned, as many would do, what they would want. First of all, they would want houses, and it would be for the County Council to see that they got them; they would want jobs, and he (the convener) looked forward with hope to the expansion of the great air field which they had, the maintenance of which would provide work for many. It was right that they should entertain that hope. He thanked his lordship on behalf of all present and called upon him to open the road.

Lord Sherwood stepped down from the platform, was handed a pair of scissors by Mr Geo. S. Barry, county road surveyor, and with this cut the tape, remarking as he did so, "I formally declare this road open." The opening was greeted with applause.

Airfield Expansion

Remarking that it was due to the Air Ministry that this road had been made necessary, Lord Sherwood remarked that he was glad to be here on this occasion as it was a case of opening a road, and not having some shut. (Laughter.) He understood he was to be entertained and he did not know what form that would have taken had it been the other way round. (Laughter.) He would like to take that opportunity of saying how much they in the Air Ministry realised the immense sacrifices they had had to ask from people in the county of Ayr and in all parts of the country due to the expansion of the air force. The R.A.F. had started quite small, and had now become one of the greatest air forces the world had ever seen. In order to carry out these preparations which were helping to win the war it had been necessary to expand, enlarge, and build countless new aerodromes, and in the process immense areas had been taken over, and in many cases people who had been on the land for generations had been deprived of their livelihood. This had meant the destruction of amenity, and of beauty, and in many cases real hard sacrifices such as they had experienced in this area. How great and how willing that sacrifice had been! He was glad that on this occasion they had been able to build this new road, and he was glad, as he was quite certain they were, that the Government had found the money for it and that it had not fallen upon the local authorities.

He was certain they would find that the sacrifices they had been called upon to make would be worth it. At that moment it was quite clear what a big project this was; the countless aeroplanes which they had seen coming in and going out, especially during the last few years, had certainly proved to them the importance of it. What the future held it would be inopportune for him to say now. Really all their energies were devoted to winning the war, and until that was done—and it was still a long way off—until this war was won, the future could not be unfolded on the lines they would wish. He was quite sure that by the claims of their place, and the interests they had here, they had proved that this was one of the great airports of this country. Applause.)

100 Years Ago

Provost Dunsmore, Prestwick, who extended a hearty welcome to Lord Sherwood, said they had been given a road which would provide an outlet from the town to the eastern part of the county area—a much needed road —and not only so, but would serve as a by-pass road for the heavy traffic which came from the north to the south. Mentioning the splendid conditions of the roads to-day, the Provost stated that it was on record that over 100 years ago the mail coach from Glasgow to Ayr which came through Prestwick was withdrawn because of the expense of the tolls on the roadways and the very bad condition of the roads. There were 10 turnpike gateways then on the road which was 35 miles in length. Had they been opening this road say 70 years ago Lord Sherwood would probably have been opening a gate instead of cutting a ribbon. (Laughter.) The latter method implied that the roads were free to all. (Applause).

Atlantic Terminal

Sir Thomas Moore, M.P., said they welcomed Lord Sherwood not only for himself but for the fact that he represented the R.A.F. to which as a nation we owed our existence to-day; and further, he represented a ministry to which, as a county, they looked forward for further development. As

had been indicated with great discretion that day they had an Atlantic terminal in Scotland—(laughter)—and they looked forward to extension in the future. They had the British stopping place of the highways of the air, and when victory brought peace they looked forward to the extension of that highway to bring many prosperous and happy associations. We were a hospitable people, he continued, hospitable to foreigners, even including Englishmen. (Laughter.) And so, he hoped when Lord Sherwood went back to London he would be persuaded by their hospitality, and by their character and capacity to be an advocate for our wellbeing in regard to the establishment of a permanent Atlantic terminal in Scotland. (Hear, hear).

Sherwood Road

Proposing a vote of thanks to Lord Sherwood on behalf of the County Council, Col. W. T. R. Houldsworth, convener of the Highways committee, presented him with a pair of scissors bearing the following inscription:—

"Presented to the Rt. Hon. Lord Sherwood, Parliamentary Under-Secretary of State for Air to mark the opening by him of Glenburn Road extension, Prestwick. 26th November, 1943."

"I am not going to say," proceeded the Colonel, "they are the identical scissors with which you so successfully just now cut the tape—they seem to me to be of more ornate design and not so adapted for practical uses—but

I sincerely trust they may be a happy reminder of the day you spent in Ayrshire and opened this road." (Applause.) They were, he proceeded, in some doubt as to what the road should be called. It was known as the Glenburn extension road, but Glenburn Rows were in the vicinity, and it was thought that there might be some confusion. Colonel Houldsworth showed that quite separately Mr Lockie and himself had arrived at the same conclusion, that the road should be called "Sherwood Road." (Applause.) After alluding to the splendid highways they had in Ayrshire, the Colonel expressed the hope that the road, opened that day, would be equal if not superior to the other roads of the county, and that it would long serve the purpose for which it was intended in this important district of Ayrshire. (Applause).

Lord Sherwood returned thanks for what he termed "this noble present." He said he felt highly honoured that the road should be named after him in this most Scottish of all places. He was delighted to be present, and he wished them all well.

In carrying out the scheme the County Council acted as agents of the Ministry of War Transport. Mr Geo. S. Barry, county surveyor, was the engineer, assisted by Mr Francis Pritty, burgh engineer of Prestwick, and the contractors were Messrs Kings and Co., public works contractors, Glasgow.

31st December 1943

Prestwick

Poppy Day. — In the Prestwick and Monkton districts Poppy Day realised £470 7s, a very great increase on last year, mainly due to the splendid effort of St Nicholas Golf Club 'at their smoking concert and auction, which produced £157 for the fund. The efforts of all who assisted in making this a record year were greatly appreciated.

31st December 1943

PRESTWICK TREAT

On Tuesday afternoon in the British Restaurant at Prestwick a Christmas party for evacuee children billeted in the town was held by the local authority. Organisation was in the hands of Mrs M. B. Dickson, official billeting officer for the burgh of Prestwick.

The party was made possible by the generosity of friends in Canada, whose donations defrayed the afternoon's expenses, and American servicemen stationed in this country provided sweets and chocolate for the children.

Some 110 children filled the restaurant from three till six o'clock, and their merry laughter mingled with music, created a happy Christmas atmosphere in the building.

A go-as-you-please competition brought forth a galaxy of talent, and among the spectators sat many proud mothers, who appeared to enjoy the fun as much as their little ones.

A dancing display by pupils of Miss Nita Allan, and Miss Jeanette Wright, the Claunch, St. Quivox Road, Prestwick, a show of lantern slides by Mr Findlay, Prestwick, and songs from Miss Nancy Campbell added to the afternoon's fun.

At the back of the restaurant stood a brightly decorated Christmas tree laden with presents, and at the end of the afternoon's entertainment Mr George Alexander, burgh foreman, in the guise of Santa Claus, handed a gift and two apples to each of the little revellers. For each there was also a packet of chocolate and sweets.

During the afternoon a lady and gentleman, who wish to remain anonymous, left a bag of new sixpences at the party and these were later distributed, each child receiving a coin.

3rd December 1943

1944

General Eisenhower became Supreme Commander of Allied Invasion Forces in Europe.

Government agreed a 4 year pact with the miners.

General De Gaulle became Commander in Chief of Free French Forces.

D. Day June 6th - Allied Forces land in Normandy.

Battle of Arnhem.

First prefabricated houses built in Britain.

Paris was liberated.

Roosevelt won fourth term in office as U.S. Presisent

Glen Miller killed in plane crash en route to France.

The Aerodrome Broadcast

The question of the broadcast by the B.B.C. in February on the activities at Prestwick Airport was raised by Mr Sloan (South Ayrshire—Lab.) in the House of Commons on Wednesday.

He described it as among the most reckless, senseless, and stupid productions that had ever emanated from the B.B.C. The broadcast had caused unnecessary alarm and indignation among the surrounding population, as the most intimate details were given. Complaints had been expressed very forcibly by the Provost, magistrates, and Town Council, and other responsible citizens of Prestwick.

The local authorities had done their best to bring the airport into operation, and also to secure it as a terminal after the war. If the horrors of war came to the county they would just have to take bombing like the others, but what they resented was this almost direct advertisement, in case the enemy might forget it, that there was such a thing as an airport in Scotland.

Mr Thurtle (Parliamentary Secretary, Ministry of Information) said no breach of security was involved. Last October, General Marshall produced his biennial report on the American Army, in which he made it quite clear that Prestwick was the Atlantic terminal for bringing over aircraft from America. The report was made public and could be obtained by enemy agents without difficulty.

The Air Ministry realised that there was no longer any effective reason for maintaining the security "stop" on disclosure of the existence of this terminal, and, as a consequence, long before this broadcast in February there was a great deal of publicity given to the terminal in Canada, America, and even in Scotland.

Sir Patrick Hannon (Moseley—U.) asked whether, before such announcements were made in America, an interchange of views took place with this country

Mr Thurtle said he did not know whether any particular communication passed between the two Governments in regard to this particular air terminal, but normally there was co-ordination and co-operation between them as to what should remain secret and what should be made public. It was the Service involved which decided whether there was a security point or not. In this case the Air Ministry was quite convinced that no question of security was involved, and therefore the broadcast might be permitted.

In reply to Mr Leslie (Sedgefield—Lab.), Captain Balfour (Under-Secretary of State for Air) said the broadcast script was carefully "vetted" for security. All the competent authorities were consulted. It was not for the Air Ministry to give any opinion on the accuracy of the statements.

South Ayrshire's Past Victories

1941—War Weapons Week.
1942—Warships Week.
1943—Wings for Victory Week.

Coming Offensive

SALUTE THE SOLDIER

DATE:
20th to 27th May

Objective £750,000

Our local regiment, the Royal Scots Fusiliers, in which so many of our near relations are serving, expect the people of South Ayrhire to contribute handsomely, so that they may be well supplied with arms and ammunition.

**They will do their bit.
Let us see that we do ours.**

Prestwick

Fruit Juices.—A new centre is being opened by the W.V.S. for the distribution of fruit juices and cod liver old for children on the second Tuesday of each month from 2 till 4 p.m. at St Ninian's Golf Clubhouse, near Prestwick Toll. The Alexandra Hall will be open as usual on the first and third Tuesdays of the month, while the Carvick Webster Hall, Monkton, will also continue to open on the afternoon of the first Thursday of the month.

7th April 1944

THE PRESTWICK AIRPORT BROADCAST

Mr A. Sloan, M.P., Denies "Poaching"

A B.B.C. "FAIRY TALE"

As briefly reported in last week's "Post" Mr. Alexander Sloan (South Ayrshire—Lab.) on the motion for the adjournment of the House of Commons raised the matter of the broadcast about Prestwick Aerodrome. The following is a fuller report.

Mr Sloan said he had put a question to the Minister of Information suggesting that in the interests of security these broadcasts ought not to have been allowed. In his reply, Mr Bracken did not question the undesirability of broadcasting to the world the locus and activities carried on in this area, he said that both these broadcasts were scrutinised by the authorities responsible for security in these matters and that they contained only information which had already appeared in the Press in Britain, in Canada and the United States of America. He also gave them the astonishing information that the Germans possess maps of Scotland, truly an amazing disclosure. He (Mr Sloan) was formerly of the opinion that no one outside Scotland knew where that country was. They might also have picture postcards of Prestwick and Ayr, and therefore the general public should be able to discuss openly our land defences, our air stations and our naval ports. He would like to remind the House—and this was the point which had come under discussion since, both here and elsewhere—that this aerodrome is entirely in his constituency. A supplementary question was put by Sir Thomas Moore which might have misled members and the public into the belief that this airport was in Sir Thomas Moore's constituency. He indicated that it was one of his brightest jewels, and he assured the Minister that if they were bombed the people in that area could take it.

Mr MacLaren (Burslem)—He would not be there.

Sir Thomas Moore

Mr Sloan said the Minister of Information described the statement as a sort of Moore's Elegy, and he might have occasion to remember it. He (Mr Sloan) did not think he should have to resort to Old Moore's Almanac to prophesy what would be the reaction of the electors in the burgh of Prestwick the next time Sir Thomas Moore had occasion to face them. The "News Chronicle" stated that he (Mr Sloan) had been guilty of a breach of gentlemanly conduct in raising matters relating to another member's constituency. The "News Chronicle" evidently had not studied those maps that were in the possession of the Germans and had disclosed an inexcusable ignorance of the geography of Ayrshire.

Mr MacLaren—It is an English paper.

Mr Sloan said there was not one of the workshops or the aerodromes, not a single inch of the runways, in the constituency represented by Sir Thomas Moore; it was entirely within the constituency of South Ayrshire. While it was inexcusable on the part of the "News Chronicle," it was entirely different in the case of the member for Ayr Burghs. He (Mr Sloan) would not expect him to know. Sir Thomas Moore was an Irishman who lived in London, and, by accident, represented a Scots constituency and was completely out of touch with the people in that particular area. He was as much a stranger to Prestwick as Prestwick was to him, and he could walk from one end to another without a dog barking at him, because he would be unrecognised. In regard to the broadcast itself, it could be classed as one of the most reckless, senseless and stupid productions that has ever emanated from the B.B.C. The whole structure of it was designed for the purpose of giving somebody a boost. If it is objectionable to advertise anybody's liver pills over the wireless, it should be equally repugnant to put on show ability which has yet to be proved. The next effect of the broadcast was to cause unnecessary alarm and indignation amongst the surrounding population. The most intimate details were given. He could say—he thought without fear of contradiction—that if any poor soul in a public-house bar, under the influence of Johnnie Walker, had said one-tenth of what appeared in that broadcast, or had disclosed half of the information given, he would have found himself in the police court on trial, and he (Mr Sloan) would say rightly so.

Must Be Consistent

To say that because the Germans had maps, or because information had been given in other parts of the world, it was quite legitimate to flaunt public opinion and give the most intimate information which would be of infinite value to the enemy, was an argument which he hoped would not be sustained by the Parliamentary Secretary. He remembered putting down a question about this airport to the Secretary of State for Air, and was informed by the Clerk at this Table that he must get the name of the locus out of the question in the interests of security. They were informed that day at question time that a secret session is to be held on the fourth sitting day to discuss the future sittings of that House. Was it suggested that the Germans had no maps to guide them to the location of the House of Commons, or did he think that the people of Ayr and Prestwick were of

less importance than members who lounge about the benches and smoke-rooms of that establishment?

We must be consistent. If it was helpful to the enemy to discuss openly the days and hours of sittings of this House it would be equally helpful for them to know the locus of a very important airport. He had the script of the broadcast, and it would serve the Minister right if he read it from beginning to end. It would be a perfect punishment for allowing it to be broadcast. [Members—"What about us?"] That was the only reason he did not want to read it all, but to give an indication of what had led to the complaints by the Provost of Prestwick, magistrates, the Town Council and responsible citizens of all classes, he wanted to give one or two quotations. One was staggered with amazement at the idea of giving to the Germans, over the air, such intimate details. Indeed our capacity for amazement was more than exhausted when we saw in prominent places the words, "Careless talk costs lives," and "Keep a guard on your tongue." Evidently those words did not apply to the B.B.C. This was one quotation:

"It is now more than three years since the first lone venturer touched down at Prestwick. Many more followed in the ensuing months until a year later we welcomed the first Lend-Lease aircraft. There was little ceremony on the airfield when the crew disembarked and to-day we celebrate the third anniversary of that significant occasion. Since then aircraft have crossed the Atlantic to Prestwick in a steady and ever-growing stream, and since September, 1941, the British Overseas Airways Corporation has maintained a continuous ferry service to take pilots back to the other side. If you went into the control tower at this minute you would see aircraft being brought in from the four quarters of the compass—British and American aircraft and so on. If you should stand for a few minutes at the reception desk in our entrance hall you will hear our receptionist welcoming and helping men of every Allied nationality, young Americans who have just brought their operational Fortresses across the Atlantic and who are on their way to bomber stations; Ferry Command pilots who have just flown across Lend-Lease operational aircraft from America; the captain and crews of British Overseas Airways Corporation, passengers and aircrews about to depart from Prestwick who will arrive at their next stop at such a variety of places as Iceland, Greenland, Labrador, Newfoundland, Canada and New York."

Could indiscretion go further than that? It reminded him of the railway stations where young women broadcast the times of the outgoing and incoming trains. Here was an implied invitation to the Germans that here was a place where a bombing operation would be very helpful to them indeed. The general tone of the broadcast, apart from the security aspect, was extremely foolish. It set out to describe how two young men overcame immense obstacles in establishing the aerodrome. The pioneers of Canada and the explorers of darkest Africa pale into insignificance compared to these young men. After listening to this description of the difficulties which were encountered the population of Prestwick and district were more hostile than the Red Indians were to the early adventurers.

A Fairy Tale

It was said that a local authority sent the police to stop the contractors from working. Was there ever such a fairy tale? Grimm completely faded out in comparison. There was only one authority which has any responsibility in the matter of planning in Ayrshire and that was the Ayrshire County Council, of which he was a member. He could assure the Parliamentary Secretary that that body never placed any obstacle whatever in the way. Was there anybody who imagined that the County Council of Ayrshire would be so stupid? If, in the B.B.C., they had had any elementary knowledge of what they were talking about they would know that no local authority was required to ask the police to stop the contractors from going on with their work. He remembered a meeting of the Town Planning Committee at which it was said that a member was able to persuade the contractors to go forward. Every assistance had been offered by the County Council in regard to this aerodrome, from its very inception. As a matter of fact, the authorities had done their best, not only to get the airport into operation but to secure it as a terminal when the war is over. Every responsible person he knew in the county had applied his mind and attention to this matter, yet this stupid statement was broadcast. One would think that the people of Ayrshire were half "barmy." The County Council closed by-passes and erected roads further east in order to get out of the way. The Water Committee of the County Council went to the extreme limit of directing water supplies into this area in their anxiety to do their best to secure this terminal airport.

The question of whether "we can take it" was entirely beside the point. In the event of the horrors of war reaching our county he supposed they would have to take it in the same way as the 51st Division faced up to the fighting they had been called upon to do since the beginning of the war. They have not yet had any figures, but the consensus of opinion was that in this war, as in the last, the percentage of casualties for Scotland would be very much higher than those for any other part of the Empire. In the event of bombing they should have to take it as others have taken it, but what they did resent was this almost direct advertisement to the Germans—in case they might forget—that there was an airport at Prestwick which might be bombed. They considered that the broadcast was silly in the extreme, and that it was a dangerous practice that ought to be discouraged, and he hoped the Parliamentary Secretary would be able to assure that such a breach of security would not be allowed to occur again.

No Breach of Security

Mr E. Thurtle, Parliamentary Secretary to the Ministry of Information, said he would like to clear away, at the outset, one or two misapprehensions under which Mr Sloan appeared to be labouring. He did not think Mr Sloan realises that the Ministry of Information were under no obligation to pronounce on the merits of a broadcast of this kind —whether it was good or bad, or whether or not the giving of the broadcast involved any breach of security, which was the point of a question which Mr Sloan put to the Minister a few weeks ago, when he asked whether action could be taken in view of the breach of security involved, as he alleged. His (Mr Thurtle's) case that day was a simple one: it was that no breach of security was involved in this

matter at all, and he will give Mr Sloan information in support of that case. If this broadcast had taken place at any time prior to October last it would have been a definite breach of security and it would not have been permitted. It was the duty of the Commander-in-Chief of the American Forces, every two years, to produce a report, and last October General Marshall produced his bi-annual report on the American Army, in which he made it quite clear that Prestwick was an Atlantic terminal for the landing of aircraft brought from America to this country.

Mr Mathers (Linlithgow)—Is this report public?

Mr Thurtle—Yes, and no doubt it could be obtained by enemy agents. When that fact came out the Air Ministry realised that there was no longer any effective reason for maintaining a security stop on the disclosure on the existence of this terminal. As a consequence, long before this broadcast, a great deal of publicity was given to this terminal in Canada, in America and even in Scotland. For example, in "The Scotsman" of November 30, there was a leading article devoted to the subject of this aerodrome. He would quote a sentence from it which he hoped would convince Mr Sloan that the fact of its existence and the kind of service it was performing was very well known to the people of Scotland and must, presumably, have been known to the world at large.

"The anniversary dinner given last night by Scottish Aviation, Limited, exactly three years after the first lease-lend aircraft landed at Prestwick, focuses attention on the busiest and most romantic air terminal in the world. The secret of Prestwick has been well guarded and it was only a few weeks ago, after General Marshall's striking tribute to the airport, that official permission was given to mention it by name in print. As Thomas Johnston, the guest of honour, said, the story of the development of this Scottish airport, when it is told, will provide an uncommonly interesting chapter in the record of Scotland's war achievements."

Sir Patrick Hannon (Birmingham, Moseley)—asked if before announcements at this stage were made in America, even at the instance of the American High Command, what exchange of views takes place between this country and the United States Government as to the particular location of an air terminal? Surely there must be some co-ordination of intelligence between the two sides of the Atlantic.

Services Consulted

Mr Thurtle said he did not know whether any communication passed between the two Governments with regard to this terminal but, normally, there was co-ordination and co-operation between them as to what should be kept secret and what should be published. He was explaining what the position was as long ago as November, bearing in mind that the broadcast of which Mr Sloan complained did not take place until three months later. He was trying to show, by means of this extract, that there was really, at that time, no secrecy involved and no question of security. That, he gathered, was the charge made against the Ministry of Information—that it permitted a breach of security regulations to take place. He (Mr Thurtle) was there to tell him that no such breach was committed.

Prestwick

Presentation. — On the occasion of their leaving St. Cuthbert's Church primary Sunday school to take up teaching in the junior department, the Misses Isobel Watson and Janet Hamilton were presented on Sunday with gifts from the primary staff. The superintendent, Miss L. Hitchcock, in handing over the gifts, spoke of both having given eleven years' faithful service, and asked that they take with them the good wishes of all. Miss Watson and Miss Hamilton suitably replied.

*"All the World's a Stage, and
Every Man must play his Part."*

To-day the stage is set for the most historic event of
all time—the triumph of freedom-loving peoples over
Nazi tyranny.

Here is Your Big Chance to "Line up" with the
Invasion Army. We will win—and win more quickly
if you play your part.

**Save as you have never done
before. Keep on Buying—**

**SAVINGS STAMPS 6d, 2'6 and 5'-
SAVINGS CERTIFICATES 15'- and 20'-**

Issued by the Scottish Savings Committee.

SALUTE THE SOLDIER and HELP SAVINGS WEEK TOTAL

GRAND FOOTBALL MATCH

In aid of Army Charities

Scottish Command

v.

Glasgow Celtic

SOMERSET PARK, AYR, SATURDAY, 20th MAY, 1944

Kick-Off 5 p.m.

ADMISSION—Stand, 3s 6d; Enclosure, 2s; Covered Terracing, 1s 9d;
Ground, 1s 6d; H.M. Forces and Boys 7d.

A CEMA PLAY TOUR

Glasgow Citizens' Theatre Company
present

"MR BOLFRY"

The New Comedy by
JAMES BRIDIE

Denis Carey	Duncan Macrae
Yvonne Coulette	Lucille Steven
Gordon Davies	Marten Tiffen
	Mary S. Urquhart

THE PLAY PRODUCED BY ERIC CAPON
SETTING BY MICHAEL WARRE

COUNCIL FOR THE ENCOURAGEMENT OF MUSIC AND THE ARTS

UNDER THE AUSPICES OF C.E.M.A.
The Citizens' Theatre, Glasgow, presents
JAMES BRIDIES' New Play
"MR BOLFRY"
In the TOWN HALL, PRESTWICK,
on
FRIDAY and SATURDAY EVENINGS
5th and 6th MAY, 1944
Doors open at 7 p.m.   Curtain at 7.30.
Admission 3s 6d, 2s 6d, and 1s 6d.
Tickets and Seats Booked at Misses Pottie,
The Cross, Prestwick.

Glasgow Herald — "James Bridie's 'Mr Bolfry' is at once the best Bridie, and among the best plays seen in the City for a long time."

Evening Citizen—"From the curtain-rise on the Manse at Larach on a wet Sunday afternoon to its fall on the Monday morning, 'Mr Bolfry' beguiles and amuses."

BURGH OF PRESTWICK.
NOTICE TO HOUSEHOLDERS.
KITCHEN WASTE.

IT IS ESSENTIAL that every scrape of WASTE FOOD should be placed in a separate utensil and put out with other salvage or refuse for collection by the Local Authority. Householders must note that it is an offence to BURN Bread and Waste Food of any kind and that this practice must cease immediately.
DON'T HELP HITLER.
SAVE ALL YOU CAN.
FRANCIS PRITTY, Burgh Engineer.
Salvage Department,
Municipal Chambers,
Prestwick, 23rd May, 1944.

"SALUTE THE SOLDIER" WEEK
20th - 27th MAY inclusive

SCOTTISH AVIATION LTD. present
A GRAND CONCERT
THE S.A.L. SHOW at BROADWAY CINEMA, PRESTWICK
SUNDAY, 21st MAY, 1944, at 7 p.m.
Doors Open 6.30 p.m.
2s 6d Saving Stamps will be on Sale at Door.

DISPLAY of ARMY CO-OPERATION AIRCRAFT and
EXHIBITION of WAR TROPHIES
At PRESTWICK AIRFIELD BUS PARK. Daily from 5.30 - 9.30 p.m.
Saturdays from 2.30 - 9.30 p.m. Sunday from 2.30 - 5.30 p.m.
Savings Stamps will be on Sale at Enclosure.

Prestwick Town Clerk

Following upon their interviewing of a short leet last week for the vacancy in the town clerkship of Prestwick, created by the death of Mr Wm. Shaw, Prestwick Town Council met on Tuesday evening in the Council chambers there, and made their selection.

The final vote was between Mr John L. Jones, depute town clerk of Kilmarnock, and Mr J. I. Wark, B.L., legal assistant, Town Clerk's office, Glasgow. Voting was equal, six for each, and Provost Dunsmore gave his casting vote for Mr Jones.

The post carries with it a commencing salary of £600, rising by biennial increments, to a maximum of £800 per annum

Mr Jones, who is 35 years of age, is the younger son of Mr Kennedy C. Jones, an engineer with Glenfield and Kennedy, Kilmarnock, and of Mrs Jones, 18 Culzean Crescent, Kilmarnock. He served his legal apprenticeship with Mr Norman J. Campbell, S.S.C., then town clerk of Kilmarnock, and took his law classes at Glasgow University. In July, 1937, when he qualified as a solicitor, he was promoted to the position of legal assistant to the town clerk, which post he held until September, 1941, when he became depute town clerk. Mr Jones is assistant secretary to the Ayrshire Council of Accident Prevention.

Mr Jones was well known in pre-war days as an amateur footballer, having been captain of the Kilmarnock Academicals, for which team he played when they won the Scottish Amateur League (Reserve Division) in seasons 1931 32 and 1932-33. He is a member of Barassie Golf Club, and secretary and treasurer of St. Marnock's Church Badminton Club. Actively interested in church affairs, he is at present elder and session clerk of St. Marnock's Church, Kilmarnock.

9th June 1944

PRESTWICK AIRPORT'S FUTURE

Increased Prosperity Hope

The possible future development of Prestwick as an airport was discussed by Mr Francis Pritty, burgh engineer, Prestwick, when he spoke to the members of the Ayr branch of the W.E.A. in the Memorial Hall of Ayr Academy on Monday night. Mr J. D. Cairns, Troon, presided.

Mr Pritty was taking the place of a lecturer who was unable to be present, and who was to have spoken on the question of light metal industries. His address followed the lines of that given by him a fortnight ago to the Institution of Municipal and County Engineers. He declared that it would be of immeasurable benefit to planners generally if some broad indication could be given by the Government at an early date as to the policy to be observed in the direction or regulation

Mr Pritty indicated that it was generally agreed that in a relatively small country such as the United Kingdom, the number of aerodromes for trans-ocean air services must be limited. It was believed that probably four in number would meet the requirements. Two of these would serve the London area; one probably in the north beyond the industrial belt; and the fourth one in Scotland, at Prestwick.

Only One Site

Numerous questions were asked at the close. In reply to one as to the claims that might be made for Dumfries, Mr Pritty said there was only one site for the trans-ocean airport and that was Prestwick on account of the fact that it was already in being, and because of the number of flying hours obtained due to the excellent climatic conditions. There would not be room for two airports of such magnitude as Prestwick. There might be a good claim for Dumfries under what was known as Class b.

A questioner said some people regarded such a project as not altogether an unmixed blessing, and he wanted to know how the "man in the street" would be affected, and whether it would be possible for him to have his summer holiday by this method of transport.

Mr Pritty said that so far as taking off and landing facilities were concerned at Prestwick there was nothing in the world to prevent people travelling by air. What the figure would be for such travel he would not like to mention.

A lady suggested that £12 10s which had been mentioned for travel abroad would take a big slice out of holiday money, but Mr Pritty said that travel to the continent in pre-war days ran away with even that sum.

Increased Prosperity

Asked about the influx of skilled people to the vicinity of Prestwick in the future, Mr Pritty pointed out that even at the present time there were boys learning their apprenticeship in connection with the aircraft industry, and in time things would right themselves. As he saw it, to establish such an airport in the area would bring something to Scotland that was much required—the lighter industries. Owing to the fact that they had all their eggs in one basket in the past—the heavy industries—there had been tremendous unemployment in the land. As the aircraft industry developed there would be increased prosperity. To-day they had something like two million people employed in the aircraft industry.

Mr P. Robb said that looking to the industrial development proposed here he thought it essential that the local authorities should have some say in its development.

Mr Pritty mentioned that it was formed in the first instance as a flying training school, and he should imagine that no one had any idea it would develop in the way it had done; it was the national emergency that had effected the big change. He pointed out that before the war the school turned out many efficient flyers and many of them knew of the part they had played in the Battle of Britain.

Asked why certain of the original people behind the development had now left it Mr Pritty said these were matters which he could not comment upon.

2nd June 1944

First Stop Prestwick For Americans After The War

"Prestwick is destined, after the war, to be one of the initial stopping-off places for Americans bound for Britain by air."

This is the estimate of Walter R. McCallum, American war correspondent, writing in the "Washington Star" of Prestwick Airport and its characteristics.

"To-day crossing the Atlantic in either direction is a routine job, almost a milk run," says McCallum. "It isn't done without a lot of careful planning, of course, but it goes on constantly and without interruption.

"The airplane, warned of storm fronts or icing fronts, simply climb above them, or drop down below icing levels. They pay little attention to even the fiercest weather conditions over that incubator of storms—the Atlantic Ocean.

London Week-End

"It is entirely possible for a New York-bound passenger to leave London to-day and be at Forty-second and Broadway within 48 hours. Air Transport Command of the United States Air Forces operates a series of shuttle planes between London and various points in the United Kingdom. One of the shuttle points is Prestwick. You can leave London at 10 a.m. and be having lunch in the comfortable Officers' Club at Prestwick at 12.30 p.m. That is around 400 air miles.

"Prestwick is destined, after the war, to be one of the initial stopping off places for Americans bound for Britain by air. Plans are under way to make the London-New York trip fairly inexpensive. They're talking now of a round trip for about §100. In other wards, a New Yorker could leave

Gotham on a Friday night, be in London the next morning and leave London Sunday night, arriving in New York Monday morning.

"Most of the air traffic east is in materials now. The big Fortresses and Liberators fly the ocean in swarms, usually without war paint.

"You see mostly American planes around Prestwick nowadays. That is because the place is what it is—a big port of call for eastward air traffic. The planes don't stay there long. They are all destined to see early action. I saw a lot of Forts take off one morning headed for South England.

The Mail Goes Through

"Urgently needed materials, such as electrically heated flying suits for bomber crews; penicillin and other drugs, even bulky stuff, all come by air nowadays if the urgency is great enough. The size of the shipments is tremendous. Tonnage, of course, cannot be revealed, but it is awesome to think of all the stuff transported over an ocean by air.

"Prestwick also happens to be the British terminus for soldier mail carried by air. You would be surprised at the figures for mail handled in the post office there. It all adds up to the fact that by the urgencies of war and lease-lend material transported by air the British have, perforce, had to build a terminal capable of handling big business. You wonder whether something of the same kind isn't in prospect around New York and whether the British will have the jump on America in that regard.

"Losses over the Atlantic route have been averaging less than half of 1 per cent. and steadily are dropping. Peace-time conditions could cut them to nothing."

9th June 1944

NEW TOWN CLERK

Prestwick Welcome For Mr J. L. Jones

Dogs and their ways, other than winning, were discussed at the monthly meeting of Prestwick Town Council on Tuesday night—Provost Dunsmore presiding.

Mr J. L. Jones, the new town clerk, took up his duties for the first time and the Provost extended a welcome to him on behalf of the Council. It would, he said, be a memorable day for Mr Jones, and he hoped the members and the officials would give him the same cordial support that they had extended to the late Mr Shaw. He trusted as time went on and he became acquainted with the work of the town that it would become congenial to him, and that he would be long spared to be with them.

Mr Jones returned thanks for the kind words of welcome, and for their confidence in appointing him to the post. He was very conscious of the honour done him, and he hoped he would prove worthy of their confidence, and that his relations between the council and the other officials would be of the best. (Applause).

When the minutes dealing with the appointment of the town clerk were being adopted Mr Duncan suggested that the terms of the appointment of the clerk should be incorporated in the minute for future reference, and this was agreed to.

Honour For Soldier

The Provost referred to the paragraph in the "Post" last week which mentioned the award of the M.M. to Corpl. McVey, of the R.S.F., and moved that the Council send their congratulations to Mr and Mrs McVey to be conveyed to their son on the honour which he had brought to the town.

This was agreed to.

Tenants' Pets

A minute of the Housing committee bore that Bailie Dunlop suggested that tenants should be notified that they must either get rid of their dogs or vacate the house. It was agreed that the convener should see the factor in regard to this matter, and ask her to notify the tenants that if they could not keep their dogs in order, action would be taken.

Mr Steele suggested that the words of the minute were somewhat contradictory. It was agreed, he thought, that the dogs should be got rid of.

Mr Sawyers said he knew that the conditions of let were that no dogs should be kept. Where dogs proved a nuisance to their neighbours he thought they could instruct the factor to institute proceedings at once and tell them either to get rid of the offending dogs or to vacate the houses.

Treasurer Kinghorn said as responsible for the drafting of the minute he would point out that the finding was as stated.

Mr Duncan said Bailie Dunlop's view was only an expression of opinion.

Bailie Dunlop said the suggestion he made arose from complaints from Glenburn where people could not get working their gardens because of the dogs.

Provost Dunsmore said the point they wished to emphasise was that unless dogs were kept under proper control extreme action would be taken.

Bailie Dougan said the dogs that damaged the gardens did not belong solely to the tenants; they came from all the airts.

Mr Steele pointed out that they would require to rescind their former decision as to lets if they were not to allow tenants to keep dogs.

The Provost said they had to be quite democratic in this matter. It would not do to enforce the conditions of let with rigour unless there were those who could not keep their dogs under control. It was only if they became a nuisance that they would enforce the terms of the let.

It was agreed that the paragraph in the minutes should remain.

Bathing Lake

A minute of the Attractions committee bore that Bailie Dougan drew attention to the fact that the Bathing Lake was used in the evenings last summer by the personnel at the First Aid Post, after it was closed to the public, and it was agreed to write and ask them if this were the case, and if so, that the practice should be stopped

The clerk read a letter he received from Mr James Ferguson, the adjutant, in which it was pointed out that the question was raised three years ago when it was pointed out that the people working at the first aid post were giving their time and leisure for the people of Prestwick and official sanction was given to the personnel of the post to use the place only after the time of closing. This had seldom been made use of by any of the personnel.

Mr Steele said the complaint was that the doors were being opened which allowed the public in to bathe.

The Provost said they had no objection to the personnel of the post using it but it meant that the other practice must be stopped.

This was agreed to.

Housing Requirements

A Housing committee minute bore that there was submitted a report by the burgh engineer in regard to future housing requirements in the burgh, together with plan shewng all land belonging to the Town Council. Councillor Adamson moved that the small Housing sub-committee appointed to go into this matter be called together now to consider the position and submit a report to the whole committee.

The sub-committee met, and the convener outlined the various proposals contained in the burgh surveyor's report with regard to suggested sites for housing schemes. After full consideration and explanation by the burgh surveyor, it was agreed that the sub-committee should visit the sites and that thereafter the surveyor should prepare plans of the various proposals excepting No. 6, and arrange for a meeting with the officials of the Department of Health to ascertain their views in the matter.

A minute of a subsequent sub-committee meeting bore that after examining the various sites and having the proposals explained by the burgh engineer, it was agreed that he should informally take up the matter with the technical officer of the Department of Health and ascertain their views as to the proposals and thereafter report.

The various sites inspected were:— Marchburn Avenue, Pleasantfield Road, Waterloo Road, land to the north-east of Marchburn Avenue, and St. Ninian's golf course.

Mr Sawyers said they could allow the whole matter to go before the Department of Health and get their views on the subject. They had gone over the sites suggested.

Mr Adamson pointed out that the report had to come before the parent committee before that could be done.

It was agreed that the usual procedure should be followed.

Post Office Hours

It was agreed to acquiesce in a request of the head postmaster at Ayr that the hours of business on the four public holidays of the year should be from 9 to 12 instead of from 8.30 a.m. to 1 p.m. as at present.

Attention was directed to the growing lack of accommodation at the public counter in Prestwick, and it was agreed that this matter might also be brought to the notice of the postmaster.

The Merchant Navy

Permission was given to hold a Merchant Navy Week in Prestwick, and to give every assistance in the way of supporting any strong committee that might be appointed on the lines of the present committee which had carried out the effort on behalf of the Y.M.C.A.

THE MARCH BURN.—At a meeting of the Lighting and Cleansing committee submitted to the Town Council on Tuesday Bailie Dunlop drew attention to the March burn being continually flooded through articles being thrown into the same, thereby spoiling the gardens in the vicinity, and suggested that it would be better to have a resident policeman in that locality. This was noted.

DUSTMEN IN BATTLE DRESS.—At the meeting of the Lighting and Cleansing Committee of the Town Council Bailie Blunt drew attention to a report which had been given at the Institute of Public Cleansing at Aberdeen in regard to uniforms for dustmen, and Councillor Duncan suggested that the burgh engineer should endeavour to obtain battledress uniforms for the men, and report to the next meeting as to his enquiries.

SWIMMING INSTRUCTION. — From a minute of the Attractions Committee it appeared that there was submitted a letter from the director of education desiring the same facilities as last year at the bathing lake for instruction in swimming to the pupils of Prestwick schools during part of the season, and this has been agreed to. There was submitted a letter from the administrative officer, Sea Cadet Corps, desiring permission for use of bathing lake on Sunday mornings at 2d per cadet, similar to last year, and it was agreed to grant them this concession again for the ensuing summer.

BRITISH RESTAURANT. — By 8 votes to 2 the British Restaurant committee of Prestwick Town Council adopted a recommendation approving of a proposal in a report by the treasurer, that the charges for meals at the British Restaurant should be increased by 1d on the meat course, 1d on the pudding, and 1d on the three-course lunch, and that the matter be reviewed again in three months' time. It appeared that the Aerodrome Canteen had been approached to see if they were willing to increase their charges, but they had stated that they not think it necessary or desirable to do so.

USE OF TOWN HALL.—From a minute of the Halls committee presented to the Town Council on Tuesday it appeared that there was submitted letter from the Rev. G. McLeod Dunn in regard to intimation received by him that the town hall was not available for the Scouts on Saturday afternoons; together with report by the hallkeeper indicating that the boys are most unruly owing to having no proper supervision. After consideration, it was agreed to write Mr Dunn that if he undertakes to see that the boys are properly supervised, they can continue the use of the hall.

Permission has been granted to the Salvation Army to hold meetings on the beach during the summer months.

The burgh gardener has been instructed to attend to the trees in Monkton Road.

HIGH SCHOOL.—The contribution of the pupils of Prestwick High School to "Salute the Soldier" Week amounted to £1175, almost doubling their target of £600. They also recently collected £55 9s. 3d. for the Barnardo Homes. It may also be mentioned that in addition to the second prize gained by Margery Bittle (Class 2a) in the second year section of the recent competition for essays on "Fires Help Hitler," special prizes were awarded Jack Alexander (Class 2a), Joyce McDonald (Class 1b) and Una McNab (Class 1a).

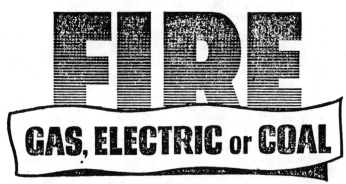

ANNOUNCEMENT BY THE MINISTRY OF FUEL AND POWER

READ THIS WARNING

before you light a

FIRE
GAS, ELECTRIC or COAL

Not next week, or tomorrow, but today, we must all put far greater effort into saving gas, electricity and coal. Here is the most important point of all — *Do not use more gas or electricity because you have less coal.*

SAVE MORE GAS and ELECTRICITY, or—

Have no doubt about gas and electricity—we must either use less now or find ourselves without these fuels at times when we may need them. Remember they come from coal and *coal must be saved for military operations that are on the way.* Face this fact every moment of the day—the Forces' need is greater than our own.

FEBRUARY COAL RESTRICTIONS

During February no domestic or other controlled premises may be supplied with more than 4 cwt. of house and kitchen coal in the South of England or 5 cwt. in the North. No delivery may be made where stocks exceed 10 cwt. or which would raise the stock above 10 cwt. In the Eastern region, where transport difficulties are already acute, stocks may not be raised above 5 cwt. Small anthracite, Welsh dry steam coal, and manufactured fuels, may be obtained where available up to a maximum aggregate of 10 cwt. during February, provided that no consumer raises his total stock of these fuels above one ton. Reserve stocks in merchants' yards must not be regarded as available for general distribution.

TODAY — NOW — start saving more

FUEL for BATTLE

11th August 1944

PRESTWICK SMASH

Many Injured When Bus Crashes Into Shop

The immunity from accident of a serious nature that has been so long a feature of 'bus traffic in Ayr and district, and indeed, in Ayrshire, was broken in rather alarming fashion on Thursday evening of last week at Prestwick, where a crash took place that caused considerable excitement in the busy centre of that town.

Around 7.30 p.m. a red bus of the A.A. Services left Boswell Park, Ayr, for towns in North Ayrshire, and, loaded up with passengers, it did not stop for any more at Prestwick Cross but kept on its journey.

Branching off the Monkton Road on which the outward and inward traffic to Ayr is carried is Alexandria Avenue, with a quaint old-fashioned gabled house, partly fronting the roadway, which is fairly wide at that point.

Suddenly, it is stated, a girl cyclist who had shaped as if about to proceed into Alexandria Avenue, came across the roadway in front of the oncoming 'bus, and the driver, confronted with this sudden emergency, swerved to avoid her, and the 'bus, continuing on its way, crashed into an unoccupied shop at the corner, and came to rest in the hole which it drove into the wall.

Many people witnessed the accident, and immediately there were loud cries of horror and dismay from the onlookers, accentuated in the next few minutes by the cries and groans of the injured.

Immediate help was forthcoming from folks in the vicinity, and the occupants of an American police car and others took charge of the situation until the arrival of the local police. When the impact came passengers had a rough time as the seats were, for the most part, torn from their bases, and the interior of the 'bus presented a confused mass of torn clothes, bleeding faces, and legs, so much so that the worst was feared.

When the first shock of the accident had passed willing hands rescued the passengers from their precarious position, some being brought out by the windows and others by the emergency door

Practically at the scene of the accident resides Mr Stevenson, the well known chemist, and his wife, and to the front and sloping ground in front of their house, many of the injured were removed, and there they received as much first aid as was possible until the arrival of ambulances and other conveyances which speedily whisked the injured off to Ayr County Hospital.

Services Help.

Good work was rendered by the A.R.P., Military police, and the Home Guard, members of the last named body subsequently taking some of the holidaymakers, still in a bewildered state, to their homes. In not a few instances members of the same family were involved in the accident, and later found themselves in hospital being cared for.

At the receiving end at Ayr the hospital staff was fully stretched to cope with such a big influx of patients, 36 or 37 in all passing through the outdoor patient department and receiving treatment. When all had been seen it was deemed necessary to detain eleven of the injured, three of whom were reckoned to be seriously injured. Nearly all suffered from abrasions and shock, and stitches had to be inserted in not a few gaping wounds.

John Doyle, the driver of the 'bus, who hails from Troon, had a marvellous escape in the circumstances although he did not get off scatheless, while Miss Stewart, the conductress, who also comes from Troon, was injured. The girl cyclist was hurt, and was among those attended to for cuts and bruises

While the actual body of the 'bus stood up well to the impact, the windows on the near side were smashed, and the front of the 'bus, and when the 'bus had been withdrawn from the wall it was found that a considerable hole had been caused in the building, which, stoutly constructed many years ago, stood up well to the blow.

Mr and Mrs Peebles, the occupants of the house and shop, were fortunately clear when the accident occurred, as the shop has been closed for some time due to the shortage of material during the war. Practically all the injured were holidaymakers, some of whom had been down in Ayr for the day and were returning home.

The Injured.

The following eleven people were detained for treatment in the wards:— Mrs Black, 63 Hawthorn Street, Springburn, Glasgow (fractured pelvis); Wm Scott, c/o Stevenson, 32 Oswald Place, Ayr (spinal injury); Mrs Helen Cunningham, 16 Boyd Street, Largs (fractured leg); Helen Farrell, 54 Holmfauldhead Drive, Linthouse, Govan (on holiday at Saltcoats); Charlotte Galloway, 35 Almswell Road, Kilwinning; David Cameron, Janefield Cottage, George Place, Stevenston; William Fisher (4), 6 George Place, Stevenston; Mrs Jeannie Bell, 18 Holm Avenue, Dumfries (her husband, John Bell, was slightly injured); Mrs Welsh, 11 Franklin Road, Saltcoats; Mrs Annie Moore, 6 George Place, Stevenston, and Francis Banner (11), 1 Langland Street, Kilmarnock.

On inquiry at Ayr County Hospital yesterday, it was ascertained that Mrs Welsh, Mrs Moore, Francis Banner, Wm. Fisher, and David Cameron, had been discharged. The more seriously injured of those who remain are progressing.

Prestwick

FOOTBALLER'S DEATH. — The death occurred suddenly on Monday of Mr Thomas Alexander Gemmell, at his home, 50 Glenburn Road, Prestwick. He was 67 years of age. In his early days Mr Gemmell was an outstanding outside left and a valuable player to Hibernian. His son, Bobby, now in the R.A.F., played for Ayr United.

PRESENTATION.—On the occasion of his retiral the congregation of John Street Church of Scotland, Glasgow, presented Mr Alexander Gilchrist with a wallet of notes in recognition of his services as secretary for twenty years, for fifteen of which he had held the joint posts of secretary and treasurer. Mr. Gilchrist now resides at 72 Berelands Road, Prestwick.

SUNDAY MEALS AT PRESTWICK.—It was reported at Prestwick Town Council on Tuesday evening that the British Restaurant was open on Sunday for the first time between the hours of 2 and 6 p.m. for teas, when over 200 were supplied, and the income was £24. The income for June showed a considerable increase as compared with the previous month, the average daily number of meals served being 297.

Ayrshire Post

ESTABLISHED 1880

No. 3519   Registered at the G.P.O. as a Newspaper   **Friday, August 18, 1944**   **Price Twopence**

GENERAL NOTICES

BURGH OF PRESTWICK.

MERCHANT NAVY COMFORTS SERVICE WEEK
19th to 26th AUGUST, 1944

PROGRAMME OF EVENTS:

FRIDAY, 18th AUGUST
SELECT DANCE in DUTCH HOUSE, 'Kilmarnock Road, Monkton, from 7.30 p.m. to 11.30 p.m. Tickets, price 10s 6d each, on sale at W.V.S. Office, Town Hall, Main Street, Prestwick.

SATURDAY, 19th AUGUST
FLAG DAY
CEREMONY OF CROWNING OF THE MERCHANT NAVY QUEEN (Miss Nan Taylor) in BOYDFIELD GARDENS. The Cross, at 2.30 p.m
ROYAL MARINE BAND in BOYDFIELD GARDENS—2.30 p.m. and 6.30 p.m.
POPULAR DANCE in TOWN HALL from 7.30 p.m. to 11 p.m. Admission 3s; Members of H.M. Forces, in uniform, 2s.

SUNDAY, 20th AUGUST
DRUMHEAD SERVICE at BOYDFIELD GARDENS, The Cross, at 3 p.m., conducted by the Rev. Luke McQuitty; Address by Rev. M. M. Macpherson, R.N. Contingents of various Service Units will attend.
WAR COMMENTARY by Mr S. A. Beyer-Pederson, and Display of Films in BROADWAY CINEMA at 7 p.m.

MONDAY, 21st AUGUST
POPULAR DANCE in TOWN HALL, from 7.30 p.m. to 11 p.m. Admission, 3s; Members of H.M. Forces, in uniform, 2s.

TUESDAY, 22nd AUGUST
BASKET WHIST DRIVE in TOWN HALL at 7.30 p.m. Tickets, price 2s 6d each (Hostess free) on sale at Town Clerk's office, Links Road; W.V.S. Office, Town Hall, Main Stareet, and Billeting Office, Main Street.

WEDNESDAY, 23rd AUGUST
FANCY FAIR and BABY SHOW in BOYDFIELD GARDENS, The Cross, at 2.30 p.m. Home Baking, Garden Produce, Fancy Goods, White Elephant and Gift Stalls; Amusements and Side Shows; Treasure Hunt. ENTRIES FOR BABY SHOW—3 classes (1)up to 6 months; (2)6-12 months; (3) 1-2 years, to be made to Mrs. M. B. Dickson Billeting Office, Main Street, by Tuesday, 22nd August. Entry fee 2/-. Tea and Refreshments will be on sale.
GRAND VARIETY CONCERT by AYR KIDDIES' CONCERT PARTY in TOWN HALL, at 7 30 p.m. Tickets, price 2s 6d, 2s and 1s 6d (children, half-price), on sale at Town Clerk's Office, Links Road; W.V.S. Office, Town Hall, Main Street; and Billeting Office, Main Street.

THURSDAY, 24th AUGUST
DANCE RECITAL in TOWN HALL at 7 p.m., by Miss Nita Allan's Pupils, supported by Local Guest Artistes, and DANCE COMPETITION for Holiday Visitors under 16 years of age. Tap, Character Highland, Ballet and Classical Dancing Tickets, price 2s. 6d., 2s. and 1s. 6d. (Children half price), on sale at Town Clerk's Office, Links Road; W.V.S. Office, Town Hall, Main Street, and Billeting Office, Main Street. Entries for Dance Competition to be made to Miss Allan at 52 St. Quivox Road on 22nd and 23rd August between 10 a.m. and 12 noon.
GRAND FOOTBALL MATCH — ROYAL AIR FORCE v. AYR NEWTON ROVERS on Prestwick Public Park, kick-off at 7 p.m. Tickets, Adults 6d. Children 3d. On sale throughout the town

FRIDAY, 25th AUGUST
SELECT DANCE and CABARET in TOWN HALL from 7.30 p.m. to 12 midnight. Tickets, price 7s. 6d. each on sale at Town Clerk's Office, Links Road; W.V.S. Office, Town Hall, Main Street, and Billeting Office, Main Street.

SATURDAY, 26th AUGUST
BOWLING TOURNAMENT on Howie Municipal Bowling Green at 2 p.m.
GALA in BATHING LAKE at 3 p.m. Admission, 1s; Children 6d.
ANNBANK, MOSSBLOWN and DISTRICT PIPE BAND will perform at the Gala in the afternoon and in Boydfield Gardens at 6.30 p.m.
POPULAR DANCE in TOWN HALL from 7.30 to 11 p.m. Admission, 3s; Members of H.M. Forces, in uniform, 2s.

SUNDAY, 27th AUGUST
GRAND CONCERT by the SCOTTISH AVIATION CONCERT PARTY in BROADWAY CINEMA, Main Street, at 8 p m Mr BOND ROWELL (by kind permission of Ben Popplewell & Sons, Ltd) will act as compere. Tickets, price 2s 6d, 2s and 1s 6d, on sale at Town Clerk's Office, Links Road; W.V.S. Office, Town Hall, Main Street; Billeting Office, Main Street, and the Broadway Cinema, Main Street Prestwick

---

OPEN-AIR DANCING at PARKING PLACE, GRANGEMUIR RD., Each Evening from 7 to 11 p.m. Admission 1s.
DARTS COMPETITION IN WARDENS' POSTS, ETC.

MILE OF PENNIES in LINKS ROAD. A HOUSE-TO-HOUSE COLLECTION will also be undertaken by Members of the W.V.S.

IF WEATHER UNSUITABLE, OUTDOOR EVENTS WILL BE HELD IN TOWN HALL

JOHN L. JONES,
Town Clerk and Hon. Secretary of Local Committee for the Merchant Navy Comforts Service.

Municipal Chambers,
Prestwick, 15th August, 1944.

BURGH OF PRESTWICK.

MERCHANT NAVY COMFORTS SERVICE WEEK.

ARTICLES required for Sale at Home Baking, Garden Produce, Fancy Goods, White Elephant and Gift Stalls in connection with Fancy Fair to be held in Boydfield Gardens on WEDNESDAY, 23rd AUGUST.

PERSONS willing to donate suitable articles should get in touch with the W.V.S. Office, Town Hall, Main Street, and arrange as to delivery.

ARTICLES for Fancy Goods White Elephant and Gift Stalls should be sent in to the W.V.S as soon as possible.

ARTICLES for the Home Baking and Garden Produce Stalls should be handed in on the day of the Sale

AS the whole proceeds of this Sale will be devoted to the Merchant Navy Comforts Service, it is hoped that householders will make every endeavour to support the Appeal by donating suitable articles

JOHN L JONES
Town Clerk and Hon. Secretary to the Local Committee.

Town Clerk's Office,
Prestwick, 9th August, 1944.

AYR COUNTY COUNCIL.

SCHOOL MANAGEMENT COMMITTEE FOR AREA No. 3.

RE-OPENING OF SCHOOLS.

PARISH OF AYR.

ST. MARGARET'S H.G. SCHOOL, will re-open on MONDAY, 21st AUGUST, 1944, at 9 a.m.

AYR ACADEMY will re-open on MONDAY, 28th AUGUST, 1944, at 10 a.m. The Junior Infant Class (i.e. Beginners' Class) will commence at 11 a.m.

NOTE.—As the Preparatory School is full and as there is a long waiting list, no fresh applications for admission can be received meantime.

ALL OTHER SCHOOLS will re-open on MONDAY, 28th AUGUST, 1944, at 10 a.m.

NEWTON PARK H.G. SCHOOL. — The Headmaster will be in attendance at 9 a.m. on Monday, 28th August, 1944, for the purpose of classifying and examining new pupils.

PARISH OF DUNDONALD.

ST. PATRICK'S R.C. SCHOOL, TROON, will re-open on MONDAY, 21st AUGUST, 1944.

TROON, DUNDONALD and LOANS PUBLIC SCHOOLS will re-open on MONDAY, 28th AUGUST, 1944.

TROON.—Enrolment of pupils will take place as follows:—Pupils from 5 to 7 years of age in ACADEMY STREET SCHOOL, and pupils from 7 to 12 years of age in the BARASSIE STREET SCHOOL on FRIDAY, 25th AUGUST, from 10 a.m. to 12 noon.

PARISHES OF
MONKTON and PPRESTWICK, CRAIGIE and SYMINGTON.

PRESTWICK HIGH, PRESTWICK PUBLIC, MONKTON PUBLIC, GLENBURN PUBLIC, CRAIGIE PUBLIC, and SYMINGTON PUBLIC SCHOOLS will re-open on MONDAY, 28th AUGUST, 1944.

PRESTWICK HIGH SCHOOL.—The Headmaster will be in attendance on FRIDAY, 25th AUGUST, from 10 a.m. to 12 noon, to confirm provisional enrolments for the Infants Department, for which no further enrolments can be accepted.

GEO. GARDINER,
Clerk to the School Management Committee.

District Office, Prestwick.

BURGH OF PRESTWICK.

MERCHANT NAVY COMFORTS SERVICE WEEK.
19th TO 26th AUGUST.

DURING the Merchant Navy Comforts Service Week, from 19th to 26th August, it is desirable that as far as possible THE TOWN SHOULD BE DECORATED. In view of present difficulties, however, it is not possible for the Organising Committee to undertake this work on its own account. An appeal is therefore made to all shopkeepers, business firms and householders, particularly those on or adjacent to the main thoroughfares to assist in this matter by displaying during the week such suitable flags, streamers, banners and bunting, etc., as they may have in their possession.

JOHN L. JONES,
Town Clerk and Hon. Secretary of Local Committee for the Merchant Navy Comforts Service.

Municipal Chambers,
Prestwick, 15th August, 1944.

25th August 1944

MEN OF THE SEA

Prestwick's Tribute To The Merchant Navy

Prestwick is holding a Merchant Navy Comforts Service Week, for which they set themselves a target of £500, the effort being organised by a local committee which has arranged events of a diversified kind as means to raise funds.

The Week was officially opened with the ceremony of crowning the Merchant Navy Queen, which took place in the Boydfield Gardens on Saturday afternoon in presence of a large number of spectators. Chosen to be Queen was Miss Nan Taylor, 4 Marina Road, a member of the Junior W.V.S. She had as ladies-in-waiting Miss Gay McEwan, 26 Allanvale Road, and Miss Margaret Welsh, 6 Weir Avenue, while the maids of honour were Miss Willa Allan, 37 Ayr Road, Miss Sadie Andrew, 65 Ayr Road, Miss Janette McGregor, 1 Alford Avenue, and Miss Elsie Lawrie, 11 Woodlands Street. Her page was Master Manrico Coia, 70 St. Quivox Road.

Preceded by the Ayrshire Company of the Sea Cadets, the Queen with her page and ladies-in-waiting drove in a landau from the Town Hall to Boydfield Gardens, the maids of honour following in a victoria drawn by a pair of piebald horses.

The Sea Cadets formed a guard of honour and presented arms as the Queen walked from her carriage to the coronation dais, where she was received by Provost R. H. Dunsmore and Mrs Dunsmore, music being provided by the band of the Royal Marines.

Every Journey a Battle

Provost Dunsmore said that during the Week they were making an appeal for funds to supply comforts and rescue kits for the men of the merchant navy, who manned our ships and kept our supply lines open whatever the cost, thereby ensuring everyone being supplied in full measure with the necessities of life, and the brave lads at the front getting an adequate supply of planes, tanks, guns and munitions from across the sea, thereby giving them a chance of returning safe and sound to their friends at home. It was very hard for us to realise our debt to the men of the merchant navy, but we must pay tribute to the thousands of men who ensured that food and supplies reached our ports. Every journey was a battle against the stormy elements and the lurking enemy; every arrival was a victory. He hoped they would never forget that we had hundreds of merchantmen at our respective invasions of North Africa, Italy, Normandy and the South of France, and that in each case they brought honour to their service. The men who manned our merchant ships were among the finest of British subjects, and were deserving of our gratitude.

Symbols of the Sea

Bailie Neil Johnston, Glasgow, Scottish representative of the Merchant Navy Comforts Service, performed the crowning. Investing her with the robe of blue as a symbol of the seven seas which our big and little ships sailed by day and night, he hoped it would bring to their minds that in spite of war, wind and weather, and in face of heavy odds, our convoys pursued their undaunted way so that the lifelines of sea communication might be kept clear for all honest sailor men.

The sceptre, which he placed in her hands, brought them gratefully to remember the officers and men who manned our merchant ships. Its crown proudly recalled that the first gentleman of this gallant and famous company—whose forefathers manned the ships which singed the King of Spain's beard—the Master of the Merchant Navy, was his Majesty King George VI.

In placing the chain about her neck, he said that each link of that silver chain was a coin of the realm bearing the King's image and in reverse a 15th century galleon. More than 135,000 of these ship ha'pennies were needed every working day of the year to pay for wool alone, which made the garments the Merchant Navy Comforts Service sent to sea.

Placing the crown upon her head, he said they paused to pay a threefold tribute: first, to the gallant men who went down to the sea in ships and gave life itself in the cause of freedom; and then they gratefully and affectionately remembered the officers and men what at that moment were sailing under the Red Ensign in our merchant navy; and lastly they gave special thanks to the Merchant Navy Queen and Provost Dunsmore and to each man and women in the community who, while doing their full share of the nation's work, and despite the anxieties of this present time, had been able to hold a Merchant Navy Comforts Service Week.

"Nan, I crown you Merchant Navy Queen," Bailie Johnston concluded, and turning to the audience said: "Good people all, I here present, properly apparelled and very rightly crowned, for your loyalty, fealty and very humble duty, Nan, your Merchant Navy Queen."

Queen's Reply

Expressing her deep appreciation of the honour just conferred on her, the Queen said she had always had the greatest admiration for the merchant navy and she felt very proud that the honour of being elected Prestwick's Merchant Navy Queen had fallen on her. This crowning ceremony was, of course, merely a symbol—a symbol of the honour due to the gallant men of our merchant navy who, since the outbreak of war had defied the perils of the sea and the dangers of dive-bombers, mines, U-boats, and other enemy craft, to keep our lifeline intact. How well and how bravely they had carried out their duties they all knew, and now, during the coming week, Prestwick would have the opportunity to show its appreciation of all that the merchant navy had done.

Mrs Dunsmore having presented a bouquet to the Queen, the Provost called for three hearty cheers, which were cordially given.

Following the coronation the Queen and her retinue proceeded to the cenotaph where she laid a wreath in memory of the brave men of the sea. She then drove to the Municipal Chambers in Links Road where she started a mile of pennies. Resuming their seats in the carriage the Queen and her attendants, preceded by the Sea Cadets, went by way of Links Road, the parking place at the Bathing Lake, Ardayre Road, Marina Road, St. Ninian's Road, Maryborough Road, Ayr Road, St. Quivox Road, Adamton Road, Shaw Road, Newdykes Road and Alexandra Avenue to the Town Hall.

A telegram received from Mr Kirkland Bridge, national director of appeals, offered best wishes in advance for a record Merchant Navy Comforts Service Week.

Generous Gesture.

On the eve of the week, Messrs Austin and McAslan Ltd. organised a dance in the Dutch House, Monkton, and as they met all the expenses the entire proceeds, amounting to £128 13s, have been handed to the honorary secretary of the committee, Mr J. L. Jones.

A flag day was held on Saturday, and in the afternoon and evening performances were given by the band of the Royal Marines in Boydfield Gardens, there being also a dance in the Town Hall in the evening.

A drumhead service, attended by service units was held at the Boydfield Gardens on Sunday, conducted by the Rev. Luke McQuitty, the preacher being the Rev. M. M. Macpherson, R.N., while in the evening at the Ministry of Information meeting in Broadway Cinema Mr S. A. Beyer Pederson spoke on "A merchant sailor's life in wartime."

A dance in the Town Hall on Monday evening and a whist drive in the same place on Tuesday evening further added to the funds.

FAIR AND BABY SHOW

Undoubtedly the big attraction at mid-week was the fancy fair and baby show, the latter of which, for obvious reasons, had to be held in the Town Hall where a large crowd assembled before the time of opening. No fewer than 102 entries were received for the four classes of the show, and many more would gladly have competed but the line had to be drawn somewhere, though no doubt some mothers were disappointed. Many of the young children were well behaved, others howled and some crowed with glee, so that there was pandemonium when Provost Dunsmore, who was accompanied by Mrs Dunsmore, declared the fair and show open.

A diversion was created and a temporary hush when the Merchant Queen and her attendants came on to the platform, their bright dresses striking a note of colour.

The Provost expressed his pleasure at seeing such a large turnout of townspeople in support of the good cause. It augured well, he said, for the final result of the effort, and showed that they were not forgetful of the men who manned their ships on the seven seas of the world. Their merchant ships, whether of a few hundred or of thousands of tons, were fine vessels, doing a splendid job of work, and the men who comprised their crews were of the best and certainly deserved their deepest gratitude. (Applause.) Alluding to the fair and the goods that were for sale he said a great deal of hard work and sacrifice were represented; the ladies had given a practical example of their thanks to the men of the Merchant Navy. He declared the event open and called on Miss Nan Taylor, the Merchant Queen, to say a few words.

The Queen said there was no need for her to go into details about the function. They all knew the debt they owed to these gallant men of the sea, and she knew they would give willingly and generously for the goods on view, and while doing so she hoped they would all enjoy themselves. (Applause).

Master M. Coia, the Queen's page, thereupon presented Mrs Dunsmore with a bouquet, which was gracefully acknowledged.

Part of the fair was held in the Boydfield Gardens in a large temporary erection, and displayed there and in the Town Hall were stalls for home baking, garden produce, fancy goods, white elephants and gifts, while there were amusements, side shows and a treasure hunt. The fair was run by the women of the W.V.S., who have been unremitting in their efforts to make the "Week" a success.

The Prize Winners.

Judges of the show were Mrs J. Read, wife of Dr. Read; Mrs J. V. Gray, Mrs A. Hogg and Miss C. R. Scott, all of Prestwick, and all ladies with experience as trained nurses. They worked on a chart which took into consideration a great many things that a baby ought to be or have. General appearance—skin, nails, hair, and scalp, cleanliness and eyes—were high pointed, as was attractiveness—curly hair, nice eyes, brightness, ears, and nose. Many other things were taken into account and the total pointage in the youngest class was 64 as against 80 in the other sections. "Some marvellous specimens," "very healthy," "lovely babies," and "no skin trouble at all" were some of the comments the judges made at the close of their big and important task, when asked to express their views on the show. The pointage of the winners reveals very close competition. Each winner received a savings certificate; there was 10s for each second, and runners-up got a 2s 6d savings stamp each. Mrs M. B. Dickson, billeting officer, had great credit as convener of the show, which proved a big success. Following are the prize winners:—

Babies up to six months—1, Desina Parker, 183 Glenburn, 64 pts.; 2, Edith Anderson, c/o 3 Wellington Street, New Prestwick, 61 pts.; 3, James Bissett, c/o Rose, 4 Ailsa Street, Prestwick, 58 pts.; 4, Carol A. Leyland, 25 New Dykes Road, Prestwick, 56 pts.

Six to twelve months—1, Elice Spens, 35 Manson Avenue, Prestwick, 71½ pts.; 2, Clive Barber, 11 Adamton Road, Prestwick, 71 pts.; 3, Tom Young 21 Elmbank Street, Ayr, 66 pts.; 4, Ronald Wilson, 9 St. Ninian's Road, Prestwick, 58 pts.

Twelve to eighteen months—1, Elizabeth Purdie, 25 Marchfield Road, Ayr, 72 pts.; 2, Gail Watson, 6 Ardayre Road, Prestwick, 71½ pts.; 3, John Nelson, 33 Mansfield Road, Prestwick, 70 pts.; 4, Patricia Kirk, 181 Prestwick Road, Ayr, 69 pts.

Eighteen months to two years — 1, Sheena Murdoch, 7 Glenburn Road, Prestwick, 78½ pts.; 2, David Alexander, c/o 104 New Dykes Road, Prestwick, 78 pts.; 3, Olga Kelly, 42b Ayr Road, Prestwick, 74 pts.; 4, Marion Gibson, 42 Waterloo Road, New Prestwick 70 pts.

Mr John L. Jones, town clerk and hon. secretary of the Local Committee, proposed a vote of thanks to the judges for their services, which was heartily accorded.

On Wednesday evening a variety concert was given in the Town Hall by the Ayr Kiddies Concert Party and attracted a large audience, the efforts of the youthful artists being much appreciated.

Other Items.

Mrs Howie, 28 Templerigg Street, Prestwick, who correctly guessed the weight of a cake, 5 lbs. 2 ozs., had it handed over to her during the course of the baby show.

There also an unexpected gift was received for the cause. It was a receptacle containing the monetary proceeds from a little sale held by the children of Mrs Dickson's helpers who have taken in evacuees in Queen's Terrace. Juana Bywaters and Sheila Rorrison handed over the gift, which was duly acknowledged.

The target was exceeded by mid-week, and it is now hoped that the support for the fund will enable the figure to be doubled.

1st September 1944

Effects Of Crash At Prestwick

Scene of destruction after the disaster which overwhelmed houses in Hillside Avenue, Prestwick, on Monday morning. These bungalows were almost completely destroyed by the plane striking them and by the fire which folowed on the accident Figures are visible on the right of the picture at work on the blasted walls. (See page 7.)

1st September 1944

PRESTWICK CRASH

Twenty-Five Perish When Plane Hits Houses

Twenty-five people were killed, including the crew and passengers of a Trans-Atlantic plane, when it crashed early on Monday morning on houses in Glenburn, Prestwick, creating a scene of havoc, and much alarm over a wide area.

Immediately following the crash tongues of fire shot into the night sky from the burning and damaged plane, and from houses which caught fire almost at once and burned fiercely, and by the light of which rescuers carried on their work.

Civilian victims of the disaster were: —Thomas George Maitland (43), 10 Hawthornvale, Leith; Thomas Kinnear (23), 25 Dunsyre Street, Kirkcaldy (the son of Councillor Thomas Kinnear, of Kirkcaldy); William Kenneth Snowden (24), 155 West End Road, Southall, Middlesex; Robert Alexander Handyside (44), Mayfield, Kelso; and Irene Haswell (5), 6 Hillside Avenue, Prestwick.

Mr Alex Haswell, who was home on leave from the R.E.M.E., and his wife, are in the Ayr County Hospital, as also Mr Andrew Haswell, a brother who resides near the scene of the accident, and who had gone to the rescue. On enquiry at the hospital yesterday it was ascertained that all three were slightly improved.

An official statement issued by the American authorities on the day following the calamity put the casualties in the plane at 20, the number including six of a crew, twelve service men, and one civilian passenger, stated to be a nurse. All were of American nationality.

The accident occurred about 1 a.m. and the plane was heard flying low just before the crash. It would appear to have struck a chimney of a corporation house at 59 Berelands Road, occupied by Mr James Hart, who saw it afterwards through his window strike the garden wall of 60 Berelands Road opposite, occupied by Mr James Anderson, it rose slightly, careered along Hillside Avenue, and finally came to rest after demolishing the houses at Nos. 4 and 6. The effect of the impact was terrific, and in all the circumstances it is surprising that the death roll among the civilian population was not heavier.

Woman's Ordeal

All four men victims, together with Mr and Mrs Alexander Haswell and little Irene Haswell, stayed with Mrs Agnes Johnston, 6 Hillside Avenue, Mrs Haswell's mother.

Badly shaken by her experience Mrs Johnston said that she and Mr and Mrs Haswell were preparing to retire for the night when the accident occurred. Irene and the four other men were already sleeping.

"I knew nothing was wrong until I heard a tremendous crash in the front of the house," she said. "Immediately the house seemed to collapse on top of us and fire broke out. Soon the house was a mass of flames, and I was pinned down by beams. I tried to kick myself free, but I couldn't do so.

"The flames were licking round me, and I had shut my eyes, fearing that I could not be saved, when the rescuers arrived."

Rescue Work

It was Mr Andrew Dougan, 103 Glenburn, son of Bailie Dougan, who rendered such valuable aid and was largely instrumental in saving Mrs Johnston and Mrs Haswell. He knew the lie of the interior of the house through having stayed there for a time, and he found Mrs Johnston practically engulfed in debris with Mrs Haswell near her. Mr Haswell was about three yards away and he managed to get his head and shoulders clear. Other willing helpers were soon assisting.

Describing Mr Haswell's predicament, Mr Dougan said the whole chimney seemed to have come down on top of his legs. Rescue squads and A.R.P. officials got a rope and pulled the chimney wreckage off him, and carried him away on a stretcher.

The Little Girl.

When the crash came and in that brief space before the house came about them, Mrs Johnston called in an agony of suspense, "Save the baby," meaning little Irene, but as she realised afterwards, her son was pinned down and could not get out. When the rescuers reached the child she was still clutching her little doll; she was alive but died on the way to hospital.

"I don't know yet how we all escaped," said Mr Anderson, the roof of whose house was sheared off and the interior went up in flames. In the house with him were his wife, his mother-in-law, Mrs Allan, his two sons, Peter (17) and Allan (12), as well as Mr Harry Smith, an airman from Nova Scotia.

"Mr Smith got out through the attic window, and the rest of us struggled from the house in our night clothes. On getting outside the house I discovered that Mrs Allan was missing. I went back into her bedroom, which is situated on the ground floor, and found that she was pinned in the room by falling debris."

Defying the flames, Mr Anderson pulled aside the burning beams and, lifting his mother-in-law from the bed, carried her to safety.

"Whole Street on Fire."

The fierceness of the flames that destroyed the four houses was described by Mrs MacGregor, 1 Alvord Avenue, whose house is situated near the scene of the tragedy.

"I was in bed when I heard the deep sound of a large 'plane coming over," she said. "It seemed to be almost at roof-top height. Then almost at once I heard a crash. I jumped from bed, rushed to the window, pulled aside the black-out curtains and looked out. The whole street seemed to be on fire—my eyes were almost blinded by the glare. I was convinced that my own house was ablaze. I rushed to the telephone and dialled the number of the local fire brigade. But there was no reply. The line was dead, having been severed by the crashing 'plane."

Her husband, Mr Ian MacGregor, ran from the house and, realising that telephone communication with the fire brigade had been interrupted, called for a volunteer with a car or a bicycle to go to the nearest telephone booth. A boy immediately volunteered for the job, and cycled to the booth. The fire brigade arrived within a few minutes.

Fire Fighting

No praise can be too high for the rescue squads of the C.D. service, the Americans and the miners, whose work was not always unhampered and for a time was hazardous in the extreme. Three of the N.E. fire brigades answered the summons promptly, and under Chief Officer Paterson soon had a plentiful supply of water playing on the burning houses, four of which were burning fiercely. Eight lines of hose were got at work, and within an hour or so the fires had been extinguished. When day dawned over the scene a spectacle of ruin presented itself, and a feeling of tragedy and sorrow was reflected on the faces of all who gathered there. Throughout Tuesday gangs worked to clear the wreckage, and hundreds of sightseers thronged round the scene of the tragedy until the police were obliged to erect a rope barrier at the area to keep the curious at bay.

Houses Destroyed

The houses destroyed, four in number, are of the bungalow type, and were of an attractive character. No. 2 was occupied by Mr and Mrs Stewart, who escaped in their night clothes by a back window when the 'plane damaged the house, and No. 4 was unoccupied at the time, Mrs and Miss Stuart having gone to Largs a day or two previously and thus escaped the horror of the scene and probably a worse fate. No. 6, the home of Mrs Johnston in which the lodgers and the little girl met such a tragic end, was completely flattened, while the home of Mr Anderson, already alluded to, at 60 Berelands Road, was gutted. One or two other houses sustained minor damage.

The remains of the four men victims have been taken to their respective homes for burial, and the little girl victim was laid to rest in Prestwick cemetery yesterday afternoon amid many manifestations of regret on the part of the population of Glenburn and district.

8th September 1944

Laid To Rest

Sad scenes were witnessed on Thursday afternoon last when the remains of little Irene Haswell (5), the child victim of the appalling plane disaster at Glenburn on the Monday, were laid to rest in Monkton and Prestwick cemetery.

During the minutes preceding four o'clock, the time of the funeral, the roads surrounding the scene of the accident appeared to be filled with people, some in deep mourning. Many of the women carried wreaths, and few of them were dry-eyed.

The cortege left the house of Mr James Haswell, an uncle, at 63 Berelands Road, in close proximity to the ruined houses, and proceeded at a walking pace to the gates of the cemetery. Here a great throng of the public had gathered to pay their last tribute of respect. The hearse, bearing the little white coffin, passed through ranks formed by her former school chums of Glenburn school. Both pupils and staff of the school had assembled at the gates and the children, still carrying their school bags and books, stood with bowed heads as the long column moved slowly forward.

At the grave the committal service was conducted by the Rev. Luke McQuitty, minister of St. Cuthbert's Church of Monkton and Prestwick, assisted by Mr F. Salter, and a part was also taken in the obsequies by Chaplain Schoech who, together with Captain Thomas and Major Shallcross, represented the U.S. authorities.

Amongst others who attended the funeral were Provost Dunsmore, Mr J. L. Jones, town clerk, and Mr F. Pritty, burgh engineer, representing the Town Council; Bailie Dougan, a friend of the family; and representatives of the Civil Defence services and the W.V.S.

Chief mourners were Mr James Haswell, Mr David Haswell, Mr Robert Haswell, Mr George Haswell, and Mr Thomas Cairns, uncles; and Mr J. Baird, Mr J. Harkness, and Mr J. Dunlop. A young cousin, Hugh Haswell, represented his father (Mr Andrew Haswell) who was injured in hospital, while another sad circumstance was that neither Mr Alexander Haswell nor Mrs Haswell, both too ill and in hospital, were able to attend.

Many floral tributes literally smothered the grave with flowers. Wreaths were there from the U.S. authorities, Town Council and Burgh officials of Prestwick, neighbouringl children, staff and pupils of Glenburn school, Prestwick W.V.S., directors of Scottish Aviation Ltd., Bethany Hall Sunday School, and Mrs Snowdon, London, widow of one of the men who lost his life in the same house as the little victim

U.S. Mineralogist

Dr Harry Berman, 42-year-old mineralogist, was among those killed.

6th October 1944

BACK FROM ARNHEM

Prestwick Hero Surprises His Mother

"A knock came to the back door on Sunday forenoon and my grandson opened it, and there was my son," Mrs Raspison, 8 Aitkenbrae Drive, Prestwick, told a *Post* reporter on Tuesday when describing the arrival of her son, Staff Sergeant Edgar Raspison, a Glider Pilot, who was through the maelstrom of Arnhem. "You can imagine how I felt," this brave mother said, "when I saw my son there, safe and sound."

A modest hero he proved to be when the "Post" interviewed him, he would say little or nothing of the part he had played in the great enterprise glider pilot, as he piloted one of the first gliders to land in Normandy on D Day for the invasion of France. He made the crossing on that occasion in darkness, and landed his load safely, but the difference there was that he took no active part in the actual fighting. He was three days on land then, and returned by sea to England.

Sergeant Raspison is proud of the fact that a few days before he took

Sergt. Raspison with his mother.

in which the 1st Airborne Division earned undying fame.

Sergeant Raspison came through the ordeal unscathed, and the few brief days he has been at home have already restored his wonted cheerfulness. He explained that he landed among the first batch of gliders in a turnip field, and immediately they were in the thick of it, and with the others he fought in different sectors of the perimeter for nine days.

Asked about the retiral under orders, the Sergeant stated that he was one of the lucky ones at the river as he got across to the other side in a boat at three in the morning.

"We were in plenty of tight corners," he said, and "when I got to the river for the final crossing to safety the whole sky was lit up with the glare from burning houses, and the din was deafening."

It is not his first experience as a off on his Arnhem mission he received his "Crown"; in other words, he was promoted staff sergeant. Raspison, who is the eldest son of Mr Robert H. Raspison, who has a boot repairing business in Main Street, Prestwick, and of Mrs Raspison, 8 Aitkenbrae Drive, joined the army in October, 1939, from Prestwick Aerodrome, where he had been employed in clerical work, and was in France with the R.S.F. in the early stages of the war, and fought at St. Valery. After a spell in this country he joined a Glider Pilot regiment, and has taken part in a number of operations, including the two which thrilled the world.

He was born at Hull 25 years ago, is now on 15 days' leave, and is off to Hull with his mother, where he will meet his father who went there on holiday before the son arrived home at Prestwick.

Rents Of Prestwick Houses

The main item of business at the meeting of Prestwick Town Council on Tuesday — Provost Dunsmore presiding—was the motion which stood in the name of Mr John Sawyers:—"That a review of the rents of Council houses be considered by the Council as from November 28, 1944."

It will be recalled, he said, that last year they had some controversy over the finance of the Housing account, and as a result of the debate that took place the rents were increased 12½ per cent. to meet the deficiency. From the statement made recently by the Finance convener it appeared that the housing account was on a much better footing than it was last year. He had gone through the figures for the nine years, and he found that they were in a healthier state, the deficiency this year amounting to about ¼d in the £. Directing attention to the abstract he pointed out that there was a slight deficit this year amounting to just over £200. He thought they were in a position now to ask that review should take place, and he would suggest that the rents of the Council houses should be reduced by 10 per cent. He did so because he thought the 12½ per cent. should run on until the end of the financial year when the deficit would be overcome. The suggested change would then come at May 15, 1945.

The Provost suggested that it should be remitted to the Finance committee as Mr Duncan, the convener, was not present. Mr Duncan was the man who had gone into the figures which brought about the increase in the rents, and he thought he should have an opportunity to reply.

This course was unanimously agreed

Another Increase.

Intimation was made of the finding of the National Arbitration Tribunal award on manual workers' wages, giving an increase of 4s 6d in the war bonus to manual workers in municipalities, the award to take effect as from September 22.

No comment was made on the award which brings the total bonus to 24s per week.

Digging for Peace.

A letter was read from Sir Robert Greig, chairman of the Scottish Gardens Allotments committee, pointing out that there could be no relaxation in the efforts to provide food on the part of allotment holders and gardeners. Previously they had been asked to dig for victory, now they would be asked to do so for peace and plenty. The Council was asked to send delegates to a meeting in Edinburgh on October 21.

Councillor Brock, the chairman of the local association, and Mr Brownlie, the gardener, were appointed to attend

Retirals.

The clerk intimated that the Provost, along with Bailies Dunlop and Dougan, were due to retire at the November term as provost and magistrate respectively. All the members would continue in office until June, 1945.

6th October 1944

MERCHANT NAVY THANKS

Prestwick's Four-Figure Cheque Handed Over

"The men who sail under the Red Ensign have placed us as a nation under a very special debt and Prestwick has said thanks to the Merchant Navy in no uncertain fashion," declared Mr Kirkland Bridge, national appeals director of the Merchant Navy Comforts Service, when on Thursday evening, in the Broadway cinema, Prestwick, he accepted a cheque from Provost Dunsmore, Prestwick, being the proceeds of the Merchant Navy Week held in Prestwick recently.

The Provost, handing over the cheque, for £1710 6s 5d, said he thought they would agree with him that the citizens of the town had done a magnificent job, and shown, in a practical way, their appreciation of the men of the Merchant Navy. Having alluded to the great task that the seamen had accomplished during the war in bringing supplies to these shores, and munitions of war to the Allies, the Provost asked Mr Bridge to accept the cheque on behalf of the people of Prestwick who wished to send with it their heartiest thanks and greetings. (Applause).

"I generally have to pay to go to the pictures," remarked Mr Bridge amidst laughter, and "I don't get a four-figure cheque for going." This was a result of which every man and woman, and every boy and girl in Prestwick could well be proud. "Thank you very much indeed, Prestwick! the Merchant Navy is grateful."

Since the war began, he continued, the Merchant Navy had not lost a minute of time nor yet one ton of material through their own fault. They had no time to go on strike, which was a grand thing because we had depended upon them in war time to bring men and materials and munitions from overseas. The men who sailed under the Red Ensign had placed them as a nation under a special debt, and Prestwick had said "Thanks, Merchant Navy," in no uncertain way.

This money, he assured them, would be put to work at once. We have sent more than three million gifts since war began, and over one million books not included in the gifts; 161,000 emergency rescue kits had gone to them; and now they were seeking to extend at a cost of £150,000 the Merchant Navy School near London which educated orphan boys and girls of the Merchant Navy. Two in that school were from Scotland, and so they started life with a natural advantage. Then there was the Red Ensign Club that held about 300 men for sleeping, and which had 600 going and coming every day. Only the day previously he had telephoned London to ascertain how many Scotsmen they had in the Club which was situated near the London docks, and was told that 50 per cent. of their customers were Scotsmen. Finally, in their post-war work they were planning to finance the erection of groups of cottage houses where the injured and the aged merchant seamen and their wives could reside in comfort. This, he added, was the kind of work the Prestwick effort was helping them to do. (Applause).

A PERMANENT RECORD

Mr Bridge thereafter presented the Provost with an engraved certificate as a permanent record of what he termed "this superb result." The document which he read sets forth the effort by Prestwick, incorporates the amount raised, and generally pays tribute to the effort by Prestwick on behalf of the men of the Merchant Navy. He asked the Provost to accept the certificate on behalf of the town as some acknowledgment of the tremendous job the town had done for the cause. (Applause).

Accepting, the Provost assured him that the memento would be treasured by them, framed and placed conspicuously in the burgh chambers so that in years to come the citizens of Prestwick would see that they had done their duty to the men of the Merchant Navy (Applause).

Laughingly, Mr Bridge then said he had three gold badges to present; they were not real gold, he explained, but they could not be bought. It was called the "Badge of Honour," and was only presented, if he might say so, for distinctive service rendered to the Merchant Navy.

He asked the Provost, Mr J. A. Kinghorn, burgh treasurer, and Mr J. L. Jones, town clerk, to accept the badges as a reminder of their gratitude for the distinctive service they had rendered, and in doing this it meant, in effect, every citizen of Prestwick. (Applause)

27th October 1944

PRESTWICK "WELCOME HOME"

Monkton Not To Join In Appeal Plans

Regret was expressed at a meeting of the Prestwick Welcome Home and Commemoration Fund Committee, held in the Council chamber there on Thursday evening of last week, that Monkton had not seen their way to be included in the scheme.

Provost Dunsmore presided over a good attendance, and the minutes of the two previous meetings were submitted and approved. Contained in these were the plans for the welcome of Prestwick's returning members of the forces at the cessation of hostilities and for the commemoration of those who have made the last measure of sacrifice for their country. These proposals appeared in last week's "Post."

At the outset' the clerk (Mr John L. Jones) said he had written Mr Andrew, Monkton, to inquire whether Monkton was prepared to join with Prestwick in the appeal that was to be made. He read the reply which stated that the Monkton Committee felt that the Prestwick programme would be of no benefit to Monkton men and women returning from service, and they would therefore carry through their own programme with funds already collected, and which would be, it was expected, considerably augmented by the time hostilities ceased. They saw no reason why appeals should be made to the same people if the committee operated in their own districts.

The Provost said they were sorry they had that reply because in every appeal made in Prestwick up to date they had always had the co-operation of Monkton.

A letter from Scottish Aviation Ltd. on the same matter stated that they should be pleased to help in assisting to raise funds, but pointed out that no direct appeal for the town of Prestwick alone could be made as many of their employees did not reside in Prestwick, and they would desire to support their own town or village effort. Prestwick would, however, have full consideration and share in any monies that it was hoped would be collected.

The Provost said that was quite satisfactory; they were assuring Prestwick that they would get their proportionate share, and under the circumstances they could not expect more.

The constitution, containing fourteen clauses, was gone over seriatim, small alterations made and adopted. In the light of the communication from Monkton the question of whether "district" should be left out was discussed, but it was agreed to leave it in.

The clause reads :—

"The aims of the committee shall be voluntarily to raise funds to provide for the recognition of the services of the men and women from Prestwick and district who have served in H.M. Forces and ancillary Services during the present war, and to perpetuate the memory of those who have made the supreme sacrifice in the service of their country."

Councillor William Duncan was unanimously appointed vice-chairman of the committee, and Mr McAlpine and Mr Mowat were appointed auditors.

Comforts Funds.

Fear that there would be overlapping on the matter of appeals was expressed when the position of the three comforts funds of Glenburn, Marchburn, and the Toll, was discussed in relation to the appeal to be made for the larger scheme.

The Provost said that at their several meetings they tried to lay down a principle that the Comforts funds would not be interfered with as far as they acted in their own districts, but if they made an appeal in the town they would be running counter to the general appeal being made.

Mr Adamson, convener of the Halls committee, said they had had an application from New Prestwick for the use of the town hall for a Sunday concert, and the matter had been continued.

Mr William Connor, New Prestwick, said his committee had pledged themselves to help the big effort all they could but they felt they should not be precluded from using the town hall as they were ratepayers. They were not going to work in opposition.

Councillor William Duncan said there appeared to be some confusion as all the gift funds committees had indicated that they were willing to co-operate with and help the Prestwick effort. He took it that the three district committees would desire to raise money for their own funds in order to continue to send gifts to the forces.

Mr H. Carse, Glenburn, emphasised the importance for them of the functions held in the town hall, and said he could show them hundreds of letters from the lads on service to show that they appreciated what was done for them. He pointed out that the town hall was available every Saturday night and every alternate Friday night. He suggested that the Welcome Home Fund should have the use of it every second Saturday and the three comforts funds would come in on the alternate Saturdays.

The Provost said that would be a matter for the Halls committee.

Finally, it was agreed that representatives of the Comforts Funds and the Entertainments sub-committee should meet and discuss the matter.

RED CROSS.—The total amount collected by the Monkton and Prestwick branch of the Red Cross Society in the penny-a-week fund was £126 14s 6d and in the P.O.W. fund £12 2s 4d.

1st December 1944

A Prestwick Man's "Nip"

"So near and yet so far," might well apply to the experience of a Prestwick man who was deprived of a "hauf" of whisky when it was almost within his grasp.

The circumstances attending the incident were brought out in evidence in a case that came before Sheriff William Garret at Ayr Sheriff Court on Wednesday afternoon, and which occupied several hours. Accused was Mary Reid Watson or Bryce, licensed hotel keeper, Royal Hotel, Prestwick, who was charged with having, on August 9, by the hands of Joseph Reid, barman, 98 Wilson Street, Ayr, imposed a condition that whisky could not be supplied to a customer unless he purchased a quantity of beer.

The charge was denied, and Mr Allan H. Lockhart, solicitor, Ayr, defended, the prosecution being conducted by Mr W. B. Norwell, depute fiscal.

Evidence for the prosecution was to the effect that two visitors to Prestwick entered the bar of the Royal hotel shortly after five o'clock, and ordered two halves of whisky and two glasses of beer, and when they had been served, the customer, who was treating, ordered another drink for a Prestwick friend who entered very shortly afterwards. A small whisky was put on the counter for the local man, but it was alleged that the head barman immediately took it back when he saw that there was no beer, remarking "if you are not drinking beer you get no whisky". The local man, according to evidence, got nothing but immediately said, "I'll fix you for that; I'll report this to the police".

For the defence evidence was given to the effect that when the barman, Reid, saw for whom the whisky had been ordered, he immediately took it back as he had told the man that he would not be served with whisky there. This, according to the barman, was because of an incident which had occurred some time previously when the local customer had, by slipping from one part of the house to another, been served with more than his quota, stated to be one "half" to each customer per session.

Tit For Tat.

Samuel A. Walker, chief inspector for the Ministry of Food for Ayrshire, gave evidence as to his investigation of the case reported to him by the police as the result of the complaint made by the Prestwick man. He had to make it clear, he said, to Mrs Bryce that what was alleged against her was conditional sale, and he gave her two instances of what he meant. Reid was present at the interview, and in her presence said "I definitely did it". Nothing was said then about this other local man being a pest. Reid told witness that the local man had promised to bring him some eggs and had not done so. (Laughter.) Mrs Bryce asked him in his (witness's) presence why he had done it, and he replied that he was in a bad mood.

Mrs Bryce also gave evidence. She said she left the attendance of the bar to Reid. She admitted she was very excited at the interview with Mr Walker and thought Mr Walker asked her if she permitted conditional sales and she said "certainly not".

Mr Lockhart submitted to his lordship that the man who was refused the drink was an undesirable customer and as such was refused, and, in any event, the sale was completed before any condition was attached. He pointed out that this was the first case of this type affecting the liquor trade to be dealt with in Scotland.

Not Proven.

The Sheriff, finding the charge not proven, pointed out that in cases of this kind where vicarious responsibility arose the evidence had to be very clear before a person charged was found guilty. The impression he had in this case was that the evidence left a considerable doubt in his mind. It had not been clearly and satisfactorily proved beyond any reasonable doubt that Reid made the remark attributed to him with regard to the beer; even assuming he did so, he (the Sheriff) did not think it was proved that both whisky and beer were ordered for this man, and tho' Reid might have made some remark about beer that would not be sufficient to imply that the accused was guilty of the charge of imposing a condition of sale at his hands.

8th December 1944

PRESTWICK PROBLEM

Cimmerian Gloom In Glenburn Homes

"Matters have got to a stage when the public will kick over the traces" was one assertion of many made in criticism of the ineffective gas supply in certain areas of Prestwick when the Town Council on Tuesday night—Provost Dunsmore presiding — discussed complaints particularly from the Glenburn area where houses were said to have no light at all.

The matter was raised by Mr Gilbert Steele, who stated that matters had got worse since last they met, and nothing short of a minor revolution would remedy things. They had to realise that most of those affected were men who were away from daylight for hours at a time, and when they came home they had to resort to candles for lighting purposes. The gas supply had been something horrible during the past week, and the more they brought the question up in council the worse it seemed to become. They would have to bring the Minister of Fuel and Power into this somehow.

Bailie Blunt said that throughout the burgh there was the same complaint. He could not see to wash his face before he came out. (Laughter.) They would require to ask authority to have electricity installed as that was the first thing that would put the Gas Company on edge.

Mr John Sawyers gave three instances of homes he had visited where there were children, and no light except candles. It was a horrible experience.

The Provost said they always heard of these complaints from Glenburn, but he could assure them that New Prestwick had cause for complaint as well. In his area for the last fortnight there had been practically no gas at all at certain periods of the day. If it was bad in that area it must be much worse at Glenburn. He suggested that they should approach the Minister of Fuel and Power.

"Downright Scandal."

Mr William Duncan said certain suggestions had been made a year or two ago but still they had the trouble. He said that something might be done if they did not take up an antagonistic attitude, and suggested that they might approach the Gas Company and hear what they had to say, and if nothing were done more drastic steps could be taken. It was a downright scandal for people to live under the conditions that had been stated in a civilised world. The matter had been discussed time and again.

Mr Steele said that while agreeing with Mr Duncan to some extent he did not think Glenburn lighting would be helped for it had been in a bad way for years, and was getting worse as time went on. The only solution, in his opinion, was the installation of electricity. It would only be putting things off by holding a meeting with the Gas Company.

The Provost said they should certainly have an expert to go with them as none of the Council members knew anything about the technical side.

Mr Sawyers said he was convinced the only remedy lay in the installation of electric current.

In further discussion, it was suggested that they might have a meeting with Ayr Town Council on the matter, and then meet the Gas Company.

Mr James Brock favoured the proposal put forward by Mr Duncan, remarking that he had not much faith in what the Minister of Fuel and Power could do in this matter. They would get far more valuable information from the gas manager.

A New Turn.

There was a new turn to the discussion when it transpired that the houses where the bad lighting conditions prevailed were owned by Bairds and Dalmellington Ltd., and the question was raised as to the difficulty of the Council in dealing with the matter.

Both Mr Steele and Bailie Blunt pointed out that the Council had responsibility for the conditions under which the ratepayers lived. Such conditions were a positive danger to the lives of the children. Bailie Blunt hinted at what might happen in houses where the gas was put on, went out, and then came on again without being turned off.

In reply to a question, Mr Francis Pritty indicated some of the difficulties of the situation, and stated that practically all the Corporation houses had electricity.

Bailie Blunt remarked that they had expended as much gas as would light Glenburn for a week. (Laughter).

It was agreed that the chairman and the manager of the Newton-on-Ayr Gas Company should be asked to meet the Council with regard to the matter.

The matter of electricity supply was mentioned, and on Mr Sawyers giving an assurance that before the week was out an application would be made to the Company from the tenants to have electricity installed, the Council decided that they could do no more at this stage.

BURGH OF PRESTWICK.

NOTICE TO FIRE GUARDS

As the Fire Guard Orders are now revoked in respect of the Burgh of Prestwick, all Fire Guards are discharged subject to the return of equipment. Such equipment must be returned to the

FIRE GUARD OFFICE, 53 MAIN STREET, PRESTWICK

as soon as possible.

Persons failing to return such equipment render themselves liable to be charged with the cost thereof.

JOHN L. JONES, Town Clerk.

Municipal Chambers,
Prestwick, 20th December, 1944.

15th December 1944

PRESTWICK AIRPORT CLAIMS

That Scotland stood solid behind the claim of Prestwick to be recognised as a sort of Clapham Junction of the world's airways was asserted by Sir William Y. Darling, former Lord Provost of Edinburgh, and chairman of the Scottish Council on Industry when he spoke at a huge meeting in the Broadway cinema, Prestwick, on Sunday afternoon.

Provost Dunsmore presided, and with him on the platform was Sir William, Councillor Hugh D. MacCalman, chairman of the Clyde Valley Regional Planning Advisory Committee, and Mr George H. Moore, president of the Prestwick branch of the Amalgamated Engineering Union.

In an eloquent speech in which he pressed the claims of Scotland he indicated the lines along which they should proceed in their post-war schemes of planning. He said that unity had come under the hammer blows of war, and in the future "Britain for the British" should be their slogan and watchword. Having remarked that Prestwick was destined to play a big part in the scheme of things he said it must remain the cross-roads of the world's airways if Scotland was to get its full share of post-war prosperity. Scotland stood behind Prestwick's claim, and in the chequered history of Scotland they had not witnessed such unanimity. There might be people in Prestwick who did not like the prospect of an international airport but they were called to world affairs by the development of widening national communications, and just as all roads led to Rome in the old days so all roads must lead to Prestwick in the future.

Councillor McCalman, a quiet effective speaker who made many points, allayed the fears of Prestwickians who might fear the extinction of the town as a seaside resort should the airport be developed. There might be some, he said, who were afraid it would interfere with their golf. He would like to tell them that it was extremely unlikely that there would be industrial development contiguous to the airport. This would be far behind Prestwick and spread all over the region among the various places that could handle the type of industry they had in mind. No one, he added, need be afraid that this beautiful little seaside town would become an industrial town.

Regional Plan.

It was important that the future of Prestwick should be known and known soon because the whole regional plan depended upon it. The communications plan at present was based on the assumption that the cause of Prestwick would triumph, and if that did not eventuate there would be little use for a regional plan for industry in this region at all. Once they had won the fight for Prestwick they must arrange for the buildings where the component parts were to be manufactured, and connect these in communications with the air base in such a way that the utmost economy would be assured. According to the White Paper, said Mr McCalman, the development areas would have priorities for building factories, and it was up to them to see in Scotland that this fleeting opportunity was seized and made of permanent value. He suggested three priorities in this order—first, a No. 1 international airport at Prestwick; second, a campaign for re-housing the people; and third, necessary factories for airport and other industries.

Mr George H. Moore stated the case for the workers on somewhat similar lines to those he urged when before the County Council not long ago. He told of one international air line in America that had found it necessary to employ 15,000 additional people now, and they visualised another 40,0000 very soon, and drew the deduction that the numbers employed at Prestwick could be substantially increased when it became an acknowledged trans-Atlantic airport. He saw great prospect for the youth in the development, spoke of the aeronautical college which might become an accomplished fact and of the contribution which he expected to see made in regard to the extension of industries in conjunction with the airport. He asked them to continue the prodding process in every avenue that might affect the Government's decision.

Full advantage was taken of the opportunity by the audience to ask questions or make observations. Unless something was done immediately, said Mr E. McCabe, convener of the shop stewards of S.A.L., Prestwick would fade away. At present there were more fears than hopes amongst the workers due to the Government's delay in post-war planning. Sir William had referred to the fact that it was destiny that had placed Prestwick where it was; but in his opinion if it was left that way then Prestwick would drift away. At the present time they were seeing the place getting smaller in so far as work was concerned. Workers were being declared redundant and that week-end the night shift had come off.

Another speaker suggested that much as they desired this airport he was afraid circumstances alone would decide. Statements made by American air line representatives he had read always mentioned London and not Prestwick. He thought they should do more to get Prestwick recognised in that way.

At the close on the call of the Provost a hearty vote of thanks was accorded the speakers.

15th December 1944

AN AYR RESOLVE

At the monthly meeting of Ayr Town Council on Monday a letter was read from the Clyde Trust asking the support of the council for the establishment of an international airport at Prestwick.

Mr T. Paterson said they were in duty bound to accept the proposals now put forward. As the letter pointed out the Council was represented at the conference of the Clyde Trust which discussed the issue and the Council was materially interested in the development of such an airport. He thought there could be little said in opposition to the proposal that it should be run either as a public corporation or under Government control. One was a bit hazy with regard to what the ultimate development of international air service might mean as the conference held abroad had been very unsatisfactory from every point of view but so far as they were concerned they were entitled to demand for Scotland an airport of the first magnitude, and he did not think there was any other place that could put forward the same claims. He moved that they give their support.

Bailie Lanham, who seconded, said they should do everything in their power to see that Prestwick was one of the new airports of the international system.

1945

Churchill, Roosevelt and Stalin met at Yalta to decide on future areas of influence in Europe.

Hitler died in Berlin.

Germany surrendered; V.E. day celebrated on 8th May.

The British general election resulted in a landslide victory; Labour 393 seats, Conservatives 213, Liberals 12 and Others 22; Attlee became Prime Minister.

The United States dropped atomic bombs on the Japanese cities of Hiroshima and Nagasaki.

Japan surrendered on 14th August; the war ended.

MINISTRY OF FUEL AND POWER ANNOUNCEMENT

COAL SUPPLIES
NOVEMBER TO JANUARY

DURING the three months, NOVEMBER, 1944, to JANUARY, 1945, inclusive, no controlled premises may be supplied except by licence, from the Local Fuel Overseer with more than 1 ton of House Coal and Kitchen Coal (including Coalite). Stocks at any premises, including any delivery made, may not be raised above 25 cwts.

During the same period of three months the maximum aggregate quantity of Coke, Small Anthracite, Small Welsh Dry Steam Coal and Manufactured Fuels (other than Coalite) which may be acquired (except by licence) at any premises is 15 cwts., and stocks of fuel in this group may not be raised above 1 ton.

These are maximum quantities, not rations. Merchants will not have enough coal to give everybody the maximum quantity and only very limited supplies of coke and anthracite are available.

The supply position remains exceedingly difficult and it is essential that the strictest economy in the use of all forms of fuel be exercised this winter if serious hardship is to be avoided during the colder weather. Consumers who have been able to build up reserve stocks should draw on these as sparingly as possible since they will be urgently needed later on.

The exemption of HOSPITALS, SCHOOLS and other EDUCATIONAL INSTITUTIONS from the restrictions will cease as from 31st OCTOBER and the only premises exempt will be those which receive a special certificate of exemption from the Regional Coal Officer.

NO CARRY OVER is permitted of quantities which have not been obtained in previous restriction periods.

ELECTRICITY AND GAS — WARNING

During exceptionally cold or foggy weather, increased consumption of electricity and gas puts a severe burden on plant capacity and labour supply which are already strained by war-time production needs. The strain as regards electricity is especially acute between 8 a.m. and 10 a.m. so cut your consumption as much as possible.

REPAIR WORK

Prestwick Town Council And New Department

Several matters connected with housing were mentioned at the meeting of Prestwick Town Council held in the Council Chambers on Tuesday evening —Provost Dunsmore presiding.

At the outset the Provost, wishing the members a Happy New Year, expressed the hope that they would be able to overtake some of the improvements which were envisaged.

Bailie Dougan moved the motion of which he had given notice, "that it be remitted to a special sub-committee to consider and report on the setting up of a Works department to undertake all work of repairs, etc., required on Town Council properties." The Bailie said he did not wish to go into the matter if they agreed to the appointment of a committee.

Bailie Black seconded.

The Provost said he was in agreement with the idea of a works department, but in preparation he thought they should have a report from the treasurer as to the amount spent on repairs.

Bailie Dougan said he intended that the committee should ask for that.

After some further talk the motion was agreed to, and a special committee consisting of the Provost, Bailie Black, Bailie Dougan and Mr J. D. Young was appointed.

Requisitioned Premises

Letters were read in connection with the premises at 8 Ardayre Road, which had been requisitioned and were now released, and the surveyor reported that the building as it existed was not suitable for adoption as separate dwellings.

Accordingly it was unanimously agreed not to ask for the transfer of the requisition to the Town Council, and the house will go back to the proprietor, whose blind sister is to reside there.

Youth Movement

Arising from a petition by the Ayrshire Cadet Committee desirous of erecting an office, store and assembly hall in Briarhill Road, it was agreed, on the motion of Police-Judge Milligan, seconded by Bailie Dougan, to grant exemption from the provisions of Section 11 of the Burgh Police Act in respect of permission for a new road.

Mr Milligan pointed out that they had only got a lease from year to year, and he believed they could vacate in three months. "We have no proper accommodation for this youth movement, and I think it is our responsibility at some time. Here is a youth movement asking on its own initiative to find a way to help them."

Bailie Dougan remarked that these boys were a great asset to the town throughout the whole of last summer, and they should be encouraged in every possible way.

Mrs Crawford—Why can't we give them the British Restaurant to carry out their schemes?

The Provost—It does not belong to us.

Mrs Crawford said it seemed awful that these boys could not get a place.

The Provost pointed out that the British Restaurant belonged to the Ex-Servicemen's Club and the Government had built certain parts which would require to be taken over.

Mrs Crawford suggested that they could negotiate with the Ex-Servicemen's Club.

The Provost said that did not arise here.

After a further statement by the town clerk and the burgh surveyor, it was agreed that they intimate to the Dean of Guild Court their finding of relaxation for one year in view of the temporary nature of the building which was proposed.

Private Enterprise

Police-Judge Milligan gave notice for next meeting: "That it be remitted to the Housing Committee to consult with the local building contractors with a view to ascertaining (1) what contribution private enterprise can make towards the provision of houses in the burgh; (2), what assistance contractors are prepared to give in the erection of state-aided houses; and (3) if the Department of Health agrees will the contractors be prepared to accept fixed prices for this work."

Entertainments

A suggestion by Mr McNair that those dealing with the matter of entertainments in the town should be empowered to bring in outsiders in order to get their views was agreed to. He suggested that bowling clubs, golf clubs and various youth organisations, and possibly hotel proprietors might be consulted.

Burgh Guide.

An entertainments committee stated that six offers had been received for the publication of a new edition of the burgh guide, and it was unanimously agreed to accept the offer of a Cheltenham firm to publish a guide of 96 pages and to supply 2500 copies free of charge, over a period of two years.

It was agreed to take no action with regard to advertising the town in two publications which were mentioned.

Public Safety.

From a minute of the Streets and Planning committee it appeared that a letter was submitted from Messrs J. and R. Thom, Ltd., Prestwick, making various suggestions for road improvements in the interests of public safety. There was also submitted a letter from the burgh surveyor, indicating his general agreement with the suggestions made, and also a report by the Inspector of Police, giving details of accidents which had occurred at the junction of Briarhill Road and Caerlaverock Road since June, 1944. After discussion, the committee agreed to remit the matter to the town clerk and the burgh surveyor to report further on the estimated cost of carrying out the suggested improvements, and to ascertain the views of the proprietors of the properties concerned on the suggestions made.

5th January 1945

Buses To Prestwick

(To the Editor, *The Ayrshire Post*)

Prestwick,

Sir,—In writing this letter I am discharging a duty not only on my own behalf but also on behalf of the many long-suffering Prestwick people who are compelled to travel to and from Ayr daily to their various places of work. A fortunate few are able to utilise the services of the railway but a great many have no option but to throw themselves on the doubtful mercy of the bus service. In the proverbial hard school of experience I have learned that not to be an aerodrome worker is to render it practically impossible to travel to and from Prestwick during business hours.

To quote a case in point. One day this week I was endeavouring to get home to Prestwick for my lunch in the one hour which I am allowed for this purpose. On arriving at my bus stop I mingled with a queue of Aerodrome workers. Very shortly a double-decker bus drew up and the conductress announced in a loud voice it was for Aerodrome passengers only. The ordinary passengers moved up to await the arrival of a service bus. After the space of about five minutes had elapsed one arrived and by that time a further queue of Aerodrome workers had formed. By the time they had all surged on to the bus it was full up and was unable to stop and lift any of the ordinary passengers who were waiting at various stops between Ayr and

9th February 1945

SINGLE SITE

Prestwick Prepares For Temporary Houses

Under a new scheme prepared by Mr Francis Pritty, the burgh surveyor, the temporary houses for Prestwick, 85 in number, are to be erected on one site.

This decision was taken at the monthly meeting of the Town Council on Tuesday night following a report and explanations submitted by Mr Pritty. Provost Dunsmore presided, and a number of ratepayers heard the discussions at the meeting.

The Housing committee had approved of lay-out plans for the erection of the temporary houses on sites in Adamton Road and facing Crandleyhill Road, and this is superseded by the new suggestions.

In his report Mr Pritty stated that the Air Ministry had intimated to the town clerk that they regretted they were not in a position to de-requisition the ground known as McEwan's field, adjoining the Biggart Home, where it was proposed to erect 67 houses. In view of the urgency of the matter Mr Pritty gave consideration to other sites, and after consultation with the town clerk prepared sketches of a layout plan on the ground situated on the south side of St. Quivox Road extending to 8.8 acres. This area, the report points out, is capable of taking the complete allocation of the 85 houses. Steps had been taken to apprise the Department of Health and the Ministry of Works of the change and they recognised the urgency.

The layout plan was before the council, and Mr Pritty explained that the ground was known as Mrs Semple's field at the east end of St. Quivox Road. They might have the type of house decided upon at any time and the question of delivery would arise.

In reply to Mr Steele, the surveyor said there were no permanent houses likely to be built on this site. All the services would be required in any event.

After further talk as to procedure the change was agreed to, and it was further agreed that offers should be invited for the construction of roads, sewers, and the laying of water mains.

British Restaurant.

A letter was read from Miss Hutton, supervisor of the British Restaurant, intimating her resignation as from February 28, 1945.

The clerk pointed out that they had to intimate the vacancy to the Ministry of Labour, who would attempt to fill the vacancy before they could advertise. He mentioned that he saw four similar posts advertised in the west at present.

It was agreed to take the necessary steps to fill the vacancy.

A Pipe Band.

A letter was read from C.-Major McBean, O/C "D" Coy., No. 3 Cadet Battalion, R.S.F., asking, in the event of the Army Cadet Corps ceasing to function the Town Council would take over the equipment as trustees, and the balance of the fund could be used for a band fund in the future. The letter stated that £125 had been raised by public subscription, and out of this the necessary equipment had been found for the band. The equipment had been insured.

The matter was remitted to the Finance committee for consideration.

C.E.M.A. Exhibition.

When a request was made for the use of the Town Hall for a C.E.M.A. art exhibition some time in the near future, Mr Steele expressed the view that if they gave up the lets of the Town Hall for the fortnight of the exhibition the other funds they were interested in would suffer. He did not think they should entertain it.

The Provost said this was a Government-sponsored exhibition and was calculated to educate people; it was not often they had an art show in the town. It was something that should not be turned down without thought.

Mr Steele said they were not drawing in nearly enough money for the Welcome Home Fund, and they were not going to improve matters if they had the hall let for this purpose.

Bailie Blunt said this exhibition would be an attraction for the young and would be instructive to them all in Prestwick. He said most of them were interested in art.

Mr Steele, seconded by Mr Adamson, moved that no action be taken.

Bailie Govan, seconded by Bailie Blunt, moved that it be remitted to the Finance committee for consideration, and on a division the remit was carried.

Need of Vegetables.

Bailie Dunlop towards the close of the meeting directed attention to the decision of the Parks committee not to proceed with the production of vegetables this year by the burgh gardener, and wished that it be rescinded. Countries which had been strong in vegetables such as France, Holland and Belgium would not be able to send any to this country yet and he thought they should encourage the growing of all the food they could grow.

Mr Steele said it would make no difference as they had received no food from these countries for five years.

Bailie Dunlop said that last year had been a disastrous one for farming in Scotland from one cause and another.

Bailie Blunt said that two years ago they had grown a lot of beet and also leeks and the British Restaurant would take none of them. If they could not get the vegetables disposed of he did not see why they should put them into the ground.

Bailie Dunlop moved the suspension of the standing orders, and this was seconded by Bailie Govan.

The Provost, seconded by Bailie Blunt, moved that they do not suspend, and on a division the orders were not suspended and the minute was allowed to stand.

16th February 1945

Prestwick Criticism Of Welcome Home Plans

Various criticisms were forthcoming at a public meeting in the Town Hall, Prestwick, on Tuesday evening in connection with the objects of the Welcome Home and War Commemoration Fund.

Provost Dunsmore presided and said it had been suggested to the Committee that the public were lukewarm, and in some respects opposed to the purposes to which the committee proposed to apply the Fund. An opportunity would be given to any persons interested to put forward their views and suggestions but the Committee felt it might clear the air if some explanation were given as to the precise purposes, and the reasons which prompted them in coming to the various decisions. He called on the hon. secretary of the Committee (Mr J. L. Jones, town clerk), to read a statement on behalf of the Executive committee.

Mr Jones, in his statement, referred first of all to the origin of the Fund and the constitution of the committee, and thereafter detailed the decisions that had been arrived at, and which have already appeared in these columns. He pointed out that the suggestion with regard to a garden of remembrance was unanimously approved by the Committee but perhaps no part of the scheme had been subjected to more criticism. It was a curious and significant fact, the statement pointed out, that of all the proposals put forward by the sub-committee the only one accepted without demur and without alteration was the one relating to this matter, and it received the unanimous support of the parent committee. It had been alleged that the general public was lukewarm or opposed to the proposals of the committee, and it might be that one reason for this allegation was that towards the target of £10,000 the total sum raised to date was between £700 and £800. This might have created the impression that the Committee was not raising the money quickly enough or that the public were refusing to subscribe. It should be borne in mind that up till now no direct appeal had been made to the public in Prestwick for subscriptions to the Fund. At the present time the weather was only suitable for indoor activities but the public could rest assured that when the better weather arrived efforts would be made on the same lines as those which proved so successful in previous ventures. Plans for various functions were at present on hand. It was anticipated that the greatest source of revenue for the Fund would be the appeal that would be made to every householder to subscribe. Concluding, the statement declared that the Committee were convinced that their recommendations would meet with the approval, not only of the majority of the townspeople but also of the members of the forces. They considered it would be a great mistake at the first sign of disapproval from what may possibly be a small section of the community to abandon ideas which were the fruit of much labour and thought

More Suggestions.

The meeting was thereafter thrown open for discussion and questions and there were some lively interchanges of opinion and views. Alternative suggestions made were as follows:—(1) that all the money collected for the Fund be divided among the returning servicemen and women; (2) that the money collected be divided equally between all service personnel who return, and the relatives of those who have died, with the proviso that a certain amount of money be retained to erect a plaque or memorial in Boydfield Gardens, which might be reconstructed to form a garden of remembrance; (3) that provision be made for the Fund being applied towards the education of the children of the men who died on service; (4) that from the money collected a benevolent fund be instituted for the benefit of widows and orphans of service personnel; (5) that a sum of money be set aside to endow the present Services Club, as reconstructed, and to provide for future maintenance; (6) that the collection of money for the Fund should proceed without the specification meantime of any detailed objects; and (7) that each returning serviceman or woman should receive a sum of £10.

It was agreed that the Committee, to which additional members were added, should reconsider the whole matter, including the suggestions made, the Committee to go into the whole matter in the light of the views expressed at the meeting.

16th March 1945

School Sites In Prestwick

Mr James Boyd, the director of education, has submitted to the Teaching and Staffing committee and also to the General Purposes committee of the Ayrshire Education Committee a report on the location of school sites in Prestwick.

At short notice, he stated, he had been asked to attend a meeting of representatives of Prestwick Town Council and of the County Council's Town Planning Committee, when there had been discussed, inter alia, the question of making provision for sites which might be required for schools.

Subject to approval by the Education Committee, sites had then been provisionally earmarked as follow:—(1) 16 acres for a Junior Secondary School on Ladies' St. Nicholas golf course; (2) 16 acres for a Junior College on St Ninian's golf course (to serve the needs of Prestwick alone, if required for that burgh's needs in view of the apprenticeship personnel employed by Scottish Aviation, Ltd., or, alternatively, to absorb the 15-18 years olds in the adjacent district of the Burgh of Ayr); (3) 1 acre for a Nursery School in a convenient part of Prestwick, having special regard to a location near a congested housing area and involving only short distances for the young children to walk.

It was agreed to remit to the architect to submit a report as to the sites provisionally selected for consideration, in the first instance, by the members appointed to deal with the question of sites for schools, etc. It was also agreed that the chairman of the Education Committee and of the General Purposes sub-committee should be invited to take consultation in the future.

9th March 1945

STREET CLEANSING

Prestwick Town Council And Temporary Houses

Tuesday evening — Provost Dunsmore presiding—a minute relating to the cleansing of streets evoked some comment from Mr Steele, who asked what decision had been reached with regard to Glenburn.

Mr F. Pritty, the surveyor, explained that the position there was somewhat difficult because of the coal that was tumbled in the gutter, which appeared to have been done generally. A man was kept constantly employed there cleaning the streets.

Asked if the difficulty was shortage of labour, Mr Pritty said it was that and lack of vehicles.

Mr Steele said he met two men who wanted to know the reason why there should be a shortage of labour as they would like to get a job.

Mr Pritty indicated that he would be only too pleased to employ anyone suitable.

The matter then dropped.

From the minute it appeared that the secretary of the Second Ward Committee had written expressing the view that the present location and method of disposal of refuse on the shore front was most unsatisfactory and asked that steps be taken to find an alternative dump. After an explanation had been given by the surveyor the committee agreed to take no action in the matter.

Temporary Houses

The Provost raised the question of the erection of permanent houses instead of temporary houses in view of the new policy indicated by the Government, and suggested that the Standing Orders might be suspended in order that they could do so. He did not see why they should go on with temporary houses if permanent ones could be completed as quickly.

The clerk alluded to a meeting held in Glasgow of the various authorities in the west of Scotland and the position was that the Government now thought they would be able to accelerate their programme to such an extent that they would be able to start building permanent houses much earlier than was anticipated, but this did not mean that they were to stop their temporary houses. The Council had intimation that Prestwick was likely to get 50 of the 85 temporary houses allocated to them by November 30. That meant they had to be ready by then for these houses.

After some further talk, Mr Steele moved that they pass to the next business, and this was agreed to.

Bus Stops

Mr Steele raised the matter of the stopping place for buses going to Glenburn, and suggested that it should be shifted nearer the Cross.

Mr Brock supported the need for a change, remarking that not only were the flower beds trampled upon but they could not get the grass to grow there.

Bailie Dougan directed attention also to the one at Grangemuir Road, where the same thing applied. Children and people who ought to know better walked on the grass.

The clerk pointed out that the matter of the bus company's stopping place at the railway station would be coming up for review when the matters mentioned could also be brought up.

Lodging Exemptions

The clerk (Mr J. L. Jones) intimated that 18 applications had been received by proprietors of hotels and boarding houses for exemption under Par. 9 of the Lodgings Restriction Order for the burgh. These were all in order.

In reply to Mr Steele, the clerk explained that such people had to reserve 20 per cent of their accommodation if such was required.

Wardens' Club

On the motion of Mr Brock, seconded by Mr McDonald, it was agreed to take back for further consideration a decision not to grant the request of a portion of the St. Nicholas Ladies' Golf clubhouse for the provision of recreational facilities for members of a proposed wardens' club.

20th April 1945

Prestwick Council Affairs

Several matters were discussed at the monthly meeting of Prestwick Town Council among them the need to protect the amenities of the shore and parks generally from abuse. Provost Dunsmore presided.

On a communication being submitted from the Ministry of Fuel and Power as to the necessity for economy, Mr Brock said the belief had gained ground that the coal trade was all right. No more dangerous misconception could be entertained, he declared. It would be their duty to economise both publicly and privately.

Bailie Blunt said it seemed ridiculous to ask people to economise when he knew of people who had not had a bag of coal for weeks. He knew of one old lady of 90 who had no fire to keep her warm.

Mr Brock said there was not enough fuel in the country, and they were already warned that next winter would be worse than the one now ended.

Mr Pritty said the suggestion in the circular was that they do not light the lamps from May until the middle of August.

After further talk Bailie Blunt moved that they continue the lighting as at present, and Mr Steele seconded.

Bailie Govan, seconded by Bailie Dunlop, moved that they have no street lighting in May, June and July.

On a division, the voting was equal. 6—6, and the Provost gave his casting vote for no lighting.

A County Levy

A letter was submitted from the joint interim county clerk in connection with a contribution in respect of the administrative expenses of the Association of County Councils.

The Provost said he could not see why they should be asked to contribute, and suggested that it be remitted to the Ayrshire Burghs' Association for their consideration.

This was agreed to.

Enforcing the By-Laws

Several members directed attention to youth activities at the esplanade and elsewhere, involving damage to property and annoyance to residents, and Mr Brock remarked that it all showed that recreational facilities in the town were insufficient, and that their post-war effort should give full consideration to that.

Bailie Dougan asked if any complaints had been received about horses being exercised at the sands, and the answer was "no."

It was pointed out that there were certain periods only when horses could be exercised.

Mr Pritty, on the question of the shore generally, said it would really require special shore police in uniform.

It was agreed to consider the whole question with a view to the enforcement of the by-laws.

No Priority

Mr Sawyers raised the question of the need of a public library for Prestwick, and remarked upon what had already been done in that connection in the County Council, and he hoped that the scheme they had in view at one time would have a priority in the post-war improvements.

Bailie Blunt thought the place to raise the matter was in the County Council.

Bailie Govan said that in point of fact Mr Watt, the county librarian, approached him the other day on the matter and indicated that there was no hope of priority for any new building. They would have to see if there was any place they could find that would accommodate the library. He (the bailie) had pointed out two places and that was as far as they had got.

Growing of Vegetables

Bailie Dunlop commented on the increased need there was this season for growing more food for home consumption. He had travelled through most of the countries on the continent and he could not see how they would be able to grow more than a small percentage of their former foodstuffs. The town Council should show an example in this matter and produce as many vegetables as possible.

Mr Brock told of what was being done. They had not sold their seedlings as they had done in former years, and he was able to state that ground on the other side of Boydfield had been planted with vegetables.

General approval was given.

Notice of Motion

Bailie Govan gave notice that at next meeting he would move that the charges for the hire of the town hall be increased.

HEAR BOTH SIDES...

The political truce, agreed by all parties for the purpose of getting on with the war, is reflected in our newspapers. With the General Election, however, the gloves will be off again, and there will be some hard hitting.

But fortunately for us all there will be no hitting below the belt. British newspapers, unlike those of some foreign countries, do not offer their columns in a black market to the highest bidder. They state their case frankly and forcefully, as is fitting in a democratic country, but always cleanly and with a profound sense of their responsibility to the public.

So when big political issues are again at stake you should read other newspapers in addition to those of the party you favour. Whatever cause they champion you can rely on their honesty of purpose.

Issued by the Scottish Daily Express

HELP THEM FINISH THEIR JOB!

VOTE LABOUR

BURGH OF PRESTWICK. — VE-DAY HOLIDAYS. — Arising out of the Government's recommendation as to Holidays in connection with the celebration of the cessation of hostilities in Europe, the Town Council recommend that MONDAY, 25th JUNE next, be observed in the Burgh as a Public Holiday.—JOHN L. JONES, Town Clerk, Municipal Chambers, Prestwick.— 7th June, 1945.

BURGH OF PRESTWICK

PRESENTATION of the FREEDOM of the BURGH to His Grace the DUKE OF HAMILTON and BRANDON, P.C., A.F.C., and DAVID F. McINTYYRE, Esq., A.F.C., will take place in the BROADWAY CINEMA, PRESTWICK, on WEDNESDAY, 27th JUNE, 1945, at 12 o'clock noon.

JOHN L. JONES, Town Clerk.
Municipal Chambers,
Prestwick, 12th June, 1945

RETURNED PRISONERS

MRS FERGUS BRYAN, 30 Seaforth Road, and Mr and Mrs ROBERT BRYAN, 70 High Street, wish to thank their friends for the kindness shown to Fergus on his return from prisoner of war camp in Germany, and to give their grateful thanks to the Red Cross for all it has done for him during captivity.

MR and MRS R. DARROCH wish to thank the ladies of the Mill Street Welcome Home Committee, also Mr and Mrs Hughes, Victoria Hotel, Kyle Street, for a very enjoyable social evening, and generous gift of money received.

MR and MRS S. DARROCH, 46 Taylor Street, desire to thank Mill Street Ladies' Social Club for social evening and gift received; also Mr and Mrs Hughes for their hospitality.

ANDY and JESSIE McALLISTER wish to thank relatives, friend and neighbours for the grand welcome home given to Andy on his return from Stalag XVIII.A., also sincere thanks to the Red Cross for parcels received during four years' captivity. —40 Nelson Street, Ayr.

MRS MARSHALL, 29 Gordon Terrace Road, wishes to thank all friends and neighbours for kind enquiries, and grateful thanks to Red Cross for parcels to her husband during his internment in Germany; also for generous gift from Glenburn March- burn Home Fund.

L/CPL. J. McINTOSH wishes to thank all friends and neighbours for gifts and kindnesses shown on his return from being a prisoner of war in Germany; also the Red Cross for all they did for him during his captivity.—62 Briarhill Road, Prestwick.

WILLIAM MORRIS, 19 Caerlaverock Road, Prestwick, desires to thank the people of Caerlaverock Road; also Members of St. Nicholas Church Woman's Guild, for their kindness and for gifts of money re- ceived on his return from being a prisoner of war in Germany.

MR and MRS S. W. PATTERSON (Sammy), desire to thank all friends and acquaintances for kind inquiries and for gifts received on his recent arrival home after five years' captivity in P.O.W. camp in Germany.—45 Lochside Road, Ayr.

MRS ROCH would like to thank all her friends for the warm welcome given to her son, Harold, on his return from a prison camp in Germany, also gifts received and for their many kindnesses shown to her during his absence; also to express her gratitude to the Red Cross and the Y.M.C.A. for their magnificent efforts on behalf of P.O.W.—13 Miller Road, Ayr.

SIGN. ROBERT WELSH, 12 Adamton Road, Prestwick, thanks all his friends; also friends, old and new, from Saunterne Road, for enquiries and gifts received, also the Red Cross for parcels received while a prisoner of war in Germany.

29th June 1945

PRESTWICK'S NEW BURGESSES

Tributes To Enterprise In Building The Airport

The Freedom of Prestwick was on Wednesday in the Broadway Cinema conferred on the Duke of Hamilton and Group Captain D. F. McIntyre in appreciation of their air achievements and of their courageous foresight and acumen in founding the Prestwick Airport.

The burgess tickets were contained in silver mounted carved oak caskets of attractive design.

Provost R. H. Dunsmore presided at the presentation ceremony, and in handing over the caskets said the actions of the Town Council did not always meet with the approval of the townspeople, but he felt their presence in such large numbers was testimony to the wholehearted support they were giving to the Town Council on this occasion. (Applause.) Twelve years ago the Marquis of Douglas and Clydesdale, as his grace was then, and Mr McIntyre had their names suddenly blazoned across the news headlines by their daring and hazardous flight over the summit of Mount Everest. That was only the forerunner of things to come, for within a matter of two years they were bound on another quest, which was in time also to make world news. They were on the search for an aerodrome, and it was not just blind chance that made them choose the spot we now knew as Prestwick Airport.

While the war interrupted the peacetime activities of the aerodrome, it also accelerated the development of the vast resources and enabled Prestwick Airport to play a major part in the struggle against Nazi Germany for air supremacy. It was the foresight and courage of the Duke of Hamilton and Mr McIntyre that made it possible. Their efforts to establish the airport as an international airport had not been easy, but they had persevered and they and the people of Scotland were determined that it should be accorded the recognition it so richly deserved. Scotland was indeed fortunate in possessing two sons of the calibre of the Duke of Hamilton and Mr McIntyre, and Prestwick felt doubly proud of claiming them as burgesses.

After the presentation the new burgesses took the oath and signed the roll.

"First of the Many"

The Duke of Hamilton, acknowledging, said this was a very significant honour which would be highly appreciated by the most distinguished person, and much more by Mr McIntyre and himself. Ten years ago the opportunity arose which resulted in Prestwick becoming the terminal airport not only of this country but of Europe, and during the critical days of the war an essential link in our lifeline. On her war record Prestwick had become famous the world over, and now Prestwick could look forward to a fair future for the peace. The progress that had taken place in the past few years could not have been achieved with the smoothness and efficiency that had become so characteristic except with the wholehearted co-operation and support of the local people. He felt the great honour bestowed on them that day was an expression of realisation by the burgh of the vital importance they attached to air power.

Group Captain McIntyre said he always remembered in 1940 when the first aeroplane from across the Atlantic landed at Prestwick how some enthusiasts rushed up to the pilot and said: "Are you the first of the few?" The pilot readily responded, "No, I am the first of the many." Even at that time the pilot was aware of the daring and skill of the great operation Lord Beaverbrook, as Minister of Aircraft Production, had planned towards bringing the output of Canadian and American aircraft factories promptly to bear on the war in Europe and the Far East; but even he did not realise how many. In four and a half years no less than 45,000 transoceanic movements were handled on Prestwick Airport. Although they were told this was a war requirement and would cease to be necessary he felt quite confident that in the transition from military to civilian traffic, these figures could be doubled. No one knew how far this thing would go. The airport was doing a good job of work now, and would do a much better one in the future. (Applause). The town of Prestwick and the airport had got off to a flying start in the air age which the people of Prestwick had so nobly helped them to usher in. (Applause.)

29th June 1945

A World Federation

At the luncheon to the youngest burgesses which followed in the Queen's Hotel, Provost Dunsmore presided, and in proposing the toast to the Duke of Hamilton and Group Captain McIntyre, said the Everest flight had shown these young men had daring and courage above the average, and in their scheme for the airport they had to overcome many difficulties, but their problems were being tackled in a way that would meet with complete success. Although Mr McIntyre was a native of Ayr he had that day remedied the fault by becoming a citizen of Prestwick. (Laughter.) The Duke of Hamilton's forbears had associations with the town, as one of his ancestors was a signatory to the charter granted Prestwick, so that in accepting citizenship he was renewing a family association with the burgh.

The Duke of Hamilton, in reply, said he had looked to see what "rights, privileges and immunities" he would enjoy as a freeman. At the time of the charter there appeared to be privileges which, unfortunately, had since been curtailed by legislation. Continuing, he said that air power, unlike other forms of transport, had no obstacles. Rivers, lochs, mountains, coastlines presented no obstructions. The air was indivisible. Quoting Tennyson's "Locksley Hall," he said that San Francisco might be the beginning of a world federation. A future Parliament of Man could only come about through the air. (Applause.) For many hundreds of years Scotland was at war with England, but he was one of those Scotsmen who believed we had gained a good deal by partnership with England — though probably England had gained a good deal more, but he did not grudge that. Wider issues were at stake. At the time of the Union, Prestwick was a good deal farther from London than they were to-day from San Francisco. In a very few years Prestwick would be nearer San Francisco than it is to London now. The air was a great source of power, and it had made the comity of nations both essential and possible. He was glad to have met Mr T. P. Wright, who was an important person in aviation in America, and to see so many American friends there. He greatly admired their system of running air transport. They believed aviation demanded that initiative should be given every possible form of encouragement.

Pull of Scottish Sentiment

Group Captain McIntyre said that had the policy of their company not been in keeping with modern thought in commercial affairs and been directed towards the good of the many rather than the good of a few shareholders they could have received in such measure the moral and material backing of all those who made up Scottish Aviation, or the support and goodwill of Scotland as a whole. The universal apathy and lack of interest ten years ago was in the light of experience the best thing that could have happened, for they had been able to apply fresh and at that time highly unorthodox thought and method in defining their policies and in creating the goodwill

and impetus which these policies had acquired in the course of years.

After five years of practice they had progressed to a stage at which there was a service every two hours in both directions between Prestwick and the capital cities of North America, taking hours where the steamship took days. The had reached the stage of having peaked as many as 72 transatlantic aircraft arrivals at Prestwick in a single hour, and on the North Atlantic routes along a transatlantic aircraft departed every twenty minutes of the day and night.

Scottish sentiment was a strong link with the rest of the world, and he thought it would be true to say that many Canadians and Americans would be happy to travel or send their goods by a Scottish airline as a matter of sentiment when they would refrain on patriotic grounds from using a Government owned and subsidised British airline. Prestwick's position was a pearl beyond price which every country must envy, and it was logical to look forward to a large proportion of the world's air travel and trade passing through this aerial gateway to Europe and the East. The story of Prestwick was as yet only half-told. There were many factors in its potential development too revolutionary and unorthodox even to be mentioned at this stage, but they would be mentioned when the time was opportune.

Friendly Competition

Mr T. P. Wright, chairman of the Civil Aeronautics Authority in America, emphasising the benefits to be derived from civil aviation, said he had been engaged in a mission which took him into Germany to assess the damage done by our air power. That was something we must see did not happen again. The aeroplane gave us a means for preventing future wars, and gave an implementation of San Francisco which we did not have at the time the League of Nations was instituted. There we had the right ideas, but there was no force to enforce peace. We must learn that lesson, and be sure that this time we kept the strength along with the good will. Air power could make the thing we had all longed for through many generations come true. He had been impressed by the aggressiveness of Mr McIntyre, which they in America relished. They liked competition, and felt that the old saying that competition was the life of trade held true. Friendly competition would build up air transport to the point where it could give true service to the public. They were glad Mr McIntyre and his associates had been successful in gaining their place in the scheme of things, in doing the impossible in breaking down the White Paper as it had come out. (Applause.) He thought Prestwick was to be congratulated in granting this honour to these two men. Flying over the Atlantic might have some retrogression in the stopping of the large war traffic, but eventually that traffic would be again built up, bringing the American people and the Scottish people closer together.

The toast of the burgh of Prestwick was proposed by the Earl of Glasgow, Convener of the County of Ayr, and acknowledged by Provost Dunsmore.

29th June 1945

POSTSCRIPTS

HAPPY CEREMONY

I must congratulate the burgh of Prestwick on the manner in which the presentation of the Freedom of the burgh to the Duke of Hamilton and Group Captain McIntyre was carried through on Wednesday. The smoothness of the arrangements spoke of very efficient organisation.

The Broadway Cinema made an acceptable place for the ceremony, and the magnificent floral display in front of the platform by the parks superintendent, Mr. J. H. Brownlie, won many admiring comments.

There was a very happy atmosphere about the proceedings both at the Freedom ceremony and at the lunch which followed, and no doubt the representatives of neighbouring burghs who were there would be taking note of the unobtrusive but efficient way everything was done.

SWEDISH HOUSES FOR PRESTWICK

Prestwick Town Council at its meeting on Tuesday night adopted a minute of the Housing committee which recommended the acceptance of Swedish timber houses to be built in the town.

From the minute it appeared that the Department of Health intimated that the Government had acquired a number of permanent prefabricated timber houses in Sweden to be transported to Scotland and made available for erection by local authorities as part of their immediate post-war housing programme. Delivery was expected to commence early in September and continue up to the middle of January next. These houses have a life of not less than sixty years and qualify equally with brick-built houses for Exchequer subsidies. The Department is prepared to allocate to Prestwick 50 of these houses.

After some discussion, the minute stated, it was agreed to inform the Department that they were prepared to accept the allocation of these houses and proposed to erect them on sites in Crandleyhill Road and Pleasantfield Road.

6th July 1945

Prestwick British Restaurant

That the town had lost no money on the British Restaurant and had never been called upon to meet any loss on its trading was asserted by Provost Dunsmore at the monthly meeting of the Prestwick Town Council on Tuesday night when figures, included in the War Emergency Services committee were under review.

A report by the burgh treasurer of the trading at the British Restaurant for the year to May 15 last and also from the opening date on March 1, 1943, until May 15, 1945, was submitted at the committee meeting. It was noted that the loss for the current year was £155 14s 4d, and the net loss for the whole period since the restaurant had been opened was £330 14s 8d. Arising from this report the committee gave consideration to the future administration of the restaurant, and after discussion, agreed to review the position at the end of August.

The Provost, commenting on the figures, said that actually the town had not lost any money; they had never been called upon to pay any money against loss on the restaurant. His piont was was that the administrative expenses charged by the town against the restaurant were greater than their loss.

Mr William Duncan said there never could be any loss to the town as this was something quite apart.

In further discussion, it was pointed out that the Ministry of Food would not refund any loss if it were solely occasioned by administrative expenses and they were hoping that by the end of summer they would have sufficient profit to make up for any loss.

Mr Kinghorn, the treasurer, said he objected very strongly to any suggestion that he had prepared a statement that was wrong.

The Provost said he was not saying that but the impression would be left on the public that the town had lost money.

The minute was adopted.

GH OF PRESTWICK. — WELCOME HOME WEEK.
13th to 21st JULY, 1945

PROGRAMME OF EVENTS:

Y, 13th JULY—
DANCE and PIN-UP GIRL COMPETITION in TOWN HALL, from 7.30 p.m. to 1 a.m Admission 4s; Members of H.M. Forces (in uniform), 3s.

RDAY, 14th JULY—
FLAG DAY.
BOWLING COMPETITION— HOWIE MUNICIPAL BOWLING GREEN, Bridge Street Commencing at 10 a.m.
DANCE in TOWN HALL from 7.30 p.m. to 11.30 p.m.
Admission, 3s 6d; Members of H.M. Forces (in uniform), 2s 6d.

AY, 16th JULY—
DANCE in TOWN HALL from 7.30 p.m. to 11 30 p.m.
Admission, 3s 6d; Members of H.M. Forces (in uniform), 2s 6d.

AY, 17th JULY—
DANCE in TOWN HALL from 7.30 p.m. to 11 p.m
Admission, 3s; Members of H.M. Forces (in uniform), 2s

ESDAY, 18th JULY—
BOWLING COMPETITION—HOWIE MUNICIPAL BOWLING GREEN, Bridge Street. Commencing at 10 a.m.
GARDEN FETE and FANCY FAIR in BOYDFIELD GARDENS, The Cross at 2.30 p.m. Chairman—Provost R. H. Dunsmore Opening Ceremony by Mrs R. L. Angus, Ladykirk. Home Baking, Garden Produce, Fancy Goods, White Elephant, Toy and Gift Stalls; Fortune Teller; Clock Golf; Putting; and other Amusements and Side Shows. Displays of Highland Dancing. Music by Army Cadet Pipe Band Teas and Refreshments will be on Sale.

SDAY, 19th JULY—
GARDEN FETE and FANCY FAIR in BOYDFIELD GARDENS, The Cross, at 3 p.m. Home Baking, Garden Produce, Fancy Goods, White Elephant, Toy and Gift Stalls; Fortune Teller; Clock Golf; Putting; and other Amusements and Side Shows. Displays of Highland Dancing. Music. Teas and Refreshments will be on Sale.
GRAND VARIETY CONCERT by AYR KIDDIES'CONCERT PARTY IN TOWN HALL at 7.30 p.m.Tickets, price 2s 6d, 2s, and 1s 6d (Children half price), on sale at Town Clerk's Office, Links Road; W.V.S. Office, Town Hall, Main Street; and Billeting Office, Main Street.

AY, 20th JULY—
GARDEN FETE and FANCY FAIR in BOYDFIELD GARDENS, The Cross, at 3 p.m. Home Baking, Garden Produce, Fancy Goods, White Elephant, Toy and Gift Stalls; Fortune Teller; Clock Golf; Putting; and other Amusements and Side Shows. Displays of Highland Dancing. Music. Teas and Refreshments will be on Sale.
DANCE in TOWN HALL from 7.30 p.m. to 11 p.m
Admission, 3s; Members of H.M. Forces (in uniform), 2s.

RDAY, 21st JULY—
GARDEN FETE and FANCY FAIR in BOYDFIELD GARDENS, The Cross, at 3 p.m. Home Baking, Garden Produce, Fancy Goods, White Elephant, Toy and Gift Stalls; Fortune Teller; Clock Golf; Putting; and other Amusements and Side Shows Displays of Highland Dancing. Music. Teas and Refreshments will be on Sale.
SWIMMING GALA and DIVING DISPLAYS at BATHING LAKE at 3 p.m. Admission, 2s 6d (Reserved Area); and 2s; Children and Members of H.M. Forces (in uniform) half price. Pipe Band of the Army Cadet Force, Prestwick, will perform at the Bathing Lake in the Afternoon and in Boydfield Gardens at 6.30 p.m.
DANCE in TOWN HALL from 7.30 p.m to 11 p.m.
Admission, 3s; Members of H.M. Forces (in uniform), 2s.

MUSIC at the Dances in the Town Hall will be provided by JOE DENHAM'S BAND.
OPEN-AIR DANCING at Parking Place, Grangemuir Road, each evening from 7 p.m. to 11 p.m. Admission, 1s.

JOHN L. JONES,
Town Clerk and Hon Secretary,
Prestwick Welcome Home and War
Commemoration Fund.

wick, 3rd July, 1945,
unicipal Chambers,

20th July 1945

WELCOME WEEK AT PRESTWICK

Sergeant-Major George Kerr, Ayrshire Yeomanry, whose home is at 9 Pleasantfield Road, New Prestwick, is in the unusual case of being sorry to have got his discharge from the Army.

For the past three months he has been managing a coal mine in Germany, and liked the job, and before that he had a similar duty in Belgium until normal conditions were restored there. Before the war he was employed as a labourer.

He joined the Yeomanry in 1921, and was with them for a number of years until he went abroad, but he was back in this country after a few years, rejoined the Yeomanry in the spring of 1939, and was mobilised just before the outbreak of war. He was with the Yeomanry when they became an Artillery unit, and it was with the 151st (A.Y.) Field Regiment, Royal Artillery, that he sailed for Normandy on D-Day. He was in the fighting from there to Venlo on the German frontier, when he was sent to hospital.

It was on his discharge from hospital that he was put in charge of three coal mines in Belgium for A.M.G., and when they were handed back to the Belgians he went to Germany where he was put in control of the coal mine at Hamm, not far from the famous marshalling yard so frequently bombed by the R.A.F.

During his stay there he had the satisfaction of seeing the output increase fivefold, and when he was leaving to come home for discharge the German miners sent three spokesmen, who thanked him for what he had done for them. They had not expected, they said, to receive the courtesy and fairness that had been shown to them. He had also received a testimonial from his commanding officer.

At first he was the only British soldier within 100 square kilometres, but afterwards some Pioneers were sent along, and the Germans did everything they could to make them comfortable, making wooden beds with springs for them, and providing white sheets which were changed twice a week.

With the return of some of the younger men to the mine he had close on 3000 workers, not including the coking plant, under him. Asked how he got on with regard to the language, Sgt.-Major Kerr said "Fine! I spoke broad Scots and they spoke German slowly, and we understood each other." Latterly he had a German secretary who spoke some English.

The displaced persons who had been working in the mine were all looking fit and well-fed. They did not give the impression of slave workers.

Ayrshire miners should send a deputation to see the working conditions in that mine, said the Sgt.-Major. The pithead was laid out like an estate, and down below conditions were ideal, the cutters standing as they worked at the face, while mechanisation made the handling of the coal simple. Each miner had a little cottage for his family, with enough ground to keep them in vegetables throughout the year.

Sgt.-Major Kerr's father was a sergeant major with the R.S.F. in the last war, and his brother, Lieut. William Kerr, had also been a sergt.-major in the county regiment before becoming small arms instructor in the Home Guard.

Most ambitious event of an attractive programme for the public at Prestwick since Friday in order to swell the funds of the Welcome Home and Commemoration Fund was the garden fete and fancy fair in Boydfield Gardens, opened on Wednesday afternoon by Mrs R. L. Angus, Ladykirk. It was continued yesterday, and concludes tomorrow (Saturday).

There was a large attendance of Prestwickians and visitors at the opening, which was presided over by Provost Dunsmore, who was accompanied on the platform by a number of those who have worked hard to make the "Week" the success it is hoped to be

Provost Dunsmore said that the fete was being run under the auspices of the local W.V.S. which had done yeomen service since the outbreak of the war. At this time the ladies were again applying their energies in the interests of the returning service personnel, and he was sure that with the co-operation of the public their efforts would again prove highly successful. They were, he concluded, privileged to have with them, Mrs Angus, a lady who for several years during the war had full charge of the local W.V.S. and was fully responsible for the successful organisation and the carrying out of the work. He had much pleasure in asking her to open the fete. (Applause).

Mrs Angus, who had a cordial reception, said it was a great pleasure to her to be there that afternoon to take a share in the fete which was part of Prestwick's great effort to raise a Welcome Home Fund. She had been particularly pleased to have been asked by the W.V.S. as she had been most happily associated with them in their work for over three years. The object of providing a fund to give their service men and women a fitting welcome home was, she was sure, one which was very dear to all their hearts. (Applause). The least they at home could do was to see that they got a very warm welcome home after all their trials and hardships at sea, on land, and in the air. Thanks to the men in all three services this country not only escaped the horrors of invasion but had emerged victorious from the European war. "We cannot forget," she continued, "that many of us here still have relatives fighting in the Far East or prisoners of war in Japanese hands, but we hope that they, too, will soon be able to claim complete victory." In declaring the fete open she expressed the hope that the event would provide a substantial addition to the Fund. (Applause).

Amid applause little Margery Jones, daughter of the town clerk, who with his wife, was on the platform, presented Mrs Angus with a bouquet.

Proposing votes of thanks to Mrs Angus, the provost, and the ladies of the W.V.S. under the leadership of Miss Black, Mrs Norman Kennedy, Doonholm, W.V.S. organiser for the county, said they all realised how difficult it was in these days to raise money from gifts of goods; the only difficulty really was to get the goods and not to get people to buy, as the public was most generous especially when it was a question of doing anything to help our soldiers, sailors and airmen.

An Attractive Display.

Boydfield gardens presented an animated appearance during the afternoon, being thronged by crowds who moved freely about displaying more than a passing interest in the goods on the stalls, of which there were quite a number. Home baked scones and cakes met a ready sale as did the garden produce displayed in large quantities. In the White Elephant stall many types of goods were on sale, and on the fancy goods stall beautiful necklaces and bangles found a place. A toy and gift stall also found favour with many and wherever articles were on view purchasers were forthcoming. Fortune telling, clock golf, putting, and booths for rolling pennies, as well as Houpla, served to amuse and at the same time afford people an opportunity of subscribing to a worthy cause. Afternoon teas were catered for and were fully taken advantage of and the pipe band of the local Cadets discoursed music while little dancers in Highland costume were an added attraction.

On Friday last there was a dance and pin-up competition in the town hall; on Saturday there was a flag day, a bowling competition, and a dance; on Monday and also on Tuesday there was a dance. On Wednesday in addition to the fete there was a bowling competition on the Howie green; last night the Ayr Kiddies Concert Party gave a concert in the town hall. As a fitting round off for the fete to-day (Friday) and to-morrow (Saturday) there will be dances in the town hall. Open-air dancing has taken place each evening at the parking place in Grangemuir Road.

9th November 1945

MUNICIPAL ELECTIONS

Labour Gains

History was made in Ayr and Prestwick as a result of the elections held on Tuesday as two ladies were returned for the first time to the council board, one in each burgh.

Exceptionally fine weather prevailed on polling day and this enabled many to walk to the polling booths who otherwise might have remained at home. While it could not be said that youth took full advantage of the opportunity extended to them for the first time to cast their vote on local affairs, the result of the polling showed that in both Ayr and Prestwick good percentages in respect of the numbers voting were attained, much better than in some municipal contests in the past, but there is room for much improvement.

PRESTWICK

Whatever the polls held at Prestwick there was bound to be much fresh blood in the new council as no fewer than four old members did not seek re-election. Even so, it must be said that the results were a surprise to many, the defeat of such stalwarts of Labour as Mr John Sawyers and Mr George Blunt being unlooked for. Mr J. B. Black, who headed the poll in the Second Ward, had already given service to the community in a former Town Council, as had Mr Frank Milligan, returned with Mr McNair for the First Ward. Mrs Crawford had the distinction of being the first woman to be returned at Prestwick, and she made no promises when she faced the music at the ratepayers' meeting. The nett result of the poll at Prestwick is that Labour's strength is decreased by two, which leaves the party with only two members to represent them.

FIRST WARD
Two Seats
Alexander B. McNair	528
Frank M. Milligan	509
Alexander Scott	417
James McGinty (Lab.) ..	144

No change.
Spoiled papers, 2; percentage voting, 51

SECOND WARD
One Seat
James B. Black (Ind.)	707
aJohn M. Sawyers (Lab.)..	456
William Boyd	211

Independent gain.
Spoiled papers, 8; percentage voting, 52

THIRD WARD
Two Seats
John D. Young..............	534
Mrs Annie Crawford	352
David Preston (Lab.) ..	286

No change.
Spoiled papers 1; percentage voting 46

FOURTH WARD
Two Seats
aMatthew B. M. Flanigan	783
John Kerr	749
David B. Smith (Lab.)..	373
aGeorge Blunt (Lab.)	351

One Moderate gain.
Spoiled papers, 3; percentage voting, 57

VICTORY TEA

On Friday afternoon the residents of Pleasantfield Road, Prestwick, entertained the children of that street and of Pleasantfield Place at a victory tea. The day being fine tables were laid out on the drying green in front of the houses, and Provost R. H. Dunsmore came along to speak to the children and join them at tea.

The festivities were made possible by a collection in the street which raised £6, and most of them joined in baking scones and cakes in such abundance that when the children had finished there was still an ample supply.

Provost Dunsmore, addressing the young people, said he thought it was an appropriate occasion to celebrate. It was not every day they would have a victory such as they had had in the past week. They were all very young, and as they grew older they would look back on that historic occasion. It was a historic occasion, because they were hoping this was the last world war they would have. Amongst us they saw American and Polish soldiers, and they thought that an every day occurrence, but they must remember that these soldiers were not here before the war. They came to help to win the war against Germany and Japan, and he would like them to remember these soldiers, because when they were as old as he was people would ask them "Do you remember the soldiers who came across from America to help us to win this war?"

1946

The British government took emergency powers to deal with the balance of payments crisis.

The United Nations General Assembly met.

Leading Nazis were sentenced to death at the War Crimes trials at Nuremberg.

The Bank of England was nationalised.

Bread rationing began in Britain.

The Reith Committee reported recommending that new towns should be built.

A Royal Commission reported in favour of equal pay for women.

2nd November 1945

PRESTWICK HOUSING DEVELOPMENT

Provost Dunsmore cutting the first sod at the development of Prestwick's housing scheme at Marchburn, where 144 permanent houses are to be erected.

18th January 1946

Airport Benefits Prestwick

The benefits which had accrued to Prestwick from the establishment of the airport were referred to by Group Captain D. F. McIntyre when he spoke at a dinner in the Queen's Hotel, Prestwick, on Friday evening, when Provost R. H. Dunsmore and Mrs Dunsmore entertained members and officials of the Town Council and friends.

The Rev. Luke McQuitty, Monkton and Prestwick Church, proposing the toast of "The Host and Hostess", said the Provost had done everything in his power to help Scottish Aviation and the airport that had been planted at their door. When our American cousins came the Provost put himself out in order to keep in touch with them and make them feel at home.

Provost Dunsmore, in reply, said he had been fortunate in having colleagues who had given him all the help he could desire. Military victory must only be a prelude to as great an effort for peace, a peace of justice between man and man and nation and nation. We must see that when the various Service personnel returned they were offered a much better life by ensuring that they had full employment, and adequate number of up-to-date houses and much better social amenities.

Group Captain D. F. McIntyre proposing "The Town and Trade of Prestwick," said Scotland appeared at last to have come to appreciate the true importance of air commerce—a point which Prestwick understood fully; and everywhere he had gone lately he had found a determination that Scotland should be well to the fore in this new means of world trade and travel, and an equal determination that we should get our affairs in order before the avalanche of air traffic begins.

Prestwick was probably the only town in the United Kingdom that had discovered how widespread the benefits of this new transport medium could be. They had seen the airport and its ancillary enterprises distributing over the neighbourhood more than a million pounds a year, a large part of which had reached the Prestwick trades people plus a further £500,000 a year in the purchase of goods and material. One Prestwick contractor alone had had contracts on the airport totalling over £500,000 since the airport was established in their midst. They had also seen the vast numbers of visitors that could be brought to these shores by air transport, and the prospect which thus opened up for the Scottish tourist industry if they were permitted to conduct their own affairs as they should be conducted.

It had many times been said that air transport knew no barriers, but there was one barrier against which they were still struggling — the political barrier which was truly formidable, and would remain so until His Majesty's Government and the leaders of public opinion attuned their mentality to the challenge of the air age. If the vast prospect which now opens before us inspires us to rise to that challenge and send Scottish air liners out over the world with the same freedom, energy and enterprise as our fathers applied to the sea carrying trade, then the town of Prestwick need never look back. (Applause).

Bailie W. S. Govan, replying, said they had not been in the fortunate position of some neighbouring towns of having people give great gifts of land. Prestwick had been ably assisted by the enterprise of Scottish Aviation, and he was sure he expressed the feelings of all when he hoped that the conference called by the Scottish Council on Industry of Scottish M.Ps., Scottish Peers and representatives of all the cities, towns and counties would be a great success, and would give Group Captain McIntyre all the satisfaction he deserved. (Applause.)

Owing to indisposition Mr William Duncan, C.A., was unable to be present, but his notes for proposing the toast of "Members and officials of the Town Council" were read by Mr James Brock; Mr J. B. Black and Mr Francis Pritty replying.

Mr J. L. Jones, town clerk, proposing a toast to past members of the Town Council, to which ex-Provost Howie replied, revealed that in seven years the Town Council would celebrate its jubilee.

Bailie F. M. Milligan proposed "The Ladies", to which Councillor Mrs Crawford replying pleaded for women to come into municipal work with the schemes and plans they had in their own homes. The best memorial they could have to the dead was not two minutes' silence, but twelve months planning for the living.

Bailie Matthew Flanigan proposed the toast to the artists, Miss Gibson, Miss Molly Napier, Mr W. R. Gould and Mr David Anderson, and the Miller-Mathieson orchestra.

15th February 1946

OBITUARY

Mr FRANCIS PRITTY

A notable figure in the daily life of Prestwick for many years has been removed by the death of Mr Francis Pritty, C.E., burgh surveyor, master of works and sanitary inspector of the burgh, which occurred on Wednesday forenoon in a nursing home there. Mr Pritty, who had taken ill about a month before his death, was the son of a former burgh surveyor of Selkirk, where he was born 60 years ago, and where, in his father's office, he had a good grounding in his profession. Later, he went to Glasgow, and was in the city engineer's office there when he was appointed to Prestwick, from some 80 applicants for the post. That was in the late autumn of 1913, and since these now far-off days, with two shattering wars between, he has played a prominent part in the making of the Prestwick we know to-day. Not only did he take an active part in his capacity as burgh engineer and master of works in bringing to completion the fine housing schemes after the first world war, but he had the plans well forward for the start on a big scale of new houses, both temporary and permanent, at the present time; in fact, building has been in progress for some time at Marchburn on a scheme of permanent houses.

Mr Pritty, for many years one of the town's representatives on the Scottish National Housing and Town Planning Council, was elected a member of the executive committee of that body. Over a long period he was closely connected with the important organisations of his profession, and few members were held in higher esteem. As a member of the Institution of Municipal and County Engineers, the high honour was conferred upon him in 1938 of Scottish vice-president of that body. Mr Pritty was a member of the Institution of Water Engineers a member of the Royal Sanitary Association, a member of the Ayr Rotary Club, and a Guild brother of Ayr. He was also a member of the St. Cuthbert's and St. Nicholas Golf Clubs, and was a past president of the United Services Club of Prestwick for ex-Servicemen. He was a member of the management board of the Prestwick South Church.

In world war No. 1 Mr Pritty served for a time with the 5th H.L.I., and later transferred to the Royal Engineers, and rose to the rank of captain, and in the great conflict, just terminated, he was in charge of rescue, demolition, and road and water repair services in Prestwick under Civil Defence. Naturally, during the war years, when important operations were carried on at the nearby aerodrome, Mr Pritty worked in close co-operation with the officials of S.A.L. and the Air Force. In addition, he was fuel overseer for the burgh and when the N.F.S. took over the fire brigade he was made an hon. section officer.

In many and diverse ways Mr Pritty had close contacts with the community, and he was held in high regard by all who knew him, and not least by his fellow officials in Prestwick. He is survived by his wife, a son (a major in the H.L.I.) and two daughters.

BURN POLLUTION

Prestwick Council To Take Action In Near Future

The pollution of the Pow Burn and the steps that should be taken to effect an improvement were discussed at the monthly meeting of the Prestwick Town Council on Tuesday night—Provost Dunsmore presiding.

The matter was raised on a letter from the secretary of the Prestwick St. Cuthbert Golf Club, which directed attention to the pollution of the burn and asked that some action be taken by the Council to remove what was a nuisance of long standing.

The Provost suggested that they might approach Bairds and Dalmellington in the matter.

Bailie Govan remarked that there had been five reports already.

Bailie Black said the question had been before the Council for ten years, and they had had many reports in that time, but they seemed to get no further. It was a positive disgrace the condition this burn had been in. They had had reports from the M.O. which had got them nowhere, and they had written the colliery firm in the past, and the County Council had also been blamed for the sewage scheme at Mossblown. Bairds and Dalmellington had told them that the water from their collieries had gone through a cleansing process which made it crystal clear before it entered the burn, and they maintained that there was no such thing as coal dust going into it.

The state of the Pow Burn at present, he continued, was as black as an Egyptian night; he could not conceive of any blackness greater than that of the burn. There was a lot of oil in it also which would appear to emanate from the aerodrome. The chances were that the pollution was caused by one or all of the sources mentioned. The matter had always been shelved in the past, to his way of thinking because of sheer laziness. He was concerned about the state of the burn, as prior to the advent of the aerodrome it was probably one of the best attractions that the burgh had. Small boys could be seen sitting by its banks in the old days fishing for flounders, but there was no possibility of even these fish surviving in it at the present time. (Laughter.) He emphasised the need for strong action and moved that all the parties be communicated with—the County Council, the Colliery Company and the Aerodrome authorities, and that if there was no improvement in two months the question of raising an action of interdict should be considered.

Bailie Milligan, seconding, remarked that something definite would require to be done before the letters were written, and he suggested that they might have a report from an engineer as to where the nuisance arose and then take action.

The Provost pointed out that half the burn was under the jurisdiction of the County Council, and he suggested that they might work in conjunction with them.

Bailie Black said the Council had a riparian interest in the boundaries which entitled them to act.

Mr Steele said that at the start of the war he was one of a deputation that went to the collieries in connection with this matter and the Department of Health was informed, but they could do nothing in war time to make a company incur expense. The war now finished and he thought the Department should be communicated with.

Bailie Govan—We could refer the Department to their previous report on the subject.

There was no amendment, and Bailie Black's motion was adopted.

Coal Under Reservoir

When a letter from Messrs Baird and Dalmellington, Ltd., was intimated concerning the working of coal under the reservoir, Bailie Govan said he would like the public to know what they are threatened with—the reservoir falling into a pit.

Read by the clerk (Mr J. L. Jones) the letter from the firm mentioned intimated their intention, under the Act, of working the coal under, adjoining, and in the neighbourhood of the reservoir and water works, and asked whether the Council wanted to secure for themselves and successors a reservation to pay for any part of the coal.

Bailie Govan said they could leave the discussion till later.

15th March 1946

STAGGERED HOLIDAYS

Provost R. H. Dunsmore, Prestwick, was named in the House of Commons on Thursday of last week as a representative of the Convention of Royal Burghs on the Standing Committee appointed under the chairmanship of Mr Thomas Fraser, Joint Under-Secretary of State for Scotland, "to stimulate and co-ordinate action on the staggering of holidays in Scotland."

Mr W. B. Scott, Ministry of Labour and National Service, who has been appointed joint secretary, was manager of the Ayr Employment Exchange from 1929 to 1936, and was later chairman of the Man Power Board at Kilmarnock until his appointment as Manager of the Edinburgh Employment Exchange.

PRESTWICK ALLOTMENTS

(To the Editor, *The Ayrshire Post*)

3 Kirkhill Crescent,
Prestwick, March 11, 1946.

Sir,—On reading the report of the Prestwick Town Council meeting in your issue of last week, I was surprised at the statement made by the Provost to the effect that the allotments at the old St. Ninian's Golf Course were quite unsuitable for growing potatoes. As a plot holder for the last three years I am pleased to state that I have had good crops from this ground and am in the happy position of never having had to buy potatoes since starting. Two years ago I lifted 4½ 8 st.-bags and last year 4 8 st.-bags. The same allotment has supplied the household with vegetables of all kinds.

In view of the recent Government directive to local authorities to assist allotment holders, I bring this to the notice of ratepayers in this area and advise them to start digging now.

In spite of the pessimism of the Provost I am planning to start soon on my fourth year.

J. GILCHRIST.

Glenburn Gas

In connection with the complaint about gas lighting in Glenburn the clerk read a letter from the Newton-on-Ayr Gas Company which stated that the inadequate street lighting was almost entirely due to lack of maintenance and repair of the lamps which was not the responsibility of the Gas Company. As to domestic supply the letter stated that gas pressure recordings taken at various points showed good pressure in the gas mains apart from two short periods when the pressure, although above the statutory limit, would be improved. With the new gas making plant now being installed a much improved gas supply might be confidently expected before the summer.

Mr Melrose, the burgh surveyor, said that since street lighting was resumed the question of supplying electricity had been on the cards all the time. Mr Melrose produced two lengths of service pipe which had been taken out and showed that they were in a hopeless state.

Asked where the gas was going, he said at that point it was going into the ground, and the men were nearly gassed.

A member asked who was responsible for that piping and the surveyor said it was the Gas Company.

The Provost said they could only hope that an improvement would be made.

10th May 1946

PRESTWICK AIRPORT

Mr E. Hughes And "Lucrative Profits"

Speaking in the debate on the Civil Aviation Bill in the House of Commons on Monday, Mr Emrys Hughes (South Ayrshire —Lab.) expressed himself delighted to hear such enthusiasm from all parts of the House for Prestwick airport, which happened to be in his constituency.

He would like to assure Major Lloyd (East Renfrew—Con.) that things were not quite so gloomy in Prestwick as he tried to make out. He (Mr Hughes) would endeavour to prove that statement, not from the evidence of any Labour man or Socialist, but from statements made by people who were the arch-apostles of private enterprise in Scotland and the people who were largely behind all the opposition to the Bill and to national ownership of civil aviation. If things were so gloomy and depressed, why did it happen that, only a week ago, the people who were now telling them that Prestwick airport would be doomed under nationalisation were saying something very different through the solicitor or agent who appeared before the Ayr licensing board, the licensing magistrates who gave two licences to hotels at Prestwick because of the rosy future that was to be opened up? Members should hear the story in detail. They had heard nothing but a story of gloom and despondency about Prestwick. When the vested interests that sought to exploit Prestwick wished to get licences for their hotels there, they could say that Prestwick was to be the hub of the universe.

Lieut.-Colonel Sir Thomas Moore (Ayr Burghs—Con.)—No. .

Mr Hughes—The hon. and gallant member says "no," but I have a report here of a speech made by the solicitor for Scottish Aviation, Ltd., when he was applying for licences for those two new hotels. Referring to the aircraft lines using the terminal airport——

Sir W. Darling—What was the date of the speech?

Mr Hughes—It was April 18. Mr Black, the agent, said that, since the beginning of the year, the hotel had been used to its utmost capacity and that even the building which had been used as overflow had been occupied to the extent of 50 to 80 per cent. of capacity.

Sir T. Moore—The Bill had not been introduced then.

Mr Hughes—The hon. and gallant member says that this Bill had not been introduced, but here is the solicitor looking forward to a rosy future.

Sir T. Moore—He had not seen the Bill.

Mr Hughes—Perhaps he had not seen the Bill, and perhaps he will now withdraw his demand for licences if he has seen the Bill. I am sure that the Ayr County Council would be pleased to take them over. Quoting a newspaper report Mr Hughes said that was the story that they tell to the Ayr District magistrates when they wanted licences. This complaint against this Bill was that it did not go far enough. He wanted an assurance from the Minister who was to reply that when the airport was taken over the two hotels which were going to offer such lucrative profits to the people who applied for the licences and who did not believe in the future of Prestwick——

Lieut.-Colonel Thorp (Berwick-upon-Tweed) asked what were the lucrative profits which Mr Hughes had mentioned?

Mr Hughes—It is impossible to give the exact figures of lucrative profits because this private enterprise concern is so private that it does not even disclose its accounts. We suggested that if the State and the Civil Aviation Bill were going to attract all this host of foreigners to Prestwick, the profits from the hotel should not go to private enterprise but to the State. What was this private enterprise they talk about in Prestwick? Scottish Aviation Limited was, he presumed, the company that would have had control of the airport if the Tories had secured a majority at the last election. The Tories would have handed the airport back to private enterprise. What was this private enterprise? Mr Wills had referred to the fact that this concern had £100,000 nominal capital. He (Mr Hughes) would not say that originally the people who invested the money in this concern did not help in some way as pioneer enterprises in aviation in Scotland, but the £100,000 capital was now in the control of four individuals. They were going to get the profits from the hotels. The leading shareholder was a noble lord, a duke, who had 43,545 shares in this company. There was the brother with 30,045 shares. There was another one with 25,910—

An Hon. Member — "Another brother?"

Mr Hughes — Not another brother; this is Captain McIntyre. Then there was the solicitor who represented the law but not the "profits" because he was only a nominal shareholder of 500 shares.

Sir W. Darling—Is it not the case that the four gentlemen whose names the hon. member has mentioned, a year ago offered to the Scottish Council of Industry their undertaking at what they agreed to pay for it? Will he tell the House that is true?

Mr Hughes—I do not know about that. I cannot explain. I do not know anything about that private transaction.

Sir W. Darling — It was a public transaction offered to the Secretary of State for Scotland, Mr Thomas Johnston, through me as chairman of the Scottish Council of Industry. Will the hon. member tell the House about that?

Mr Hughes, continuing, said he was quite aware that these revelations would not be received with enthusiasm by the supporters of private enterprise, but here was a state of affairs that this company, 73 per cent. of whose capital was owned by two noble lords—("Why not?")—I suggest that we should not hand over Prestwick to private enterprise and that the time had come, when £2,500,000 or £3 million of State money is in Prestwick, that its future must depend entirely upon development by Government and public enterprise. There was absolutely no other way to make Prestwick a success than to make it publicly controlled and run in the interests of the nation. After all, it was not a couple of people whose enterprise made Prestwick. Prestwick was built during the blitz and the blackout by thousands of people during the war, and later on the hon. gentleman who was to reply could tell them how much State control had invested in Prestwick. As trustees for the people who helped to build Prestwick, multitudes of unknown men, it would be criminal for Prestwick to be handed over to private enterprise and for all our civil aviation in future to be handled by private enterprise.

After all, why should we be defeatist and say that the people who went in the bombers and the fighters could not run civil airlines? The future of civil aviation would be safer under public enterprise than under private enterprise, which worked for profit and exploitation, and the great majority of public opinion in Scotland and throughout the country would welcome this Bill as a statesmanlike Bill, putting civil aviation on its feet in the interests of the country.

Prestwick

"THE BROWNS" IN U.S.A. — A Moultrie, Georgia, newspaper to hand tells how a "bonnie" war bride and her 11 months' old son have adjusted themselves to conditions "over there." In an interview, Mrs Andrew Brown (a daughter of Mr and Mrs Kennedy, 25 Pleasantfield Road, New Prestwick), who has been re-united with her husband, whom she met when he was serving in Prestwick with the United States Air Force, expressed herself as surprised that the stores had so much to sell, and her greatest surprise was to be able to buy bananas, something she had not seen for six years. The people are very friendly, and she can understand them without much trouble, "but you should see the looks on their faces when I begin to talk," she told her interviewer. During the war Mrs Brown, then Miss Kennedy, was employed for a time with the Royal Observer Corps. Within two days' journey of Mrs Brown's home is another sister, who also married an American soldier, Sergt. William Culp, and they hope to see each other again soon.

7th June 1946

Prestwick B.R. Into Factory

It was revealed in a minute of the Streets and Planning committee submitted to Prestwick Town Council on Tuesday that a petition against a proposal that the British Restaurant should be used for factory purposes had been lodged.

The minute which related to town planning stated that a letter from Mr Alexander Cunningham of the Clyde Hosiery Co. (Glasgow), Ltd., Irvine, was submitted, stating that he was contemplating acquiring the premises formerly used as the British Restaurant, for use as a hosiery factory and enquiring what the Town Council's views were from the point of view of town planning. He stated that the power to be used in the factory would be electricity.

The town clerk reported that a petition had recently been received from a number of residents of properties adjoining the British Restaurant protesting against any proposal that these premises should be used for factory purposes.

After discussion, Councillor Crawford moved that the matter be continued for further consideration meantime. Police-Judge Dunlop seconded. Councillor Young moved, as an amendment, that the Council inform Mr Cunningham that, from a town planning point of view, they saw no objection to the proposed use of the premises. Bailie Dougan seconded. On a vote the amendment was carried by 4 votes to 3.

Mr A. B. McNair said he felt this was a challenge to the Council. Since the meeting of the committee he had found that Mr Rosie, the town planning officer, had pushed this thing more or less on to the Town Council, and this might have been brought about by a remark he (Mr McNair) had made when Mr Rosie was present at the special meeting. Mr Rosie considered

his job was housing and he would not interfere with the planning of the burgh. In this case he (Mr McNair) felt that to give a blessing to such a thing, something that was actually in a residential area, would be a very poor start to their planning of the burgh.

Bailie Black moved that it be remitted back. Since the matter had been before the committee he had discovered there were certain peculiarities about the building which had to be got over. It might be that the Youth committee wished to acquire it; on the other hand part of the building belonged to the ex-Servicemen and another part to the Ministry of Supply. Far too much time and attention had been given to recreation facilities, and he reminded them that there were many young girls in the district who had only Prestwick laundry and they should encourage light industries to the place whether here or somewhere else. He had always been led to understand that the whole of the town was a residential area.

Mrs Crawford seconded.

Mr Steele moved the adoption of the minute because, he said, he was firmly convinced, like Bailie Black, that they needed light industries in the town. When there was a likelihood of work for young girls in the town they should grasp the opportunity.

Bailie Govan seconded. He sympathised with the idea of a factory. A condition laid down for town planning was that there should be no smoky chimneys, and in this instance it was to be a matter of "all electrical." They should remember that the railway ran alongside and it was the most industrial thing they could have, and he did not think it could be claimed that this was a residential district entirely.

On a division, the minute was carried by 6 votes to 3.

ARMY CADETS. — After many months without a home, the Army Cadet Force in Prestwick has resumed parades in the Cadet Hall, off Briarhill Road. In addition to one hour's cadet training, the boys now have a club and already sections have been formed in football, cricket, swimming, chess and table tennis. The Pipe Band, despite losses to the services and to senior bands, continues to enhance its reputation. The main problem is lack of leaders and it is hoped that young men fresh from the services will assist either in the cadet training or in the club.

BARNARDO HOMES.—The pupils of Prestwick High School have for many years been enthusiastic collectors in aid of Dr Barnardo's Homes. They have this year, by means of a flag day on Saturday, May 4, collected the sum of £49 0s 10d, which has been forwarded to the treasurer. The work of the collectors was organised by Mr McBride.

26th July 1946

SOCIAL AMENITIES FOR PRESTWICK

Escalda,
9 Bank Street,
Prestwick, Ayrshire
22/7/46

(To the Editor "The Ayrshire Post")

Sir.—I would like to associate myself with your reader's remarks in his letter of last week under the heading "Prestwick Attractions", and would like to go a little further by saying that not only should Prestwick provide better attractions for its visitors, but also for its residents as well.

I appreciate that it is easy to sit on the fence and criticise, but I feel that Prestwick is lagging far behind in its catering for the community in general.

We all know of course that it is not easy these days to do everything that one would like to do. At every turn one is hampered by red tape, permits, special licences, and a shortage of materials.

The local authority's efforts in trying to make Prestwick attractive for its holidaymakers this season are in the right direction and they should be complimented but it needs more than this to make it worth while for the average visitor and certainly a more strenuous effort should be made to provide all-the-year-round attractions whereby the community in general would have their share.

I would like to see on the agenda of the local authority's next meeting some things like these: (1) The Town Hall to be opened all the year round for good concerts (Sundays included). (2) Dancing and concerts by local talent and sponsored by the merchants and shopkeepers association. (3) Arrangements to be made to form a boxing and sports club. (4) Facilities for annual sports events for visitors and rseidents, young and old. (5) Facilities for open air dancing with proper accommodation and band at evening sessions. (6) An amusement park on the sea front. (7) Larger refreshment kiosks on sea front. (8) A band stand to be erected on sea front.

These suggestions added to those of Mr Wm. Boyd are only a few of many which would help to make Prestwick something like an attractive place not only for its visitors but for the community in general. If the local authority is keen to get on with the job then criticism from the public will not be necessary.

C. H. White.

19th July 1946

ATTRACTIONS

the Editor, *The Ayrshire Post*)
5 Aitkenbrae Drive, Prestwick,
For free publicity

it must be the envy of every coast resort in Britain. I will offer a few suggestions for improvements:

First, as boating is considered to be the essential attraction, of any coast resort worthy of the name, surely a good jetty could be laid down to facilitate the getting out and in the boats.

Second, a model yacht pond is required badly and could be laid down at no great cost. Hundreds of children come to Prestwick every summer, and to most of them their first thought is, where to sail their boat. At present the open sea is the only place.

Lastly, why can't we have a service of small buses running between the Beach and the Cross? Little open cars, of the toast rack type similar to what they have in Blackpool are best. It would be a decided help to the shopkeepers.

WM. BOYD.

2nd August 1946

Prestwick Woman's Bequests

A large number of bequests and the setting up of a holiday home for missionaries are disclosed in the will of Mrs Amy Florence Tate or Marshall, widow, late of 12 Ailsa Street, Prestwick, which is among those recently lodged with the Sheriff Clerk of Ayrshire at Ayr.

Mrs Marshall left estate of the value of £26,204, and a considerable portion of it is to be devoted to religious works. She has directed that her home, Redcroft, Ailsa Street, Prestwick, is to be administered and managed as a home for missionaries who are on furlough or are sick, their children and dependants. The home—to be known as the Marshall Home—is to be for "the benefit of both home and foreign missionaries, or both, connected with the assembly of Christians in Scotland, known by others as Brethren or Christian Brethren.

In her last will and testament, which is of considerable length, Mrs Marshall has laid down strict stipulations regarding the religious beliefs of those enjoying the use of the home. She adds that wherever possible, preference is to be given to widows and single women.

She has also made provision for the eventuality of her intentions not being practicable or, by the time of her death, unnecessary, and has stipulated that, in those circumstances, the house is to be disposed of and the proceeds accrued are to be distributed by the trustees for the benefit of the missionaries for their benefit when on furlough or sick leave.

In addition, Mrs Marshall has made a number of private bequests to relatives and friends, both in this country and Canada, and a number of servants, who were with her at time of her death, or during her later life.

To the following organisations she has bequeathed £50 — The Retired Missionaries Aid Fund, c/o "Echoes of Service," Bath; The National Bible Society of Scotland; Miss Smallwood's Society for Poor Ladies, Lancaster House, Malvern; the Oversight Brethren of Bute Hall, Prestwick, in trust for the poor of the assembly.

Others who attended her in the latter days of her life are not forgotten, and are to be recompensed at the discretion of her trustees.

27th September 1946

POLLUTION OF POW BURN

The Department of Health's chief inspector under the Rivers Pollution (Prevention) Acts having inspected the Pow Burn, has made a report in which he makes the following recommendations:

The discharge from the sump at Glenburn Colliery of water heavily charged with coaly matter should be prevented by insisting on the sealing up of the overflow from the sump;

The sludge settling ponds at Glenburn Colliery should be deepened and extended in area;

If possible, the drainage from the pit baths at Glenburn Colliery should be connected to a sewer in Glenburn village;

The sewage from Mossblown village should not be allowed to discharge in its present polluting state into the Mossblown Burn for longer than absolutely necessary;

The drainage from the pit baths at Mossblown Colliery should be connected to the proposed sewer when it is constructed;

The Burgh of Prestwick should extract the suspended matter from the filter washings from their water works before discharging the washings to the Raith Burn;

The possibility of taking some, if not all, the Pow Burn effluents into the proposed sewer connecting Mossblown to Monkton should be investigated.

The County Council is to ask the interested parties to consider the recommendations contained in the report.

18th October 1946

PRESTWICK PLANE'S MISSION OF MERCY

In dramatic fashion the life of a passenger suffering from thrombosis of the heart was saved through the timely arrival of a drug flown by a Dakota from Prestwick on Sunday.

The patient thus relieved was C. E. Wickman, aged 59, bound from America to Gothenberg in Sweden on board the Swedish-American motor ship, the Gripsholm, known to many in this country as having brought back repatriated prisoners of war. The patient's condition was regarded as critical, and an SOS was sent out on Friday night to Swedish Legation in London. A Glasgow man, Mr R. McK. Lawrence, acting for the Swedish consulate, was contacted and he chartered a plane from Scottish Airlines at Prestwick. Meantime a country-wide search had begun for 50 c.c's of a drug known as Heparin, and this was eventually obtained from a chemist in Edinburggh, and rushed by train and motor to the airport. Then the Dakota, piloted by Wing Commander John Dawson, with a special crew, set off on their errand of mercy. Having previously checked the vessel's position the aircraft some two and a quarter hours after leaving Prestwick picked up the liner 135 miles north-east of Aberdeen in the North Sea.

Shortly after noon on Sunday the vessel was sighted and a few minutes afterwards a boat was seen to leave the liner in order to secure the precious drug, contained in a special kitbag. The Dakota roared over the ship and coming lower and getting into position the bag was dropped and landed in the sea near enough to the small boat to be retrieved immediately.

Crew and passengers lined the vessel's decks and cheered lustily at the thrilling spectacle, and having received a "thank you" radioed by the captain of the liner, the plane turned for home and on the way back received a further message which gratified all on board that the passenger was much better.

Just another story of the gallant men of the air, and a reminder that the plane can be made to serve a noble purpose, the alleviation of suffering.

FOOD FACTS
BREAD for the HOLIDAYS

Home . . . . . .

Keep your bread in a bin with the lid tilted. Or wrap it in a clean, dry cloth and put it on an airy shelf. It will keep fresher. Don't leave it about after a meal. Put it away again as soon as you can. Bread goes stale quickly when it's exposed to the air.

. . . . . . and away

See that you have enough BU coupons. Manage with those you have kept if you can and only get back some of those you have deposited if you really need them.

And Two Ideas for Picnics

MAKING SANDWICHES?

Then don't forget that sandwiches keep fresh and soft if you wrap them in a damp cloth. Easier still, take the whole loaf. You can then make "open" sandwiches — one piece of bread heaped with a savoury mixture. Here's one —

Beef Mixture. Mix together 2 oz. corned beef, a dessertspoon of chutney, ½ teaspoon of Worcester sauce and a teaspoon of chopped parsley.

Quick Salad Dressing. 2 oz. flour; 1 oz. margarine or cooking fat; ¼ pint of milk; ¼ pint of water; 1 teaspoon dry mustard; salt, pepper, vinegar to taste. Melt fat in pan, stir in flour and mustard; boil 5 minutes. Add liquid gradually, stir-

ring well. Add salt and pepper and vinegar to taste.

SHORT OF BREAD?

Then boil a pound or two of new potatoes, all about the same size, smallish if possible. Don't overcook. Make quick salad dressing (recipe on left) and beat in some finely chopped mint or coarsely chopped parsley—mint's the most refreshing.

Take the potatoes and salad dressing separately. Dip the potatoes in the dressing or pour it on to them just before eating.

Delicious and very easy. Carrots taste good this way, too.

Whole tomatoes and a whole lettuce are also easy to carry. Wrap the lettuce in a damp cloth after you have washed it.

BREAD- SHOPPING REMINDER	BREAD: 1 small loaf (14 oz.)	2 BU's
	1 large loaf (1 lb. 12 oz.)..	4 „
	FLOUR: 3-lb. bag	9 „
	1-lb. „	3 „
	CAKES, BUNS, SCONES, ½ lb...	1 BU

COUPON VALUES: L=1; M=2; G=6; J=6; F=2; BUX=4; BUY=2.

CUT THIS OUT AND KEEP IT

ISSUED BY THE MINISTRY OF FOOD, LONDON, S.W.I.   FOOD FACTS No. 317

8th November 1946

LABOUR LOSS IN PRESTWICK

Less than 50 per cent. voted in Prestwick where three seats were being contested and the result of the municipal election was a gain for the Moderates of one seat from Labour. This was achieved in the second ward where the retiring member, Mr James Dougan, was defeated by Mr Thomas J. Ross. Mr Dougan has served in the Council since 1930 and was convener of the Housing Committee. The composition of the Council now stands at Moderates 11, Labour 1.

FIRST WARD

aThomas Cameron Stewart Clarkson (Mod.), unopposed.

SECOND WARD (One seat)

Thomas Johnston Ross (Mod.) 767
aJames Dougan (Lab.) 559
Moderate gain.
Spoiled papers 6. Percentage voting 49.6.

THIRD WARD (One seat)

William Shaw Moir (Mod.) .. 684
Elliott Purdom (Lab.) 245
No change.
Spoiled papers 1. Percentage voting 47.5.

FOURTH WARD (One seat)

aJohn Kerr (Mod.) 878
Alan Muir Campbell (Lab.).. 172
No change
Spoiled papers 5. Percentage voting 48.6.

TROON

There were two contests at Troon where an Independent gained a seat at the expense of Labour. Following is the return:—

FIRST WARD

R. Doig (Ind.) 627
G. M. Chalmers (Lab.) 397
A. M. Jamieson (Comm.) ..:. 382
Independent Gain.

SECOND WARD

aJohn Hood (Lab.) .. unopposed.

THIRD WARD

J. F. Smith (Mod.) .. unopposed.

FOURTH WARD

Dr. J. M. C. Clark (Mod.).... 426
A. Thomson (Ind.) 390

29th November 1946

Prestwick In The Future

What about the Prestwick of the future? This, in effect, was the question which came in for some discussion at the monthly meeting of the Town Council there on Tuesday evening—Provost Dunsmore presiding—when a motion by Bailie Black was adopted.

The Bailie's motion, which had been continued from last meeting, was, "That the Council determine, so far as possible, the future development of the burgh, having regard to all the existing circumstances". He was greatly concerned, he said, as to the future of Prestwick. He was fully aware of the fact that there were two sections in the community, one anxious to see the town forging ahead and taking a foremost place as a health resort, and another which comprised retired people who desired to be allowed to end their days in peace without any increase in the rates. It was for the Council to determine what policy would be followed in the future, and he advocated a bold policy so that the town could compete with others in the British Isles. At this juncture he suggested the formation of a small committee which could go into the question of the golf course, the question of stopping the cartage of sand which was spoiling the foreshore, and the matter of encouraging hotel proprietors to have indoor pastimes for visitors in the event of inclement weather; and to consider how best the bathing lake could be dealt with. It had also been suggested that a service might be run for old people from the Main Street to the shore. He suggested that the committee which might be appointed could have powers to co-opt outsiders.

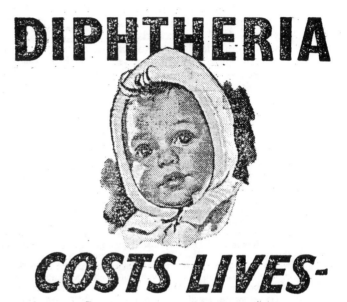

DIPHTHERIA
COSTS LIVES-

YOU WOULD NEVER FORGIVE YOURSELF . . . if a simple precaution would have saved your child's life—and you had left it too late. The parents who have had their children immunised can be happy in the knowledge that they have given them the best safeguard that medical science offers.

The child who has been immunised is twenty-six times less likely to die from diphtheria than the child who has not. Any child—rich or poor—is liable to attack. The most dangerous years of all are up to five. So take your child early to be immunised. The best time is just before his first birthday. If he is older take him at once. Ask your local Council Offices, School or Welfare Centre for full advice. **DO NOT LEAVE IT TOO LATE!**

6th December 1946

FRUSTRATION OF PRESTWICK

"You here in Ayr would really know what prosperity was if Prestwick got a square deal", said Wendy Wood when she was addressing a meeting organised by the Ayr Branch of the Scottish Nationalist Party at Young's Tea Rooms on Thursday evening.

Wendy Wood, who had been introduced by the chairman, Mr D. Johnstone, was speaking on "Scotland Today and To-morrow" and she stressed that there was no economic reason why Prestwick should not be one of the very greatest international airports.

She had spent the whole day there and the only 'planes she saw were one from London for servicing and one for Iceland which had "Hired from Scottish Aviation" on it.

The frustration of Prestwick, she said, was determined from the South. There was a deliberate effort to create jealousy between Prestwick and Renfrew, but she did not think Renfrew was going to be played against Prestwick, which could employ three times as many people as it did at the moment. If the aerodrome was serving the whole of Europe Ayr would be four times as big, and the whole district could be enlivened. Business men at present were taking their trade through Scotland to Oslo and further. There should be, Miss Wood contended, offices near the aerodrome to catch this trade.

"None of our money stops here," she continued, "it goes out from Prestwick into England and France—all large incomes are running into England. If only we could stop this drain-pipe running our people and wealth clean out of the country."

GLENBURN PIT STRIKES

Men's Attitude To Suspension By Miners' Union

"Per man shift that is the best pit in Scotland and it is about 9 cwt. per man shift better than the average output in Scotland" said Bailie Gilbert Steele, member of the committee of Mossblown and Prestwick Branch of the National Union of Mineworkers (Scottish Area), when discussing with a representative of "The Ayrshire Post" the grounds for dissatisfaction leading up to the latest stoppage on Tuesday of last week at Auchincruive No. 4 and 5 pits, Glenburn.

"A lot of unofficial stoppages," he went on, "have been for no reason at all, but this one is a result of a dispute of two years ago over dirty coal, that is, thick plies of dirt running in the coal, and wet conditions in No. 4 pit."

Miners numbering 550 at the two pits have come under a suspension order from the National Union of Mineworkers following a number of unofficial stoppages, and on Wednesday of last week a wire was received from Lord Balfour, Regional Controller, threatening to shut down the two pits, which are worked by Bairds and Dalmellington, Ltd., and have a daily output of between 850 and 900 tons.

The stoppage lasted for one day, Tuesday, and as far as the suspension from the Union was concerned, Bailie Steele said that at a meeting on Thursday of last week the men had by 25 votes to 12 agreed to send in an application to Union headquarters asking for reinstatement and they were now awaiting a reply.

The men realised the loss of production through stoppages, he went on. The Union policy was for no stoppages as there was machinery set up for airing grievances, but this machinery in the men's opinion, was not operating quickly enough and they had had to wait as long as seven months on occasions before a decision was given. "As a general rule they take too long," he added.

It had apparently been in No. 4 pit that there had been the greatest dissatisfaction, No. 5 coming out in sympathy. Bailie Steele describing No. 4, said it consists of three sections, two of which are worked by machinery, and these were "dirty." Two years ago an agreement had been reached that the Walker section got 2d per ton extra for dirty coal, but men in the other section, Fairfield, got nothing, even after an examination of the section by a deputation of the men and the management.

This had caused a lot of dissatisfaction and two or three weeks ago, there had been a demand for sixpence a ton extra for plies, which was refused. The men asked their committee to approach the mining agent and he agreed to meet the committee. On Monday of last week he had agreed to go and examine the section, after which, it was admitted there were dirty plies, and there was an offer made of 1½d per ton for two places out of about 16 in the section.

This offer of 1½d had been for the two sections where the coal was thin.

This had apparently been the last straw, and the men, already dissatisfied, and numbering about 550, stopped work on the Tuesday morning. The president of the local branch and Bailie Steele had tried to get as many men back as possible, but at a pithead discussion it was thought the men had a just grievance. Ultimately they had got the men to agree to making it a one day protest and to return to work the following day as they saw the far-reaching effects on production that a protracted stoppage would mean. On Tuesday had come the suspension wire from the Union and the following day there had come the threat of closure of the pits from the Regional Controller.

Bailie Steele's statement that the pits at Glenburn were so far ahead of the average pit production in Scotland prompted the question as to how the men felt about the threat to shut down and to this he replied that their attitude now appeared to be that the loss of the pit's production cannot be afforded.

There has apparently been every effort made by the local committee officials to point out to the men that they would suffer, and meantime the men are all back at their work again and awaiting the reply of the Union about their application for re-instatement.

27th December 1946

BAN ON GLENBURN MINERS LIFTED

The Executive Council of the National Union of Mineworkers (Scottish Area) have acceded to the request of the Glenburn miners to be readmitted to membership, and in view of the assurance that they will in future conform to union policy the ban which had been placed on them has been removed.

This was announced in Edinburgh on Monday by Mr Abe Moffat, president of the Scottish area, following a meeting of the Executive Council.

Mr Moffat pointed out that the suspension step was taken only after much consideration, and that 6000 tons of coal had been lost in one month by unofficial stoppages at the colliery concerned. A request for readmission made by the men and signed by all the local officials undertook to submit future disagreements to the established conciliation machinery, and that had been accepted.

1947

The coal industry was nationalised in Britain.
Britain suffered a severe fuel crisis; newspapers
were reduced in size to conserve supplies.
The 'New Look' Dior fashion collection was shown
in Paris.
U.S. Secretary of State George Marshall proposed
a plan for European recovery (Marshall Aid).
British rule ended in India; the independent states
of India and Pakistan were formed.
Princess Elizabeth married Lieutenant Philip
Mountbatten.

17th January 1947

"DECADENCE"

(To the Editor, *The Ayrshire Post*)

Sir,—I notice in a recent "Post" the decision by Prestwick Town Council to offer ground on our shore front—between Ardayre – House and the Queen's Hotel—for the erection of a miniature railway. The assessable value of the houses between Ardayre and the Queen's is over £1100, and the local rates thereon are over £950. Surely the Council should offer some other than the finest residential area in the-town.

During Glasgow Fair Week last year, Ayr Town Council allowed a similar show on the Low Green, and a protest has been lodged by adjacent householders—the nearest at least 200 yards from the vast attending crowds—against a repetition of what was to them an abominable nuisance.

Our shore front, with its charming prospect, is our principal attraction to visitors and if kept in proper order would be unsurpassed, and I earnestly hope our Town Council will rescind their decision and preserve our "Little Scottish World" from the vulgarities common to some Clyde resorts.

—PRESTWICKIAN.

I was a miner. I'm going **back to the mines** NCB

● Things have changed since I left . . . That flag above the mines has a lot to do with it . . . It means National ownership and National responsibility for the well-being and the future of the miner.

7,837 ex-miners have already returned this year.

Your old pals want those who were with them in the hard times, to share the solid benefits and high prestige of mining today. Write to one of them. He will tell you.

Pride and Prosperity

have come back to the

MINES

THE NATIONAL INDUSTRY WITH AN ASSURED FUTURE

Issued by the Ministry of Labour and National Service in conjunction with the National Coal Board

17th January 1947

32 Ardayre Road,
Prestwick, 6/1/47.
(To the Editor, *The Ayrshire Post*)

Sir,—While commending the enterprise of the Prestwick Town Council in arranging as a summer attraction an exhibition of a model railway, I think that their selection of the ground between the Putting Kiosk and Burgh Road for this enterprise is particularly unfortunate. Many visitors consider the stretch of ground between the esplanade and the houses facing the sea as one of the chief attractions of the town, as they can walk or sit there for several hours while their families play around them, and its usefulness in this respect has been increased by the present deteriorated condition of the beach. In recent years a large section of this ground has been occupied by the putting green and the decision of the Entertainment Committee to offer the above site for the model railway means that the entire northern half of this stretch of grass will no longer be available to the public in general, as distinct from those interested in putting or model railways.

I am of the opinion that a more suitable site for this venture would be adjoining the children's recreation ground towards the southern end of the esplanade and I trust that the Town Council will finally settle on a site in this neighbourhood. Their present decision only substitutes one kind of attraction for another and does not add to the general attractiveness of the seafront.

G. M. BAIRD.

28th February 1947

POINTS SCHEME

Prestwick Criticism Of House Allocation

A motion by Mr T. J. Ross to Prestwick Town Council on Tuesday night, that the Council reconsider their decision with regard to the housing allocation, was defeated by the casting vote of Provost Dunsmore.

Mr Ross, in moving the motion, said he understood it was suggested to objectors to the present allocation scheme that it should be given a trial and he thought it had shown, very definitely, its weaknesses. The condition that houses were to be granted to natives of the burgh, he pointed out, meant that a person could be born in the burgh, leave at the age of one year and come back at the age of 40, having a qualification for a house.

Persons who had resided in the burgh for more than 15 years could qualify, a statement which was much too simple in respect that there was one particular case where a man residing in the burgh for 19 years, continuously, from the time he was 10 until he was 29 years of age, was then unable to obtain employment here and had to leave the district. He returned after service to Prestwick and was now working at the aerodrome. On applying for a house he was informed he had not the qualifications. "I submit he had the qualification according to the wording of the order," said Mr Ross.

"Anyone working permanently within the burgh" carried the implication "for ever more", but if it was discovered during the waiting period that the applicants were no longer working in Prestwick—there were such cases—were they still to have houses? They had dozens and dozens of their own people who were not getting houses, and they were their main consideration. Prestwick was a residential area and anyone could come to Prestwick if they could get a job in the burgh. There were people who came to Prestwick, had been put on the housing list under that particular heading, and were no longer within the burgh and yet were still on the list. That was unfair and unreasonable.

Priority was given for cases of extreme hardship or where the person was residing in an unfit house. Mr Ross confessed he did not know the definition of "unfit". Were the Town Council of Prestwick going to make it their business to see that the people who had been re-housed out of unfit buildings were not making room for someone else to occupy these so-called unfit houses?

He had absolutely no objection to sub-tenants being allowed points and said that if he were making a suggestion for alteration it would be that they be allowed more than their 10 points because he considered that the young man and wife and two or three children, struggling along, having been married 8 or 10 years and having never had a home of their own—in perhaps insanitary and depressing conditions—should have more than that.

On a point of previous application, old records were not available any longer and it was largely a question of taking the applicant's word. He thought they should have tried to get corroborative evidence of some kind—even a statement from a neighbour or someone else who had applied for a house.

On the grounds of war service, Mr Ross said, he did not wish to deny that the fighting men undoubtedly played a big part, but he submitted that there were many ratepayers and many applicants for houses in Prestwick who had an equally important job to do in the war in supplying the materials that made our existence possible. The mining community, engineers, electricians, these men were all in reserved occupations. They did not, whether they had the fancy for it or not, have the opportunity to join H.M. Forces and not having had the opportunity they were denied the right to earn points which those members who had served in H.M. Forces were entitled to and this was unfair.

Bailie Steele seconded.

Mr J. D. Young moved, as an amendment, that no change be made until the present allocation was completed. To make any change at the present time would create further discontent and the position would become chaotic, said Mr Young. It was in the interests of all concerned that the position should remain unchanged in the meantime.

Bailie Black, seconding, said it was quite obvious they could not go back on the points scheme when they had, in fact, intimated to several people that they were to get houses, and they had made arrangements, committing themselves to the purchase of furniture, etc. The people who had got the houses on the points system agreed to by the Council were not in any way to blame for that system. Mr Ross was merely trying to find pin-pricking faults with the present points system. It would take a Solomon to create a system that would give fairness and satisfaction to everyone.

On a division 6 members voted for the motion and six for the amendment, and the Provost, as stated, gave his casting vote for the amendment.

11th April 1947

PRESTWICK TOWN COUNCIL

To The Editor, "The Ayrshire Post".
5 St. John Street,
Prestwick, April 6, 1947.

Sir,—In your last issue you gave a report of Prestwick Town Council's most recent discussion on the vexed question of housing. Your report, however, did not convey the extent to which Bailie Milligan went in order to decry and deride the policy of the present government. Not only did he attack the government for their housing policy, but also for their handling of the questions of food, clothing, employment, demobilisation, and nationalisation. Bailie Milligan further suggested that our Scottish representatives at Westminster were feathering their own nests.

Councillor Mrs Crawford approved of these accusations and spoke of self-government for Scotland, at the same time claiming to be not the least interested in politics.

There is one Labour representative on Prestwick Town Council, namely Bailie Steele. He attempted to reply to Bailie Milligan's statements, but was ruled out of order by the Provost, and not permitted to speak—an obvious case of political discrimination. The intriguing thing is that all the other councillors were elected on a non-party ticket, most of them claiming there was no place for party politics in local government. Surely this incident shows us that everyone has his political bias and, whether it be to right or left, will undoubtedly influence his statements and actions inside the Town Council and elsewhere.

Andrew L. Dunlop.

18th April 1947

PRESTWICK TOWN COUNCIL

(To the Editor, *The Ayrshire Post*)
8 Whinfield Avenue,
Prestwick, April 14, 1947.

Sir,—With reference to the letter from Andrew L. Dunlop in your last week's issue, I would remind him that the Provost objected to the references made by Bailie Milligan. However, in all fairness to Bailie Milligan I would like to add that his comments principally referred to the present handling of housing, and that no matter what Government held office, similar criticism would have been meted out to them. It was not a question of Party against Party, and so long as matters are handled or mishandled by the Government in office, that Government must bear the responsibility.

The majority—if not all, members of the Council—deplore the introduction of politics in our deliberations. We were elected by the ratepayers and therefore set ourselves out to represent their best interests, no matter what the ratepayers' personal political or religious views may be.

We are certainly not swayed in our decisions by political bias, and I cannot too strongly emphasise this point.

JOHN KERR.

25th April 1947

New R.C. Hall For Prestwick

The history of the Catholic Church and congregation in Prestwick was recalled at the official opening of the new Roman Catholic Hall in St. Quivox Road on Wednesday evening.

The Rev. Laurence Breen said that when he came to Prestwick the present church was being used for all activities, and he stopped that. Looking back over six years he was sure every one of them would agree that his decision was the right one. They would rather pray than dance, and they had one of the nicest churches in the whole of Scotland, which would have been impossible had they been using it as a hall.

Towards the end of the war, Father Breen said, he started looking round, got in touch with divers persons, and was promised an army hut. Outlining the setbacks they had received, and the help forthcoming from Mr J. Crowley and Mr J. Wilson, he said he eventually succeeded in getting a hut from Dam Park. A week after the hall was put up there, the squatters walked into Dam Park. Thanking Mr Crowley for his help and advice, Father Breen said he had sent his own workmen to take the hut down, erected it by the church, put on a new roof and made a passage to the church, and finally had said "Accept it as a gift to the parish." Father Breen expressed his personal debt of gratitude to Mr Crowley for all his kindness and help during the past. The proceedings with the Town Council, Dean of Guild, and so on, had been taken off his shoulders by Mr Wilson.

In thanking all who had contributed to get the hall into its present condition, he mentioned Mr Andrew Connor, a miner, who was in hospital, and who had executed all the painting. The curtain material, which did not require coupons, arrived on Thursday evening and was made up in one day. The linoleum had been laid the day before the opening. "I think the hall is one of which we can be proud," he remarked, adding that it would take over 200 people.

Mr P. Power, who spoke as someone who had had a hand in the beginning in building the church and had seen the growth of the parish, recalled that they had raised over £4,500 in a matter of less than a dozen years. He could remember a time when Mass was held once a week, sometimes in the Town Hall, or in Prestwick Public School, and on one occasion in a loft over a garage.

Father O'Connell, Girvan, congratulated Father Breen and the Catholic people of Prestwick who had co-operated with him in getting their hall. He wished them every happiness and blessing with it.

The evening's entertainers were all members of the congregation, introduced by Mr H. Bradley, and included Miss B. Wilson and Mr J. Wallace, Mr J. Hill (accordeonist), and 9-year-old Violet McLaughlan (dancing), 14-year-old Marion Graham (singing), 16-year-old James Murphy (pipes), and Master Tommy Dunlop (Scots songs).

25th April 1947

PRESTWICK TOWN COUNCIL
To the Editor, "The Ayrshire Post"
5 St. John Street,
Prestwick, April 21, 1947.

Sir,—In replying to my recent letter Councillor Kerr claims that the Provost objected to Bailie Milligan's statements —a claim which is without foundation. Bailie Milligan made his statements without interruption and then Mrs Crawford, Mr McNair, and Mr Kinghorn were heard. Finally Bailie Steele got his chance. He began to answer Bailie Milligan and was soon interrupted by the Provost, who objected to his remarks and declared him out of order. Bailie Steele protested and was supported by two councillors. At this point the Provost admitted that he ought to have objected to Bailie Milligan's statements—quite a different matter.

Councillor Kerr next claims that Bailie Milligan's comments referred principally to housing. I witnessed the whole exhibition and formed the opinion that the housing situation was used as a pretext for an all-out attack on several features of Government policy. When Councillor Kerr states that similar criticism would have been meted out, no matter what government held office, he is admitting that politics cannot be kept out of local affairs and that local and national affairs are in some instances inseparable. Yet he joins with the majority of his fellow-councillors in deploring the advent of politics to Town Council deliberations. Councillor Kerr should make up his mind; he cannot have it both ways.

I am convinced that there are times when local and national affairs are inseparable, as in the case of housing. There is no councillor, I am sure, who can keep strictly to the path of neutrality on such occasions. He is bound, from time to time, to digress to one side or the other.

Andrew L. Dunlop.

13th June 1947

PRESTWICK TOWN HALL
(To the Editor, *The Ayrshire Post*)
8 Ferguson Avenue,
Prestwick.
June 7, 1947.

Sir,—The function of a Town Hall is to serve as a focal point for the social and cultural activities of the community. In a growing town such as Prestwick the need for such a centre will become greater and not less. All the arguments put forward in the public meetings of Prestwick Town Council are mere sophistries, not one of which carries any weight with the average citizen so the question arises, 'Who is going to profit from the sale of the Town Hall?'

Who wants to sell the Town Hall? Have the people of Prestwick demanded the sale of the hall, or is it a small group of individuals? If the Town Council have only the public welfare at heart why not have a plebiscite and let the people decide?

Robert Picken.

BURGH OF PRESTWICK.

ST. NINIAN'S GOLF COURSE.
TICKETS for St. Ninian's Golf Course are now available and may be obtained at the CLUBHOUSE. The charges will be the same as formerly, viz.:—

	Adults	Juveniles
One Round	1s 6d	1s 0d
Day Ticket	2s 6d	1s 6d
Weekly Ticket	11s 6d	4s 0d
Two Week Ticket	15s 0d	7s 6d
Monthly Ticket	25s 0d	12s 6d
Season (Ladies & Gent.'s)	35s 0d	20s 0d
Lockers	2s 6d	

JOHN L. JONES, Town Clerk.
Municipal Chambers,
Prestwick, 22nd April, 1947.

AYR COUNTY COUNCIL.

COUNTY LIBRARY—PRESTWICK BRANCH.
The Prestwick Branch of the County Library will be OPEN to people residing in Prestwick and Monkton Area on THURSDAY, 1st MAY, 1947. The hours of opening can be seen in the Notice Board at the Library in Bridge Street, Prestwick.

Books still on loan to readers from County Library Headquarters, County Buildings, Ayr, should be returned there immediately.

23rd May 1947

Prestwick Lake Gets Ready

Prestwick Bathing Lake will be opened to-morrow for what is anticipated will be a bumper season. There will be no ceremony. The hours will be as formerly, from 10 a.m.

The lake has undergone a deal of preparation and repair, quite apart from the usual repainting operations, which current shortages of material have impeded.

The re-constructed dressing accommodations will cater for 300 bathers at present. Instead of the old locker-type of accommodation, the lake now has rows of changing-rooms, the system being on the lines of an ordinary cloakroom. Patrons will change in a cubicle, put their clothes in a basket and collect them again from the attendant when finished swimming. The doors and other fitments have been adapted from wood, which, last year, made up the locker-framework.

Watching the water being pumped into the lake on Tuesday, Mr John T. Morson, superintendent and instructor, with his assistant, Mr Victor Marfarlane, anticipated a brisk season. Both were P.T. instructors with the R.A.F. and they plan to do their best to show what the Bathing Lake can do, possessing ideal swimming facilties. The accent will be on diving in the special features (mostly at weekends) that are being fixed for the season's programme.

The Lake will hold a million gallons of water and down in the pumping room the various processes of purification take place, from the time when the water is pumped in, passes through the filtering actions, and receives the addition of certain chemicals, until the time when it emerges, eventually, free from seaweed, sand and all other impurities, fit to drink. The complete circulation of water in the pool takes 24 hours.

Last year there were over 1,000 pupils for swimming, but this year it is hoped to hit a far higher figure. There is plenty of scope, for there is room for 4,000 spectators and 1,200 bathers, and while the emphasis will naturally fall on those who take an active part in the sport, both spectator and swimmer will find their interests catered for.

BUILDING.—At recent meetings of Prestwick Dean of Guild Court, the following petitions were submitted and granted: John Martin, to erect a dwelling house in Whinfield Avenue, Prestwick, at an estimated cost of £1,250; Hugh Higgins, to alter and erect bedrooms at Monkton Road, Prestwick, at an estimated cost of £400; Messrs W. P. Lawrie, to erect factory extension in Boydfield Avenue, Prestwick, at an estimated cost of £90; Ayr County Council, to erect additional classroom accommodation in Newdykes Road, Prestwick, at an estimated cost of £8,410; and Messrs Gardiners (Prestwick) Ltd., to alter shop front in Main Street, Prestwick, at an estimated cost of £943.

27th June 1947

PRESTWICK SHORE MEETINGS

"We have several political parties to-day and likewise, several religious bodies and if the Council agree to the holding of religious meetings on the shore, I do not think we are at all entitled to cut out the political issue," said Mr T. J. Ross at Prestwick Town Council meeting on Tuesday evening, when Bailie Steel had raised the subject of meetings on the shore.

The minute the bailie was referring to stated that the Parks Committee had unanimously agreed to recommend that permission be not granted to Prestwick Labour Party to hold evening meetings on the shore one night per week during the months of June, July and August.

The bailie asked for reconsideration of that point on the grounds that it was not fair. With regard to the alternative of holding meetings in the public park, he said it was only putting a gag on it. They would not attract the public.

Bailie Black said they had either to give to none or to all.

The Provost said they had been trying to keep clear of political meetings on the shore—they had never been held there before and this would be the start. He moved that they adopt the minute and Mr Kerr seconded.

Mr McNair said he had no objection to any political party holding meetings in the public park, but he had a decided objection to their being held on the foreshore because they, as a Council, were making an endeavour to bring about a reasonably good standard of holiday resort in Prestwick.

Bailie Milligan said obviously, they wanted, in the first instance, to have harmony with their visitors and residents, and he was afraid if they brought any subject of a controversial nature into public discussion that harmony might be upset. Bailie Milligan said he met Bailie Steele on the front and in the Lake and enjoyed the bailie's company and his crack, but under other circumstances they might come to fisticuffs and for that reason alone he would not have any meetings which might introduce heated controversy.

The Council voted 7 to 4 in favour of the Provost's motion for the minute.

Sunday "Trains"

A minute dealing with the running of the model railway on Sundays drew a comment from Mr T. J. Ross, who said they had just had an example of keeping the foreshore clear for the quiet Sunday entertainment of their visitors and residents and he thought that this question might be worthy of a little further consideration. The foreshore, in days gone by, was always the model of quietude and rest, where people could go and enjoy a quiet, leisured afternoon. There was no doubt the model railways had its attractions, but, at the same time, he thought it was creating a certain amount of stir and disturbance they could well do without.

Provost Dunsmore, seconding, said he could foresee the introduction of shows on the green. It was no different from roundabouts and if the running of the railway was granted there was no reason why the ordinary roundabout should not run on the shore alongside.

Bailie Steele said he did not see any more disturbance on Sunday than was caused by driving motor cars.

Bailie Black moved approval of the minute, saying he had asked in what way any nuisance or annoyance was created by the miniature railway but he had had no satisfactory reply. He agreed it was wrong that people entering into an agreement with the burgh of Prestwick, should, after they were here, want to amend it to their own interests, but that did not apply in this instance to the same extent because the rental was not a fixed one and was based on their getting 20 per cent. of the gross takings of the railway, and if there were profits on Sunday, they would benefit accordingly.

Mr McNair seconded.

Voting was 9-2 in favour of the minute allowing the railway to run on Sundays.

25th July 1947

PRESTWICK YOUTH CENTRE

Prestwick Youth have an outstanding opportunity in their centre in Templerigg Street—described as about the best to be seen in Ayrshire, with central heating in the building and tennis courts at the back—but if they want their centre, Prestwick's young men and women must work for it.

The County Council have agreed to equip and maintain the centre, which was formerly the United Services Club and latterly a British Restaurant, when it has been put in order, and Prestwick Youth Panel are tackling the problem with voluntary helpers, of whom many more are needed.

Among the amenities of the centre is a large hall to be used for sports and functions—probably, too, dramatic shows, since there is to be a stage erected and a dressing room is already installed. It is nearly 60 ft. long 35 ft. wide. Behind the hall there is a billiards room, which is waiting for the attention of young men helpers who can plaster, as well as for other helpers to put it in order. There is a kitchen with plenty of shelf-space, an outside shed for woodwork, joinery, and other hobbies; a common room, a quiet room where it is hoped to build up a good library, and plenty of cloak room accommodation. Contributions of chairs, tables, bookcases, and other furniture and equipment are being asked for. Those who are working with the young people are doing so with a six weeks' deadline in view—they want the centre to be open by September.

11th July 1947

PRESTWICK CALL SUSTAINED

Ayr Presbytery at its meeting on July 1 — the Rev. E. W. Wallis, Waterside, moderator — sustained the call to the Rev. Donald M. Caskie, Coats Church, Coatbridge, by the St. Cuthbert's Church of Monkton and Prestwick.

The clerk laid on the table the papers relating to the call which had been signed by 315 members and 20 adherents, and the letter of acceptance by Mr Caskie.

Commissioners present to prosecute the call were Mr Peter Haining, interim session clerk, and Mr G. F. D. Bryce, elder to the presbytery. Mr Haining said he regretted to say that the voting at the election was small, and the signatures to the call represented only 20 per cent. of the number of communicants on the electoral register. That had given him as session clerk and clerk of the Vacancy Committee some anxious moments, but when last evening he attended the kirk session meeting, the doubts which he had formerly had in his mind as to what he might say, if he were asked to prosecute this call before the presbytery, disappeared.

He explained that there had been also some misunderstanding among members who thought that, having voted, they did not require also to sign the call. There had been some hesitancy on the part of the congregation to accept the sole nomination, because, as the presbytery would understand, "old tradition dies hard". He thought they would agree that it would have been disastrous, in a church the size of St. Cuthbert's, to have had a "preaching competition"—it could only be regarded as that. Some, in the exercise of their presbyterial rights, would have preferred someone else, but in the true atmosphere of a court of the church, the kirk session feelingly and frankly discussed the points which had been brought to their notice, and, he could say, quite truthfully, that the feeling was that no point raised created a barrier to Mr Caskie's ministry or pastorate in St. Cuthbert's. He assured them that the opinion of the kirk session, representing the feelings of the congregation, was, he believed, that there was much greater unanimity in the congregation than the signatures of the call appeared to indicate.

Mr Bryce, and the interim moderator, the Rev. R. H. S. Budge, Troon, spoke in support of the call.

The call was unanimously sustained and Wednesday, September 3, was fixed as the date of the induction, the moderator to preside, the Rev. H. R. Taylor, Catrine, to preach and the Rev. And. Burnett, New Cumnock, to give the charges.

25th July 1947

TOWN CLERK OBJECTS

Mr J. Kerr at Prestwick Town Council on Tuesday said he had had a serious complaint from residents in Douglas Road off Maryborough Road, "quite an important part of the town," that it had been made a public dumping-ground. Mr Kerr said that when he took it up with Mr Melrose some twelve months' ago a board had been erected to the effect that dumping was not permitted on this ground. There were old prams, bottles, tiles and all thrown against the very board that prohibited rubbish being dumped there, and grass was growing waist-deep. One of the house-holders had given the names of people guilty of dumping rubbish and Mr Kerr said that prosecution was the only thing to put a stop to the habit.

The town clerk (Mr John L. Jones)—I want to object to notices being put up with my name on them—we have no right to put any notice on that ground when it does not belong to us. There are far too many notices being put up, without my authority, with my name on them.

After further discussion regarding the local position with ground not belonging to them, the town clerk said that the owner of the ground had his remedy in the civil courts. It was decided to leave the matter in the hands of Mr Melrose.

OVERCROWDED.—In his report at the closing of Prestwick High School Mr James W. Scott, headmaster, said that, due to the raising of the school leaving age, the High School, already grievously overcrowded, was to become more so. Next session partial relief was to be provided by sending one of the primary classes to Glenburn School, until extra classrooms were built. The breaking up of a very happy family circle was very unpleasant to all concerned, and he appealed to the councillors present to use to the uttermost their influence to have the school extension proceeded with, without further delay, so that an early re-union could take place.

29th August 1947

Prestwick Man In Rhine Army

By a Military Observer

"The 2nd Battalion The Royal Scots Fusiliers run an educational scheme which should be emulated by all regiments in the British Army".

This statement was made to a Military Observer by 19-year-old Fusilier R. Pollock, a former student of Fettes College, whose father, a market gardener, lives at Overdale, Prestwick.

Outlining the scheme, he explained that six weeks before men left the Battalion for demobilisation, they attend school for a series of lectures which are designed as a provisional re-settlement course. The idea behind the scheme is not to cram the three "R.'s" into pupils' heads but to brush up their general knowledge, and, most important of all, to advise students on how to adapt themselves to conditions prevalent in Great Britain today.

Fusilier Pollock is one of the cadre of potential instructors. His special subject is mathematics, but he is also a fount of information on horticulture. This is his secondary subject and men returning, or hoping to start market gardening, have discovered that this youthful lecturer speaks from a wealth of experience, gained from his father and advanced study while attending college.

Lectures on horticulture are very infrequent, however, and Pollock spends most of his time polishing off the rough edges of his classes' mathematical knowledge. His own principle of instruction is that the shortest distance between two points is a straight line and by adopting this principle the most problematical sum can be successfully worked out. In simple addition, subtraction or advanced algebra, Fusilier Pollock is fully at home, and his pupils benefit greatly from his direct methods of teaching.

When released from the Army he intends to enter Reading Agricultural College to study advanced theoretical and practical horticulture. If he qualifies successfully, his father will accept him as a partner.

5th September 1947

Monkton Church Induction

There was a large attendance of the congregation of the church together with a good representation of members of Ayr Presbytery and friends of the new minister at Prestwick St. Cuthbert's Church on Wednesday afternoon when the Rev. Donald M. Caskie, M.A., was inducted to the charge in succession to the late Rev. Luke McQuitty.

At the induction service which followed along the usual lines, the Moderator of Ayr Presbytery, Rev. Dr. E. W. Wallis, Waterside, presided. The Rev. Andrew Burnett, New Cumnock, addressed the newly inducted minister and the congregation and the Rev. Hanry Raymond Taylor, Gordon Memorial Church, Catrine, conducted public worship.

Mr Caskie, who is a native of Glasgow, comes to Prestwick from Coates Church, Coatbridge. He is 39 years of age, and in addition to his parochial experience in Coatbridge and Millport he served with the 15th Scottish Division during the war, some of his experiences being related by the senior chaplain of the Division, Rev. W. D. Maxwell, Hillhead, who said that Mr Caskie had been chaplain to a battalion of the Argyll and Sutherland Highlanders, and later became senior chaplain of a brigade. He had proved himself to be a man not only of moral but of physical courage.

At the outset of the evening's proceedings, the Rev. Ronald H. Budge, Troon Old, occupied the chair and in a short address said that with the appointment of the new minister, they all, Vacancy Committee, Kirk Session and congregation felt that the foundation stone had been laid for the good work that was to be done in the coming years.

Mrs J. Mair, vice-president of the Woman's Guild, made the presentations on behalf of the congregation. St. Cuthbert's, she said, had always been a happy church and fortunate in its choice of ministers, and as an earnest of their good will to the minister and his wife she handed over a wireless set to Mr Caskie and a handbag and cheque to Mrs Caskie.

No Rash Innovator

Mr Caskie, in reply, said that they all knew that new brooms swept clean, but he hoped that the new broom in the parish would not raise too much of a dust. In their new minister they would find no rash innovator. We were, said Mr Caskie, very conservative at heart, particularly with regard to our religion, and he was convinced that it was very rarely that a change merely for change's sake was a good thing. Neither would they find in their new minister a slavish imitator, "for", said Mr Caskie, "I would be false to myself and to the trust you have reposed in me if I were to model myself on anyone who has gone before. This is a parish that is rich in history and lustre. Each one of those who went before me was himself and added his own bit to that history in which you can take so much pride to-day".

He appealed for their co-operation and understanding even in matters in which they might not fully agree, and, citing the example of a time when the head of the household before going to Sunday worship with his family prayed for the minister to teach and the congregation to understand, said that without a praying people there could be no fruitful ministry.

The Rev. J. Calmers Grant, Dunblane Cathedral, a boyhood friend of Mr Caskie, told the congregation that while their minister was not old in years he had already graduated with honours in the university of life. "If more men in the Church of Scotland", he said, "had his vision and understanding, our days of austerity in the Church would be over".

Ayr-Prestwick Unity

Bringing the good wishes of the neighbouring churches, the Rev. R. D. M. Johnston, Sandgate Church, who is the interim moderator in the South Church, Prestwick, remarked that though Ayr and Prestwick were not yet one he felt that in church circles they were one. They were lucky to have a man like Mr Caskie, who was of a friendly nature, and he was assured of being made to feel at home in Ayr Presbytery.

The other denominations were represented by the Rev. Ernest Jauncey, rector of St. Ninian's Episcopal Church, Prestwick, and addresses were also given by ministerial friends of Mr Caskie, including the Rev. W. W. Dornan, Coatbridge, who was moderator of the United Free Church Presbytery of Ayr 18 years ago, and by the Rev. R. G. McConnachie, Airdrie, moderator of the Presbytery of Hamilton.

"Stop being pessimistic about the Church going down" Mr McConnachie said. There was nothing that aroused him so much as to listen to people complaining about the church not being what it was. Mr Caskie had that optimistic outlook that would carry him through.

Work Remembered

In making the presentation of a cheque to the interim-moderator, Mr R. L. Angus of Ladykirk, convener of the Vacancy Committee, said that he was the only one on the Vacancy Committee who had also been on the committee when their late minister had been appointed to the church. They would never forget Mr McQuitty for the work he had done in building up St. Cuthbert's. There had been 107 applications for the position and the committee had done their task with the sole desire of procuring the best possible man and that they had succeeded he was quite sure.

Mr Budge expressed his appreciation for the assistance that he had received from the committee and the kirk session and said it had been a real pleasure for him to undertake the work.

Mr James A. Kinghorn, church treasurer, presented a cheque to Mr Peter Haining who, in addition to being session clerk, also undertook the duties of clerk to the Vacancy Committee.

Another presentation was forthcoming to Mr A. M. Duncanson, ex-session clerk, late headmaster of Prestwick Public School, which was made by Mr Robert Stevenson, one of the senior elders in the church.

During the evening entertainment was provided by the choir, a solo by Mr Whannell and a quartette.

26th September 1947

Prestwick Rates As Last Year

Prestwick rates 'for 1947-48, passed at the meeting of the Town Council on Monday, are:—Consolidated rate of 16s 8d per £—7s 6¼d on owners and 9s 1¼d on occupiers in Prestwick; and a consolidated rate of 15s 4½d per £—6s 10¼d on owners and 8s 5½d on occupiers in New Prestwick district. The rates remain the same as last year.

A letter from the County Clerk, Ayr, stated that notification had been received of an increased grant to be paid by the Scottish Education Department to education authorities and that it would be possible to reduce the County Council's requisition to £51,964 9s 2d, although the question of the reduction had still to be decided by the County Council. After discussion and presuming approval by the County Council of the reduction, the Finance Sub-committee agreed to recommend approval of the following statement showing the estimated net expenditure falling to be met out of consolidated rates:—

	Owner	Occupier	Total
Lighting	—	£2.300	£2.300
Cleansing	—	6.590	6.590
Public Parks	£5.130	5.130	10.260
Roads	2.665	2.665	5.330
Drainage	1.460	1.460	2.920
Public Health	1.395	1.395	2.790
Housing	1.495	1.495	2.990
Water	4.125	4.125	8.250
Miscellaneous Services	835	835	1.670
Town Council	£17.105	£25.995	£43.100
County Council	25.982	25.982	51.964
Total net expenditure	£43.087	£51.977	£95.064
Less General Exchequer Grant	3.496	4.218	7.714
	£39.591	£47.759	£87.350

Approval of the minute at the Finance Sub-committee meeting in August was moved by Bailie Black, seconded by Bailie Milligan and an amendment that the matter be reconsidered with a view to making a reduction in the estimates of expenditure for the current year, was moved by Mr T. J. Ross, seconded by Bailie Steele. On a vote being taken, the motion to approve the sub-committee's minute was carried by nine votes to two.

At the Town Council meeting on Monday Mr Ross again oppossed the minute when it came up. Referring to an item of £1,000 which had been rated for in 1946-47 estimates for the purchase of a motor vehicle which had not been made, and which had been included again in this year's estimates, he held that by not including this sum this year, they would have been justified in a reduction of the rates at this time. There were many old people in the town who had had their incomes reduced and were paying out much more, and with a balance of £4,629 on hand from last year surely they were justified in making a reduction this year, and not next year or the year after. Mr Ross proposed that it be remitted back for further consideration, either to the next committee meeting or to a special meeting of the Finance Committee. Bailie Steele seconded.

Bailie Black moved the minute, seconded by Mr McNair, and this was carried by nine votes to two after members had pointed out that contingencies could arise during the year which had to be taken into account in the estimates.

31st October 1947

WAGES SPIRAL

Local Authorities Competing For Labour

At Prestwick Town Council's monthly meeting on Tuesday night—Provost Dunsmore presiding—reference was made to the danger of a wages spiral arising through the action of some contractors offering higher conditions than those laid down in the wage agreements and enticing labour from other schemes.

The matter was raised in a letter to the Town Council from Mr James Melrose, burgh surveyor, who reported on a meeting of contractors' officials on the Marchburn housing site. A point discussed was the difficulty of obtaining labour in certain trades. "Contractors maintain," he reported, "that certain authorities, including Ayr County Council, were enticing men from their sites by offering a 44-hour guaranteed week, compared with the 32-hour week offered the men here."

"It is coming to another winter," said Mr Melrose. "That is when the men are looking for guaranteed time. We are only guaranteeing them a 32-hour week, whereas, if it rains for the whole week at the County Council site, the men still get their full 44 hours' pay."

It was agreed to remit the matter to the town clerk and burgh surveyor to ascertain the position in the district.

A letter from the architects referring to the enticements being offered was also submitted. In order to retain them the plasterer at Prestwick Town Council's site had agreed to his men working an extra half-hour a day at extra rates. "That", the letter pointed out, "commences a wages spiral." Unless some settlement was reached on the question, it added, the schemes at Prestwick would suffer from lack of labour.

In further explanation, Mr Melrose said increased payments might lead to good results for a short time, but he did not see that they were going to benefit in the long run, because such increases would gradually spread like a disease. They had asked the contractors to explore every possible avenue in order to see that the Council's houses were finished and they reported that they were finding difficulty in obtaining labour to finish the houses, when in adjoining towns and villages, men were being offered 3d an hour extra and a guaranteed 44-hour week.

In answer to questions put by members of the Council Mr Melrose thought these improved conditions were being offered at Dalmellington. At Patna, where the Scottish Special Housing Association had a contract, it was in force

19th December 1947

Prestwick Youth Centre

The official opening of Prestwick Youth Centre by Mr A. B. Cameron, M.A., assistant director of education, took place on Wednesday evening, Provost Milligan, the magistrates and councillors of Prestwick attending as did many local ministers. Over 350 people packed into the hall.

Mr D. MacBean expressed the gratitude of the club to Prestwick Town Council, Ayr County Council, and members of Prestwick Ex-Servicemen's Club, whose energies and efforts had permitted the establishment of the club.

Mr Cameron, who formally handed over the premises to the youth of Prestwick about a month ago, said he was delighted to see what an excellent job had been made of the premises. The centre had been bought and they hoped to fit it out for the youth of Prestwick; he was very pleased indeed to see that so many clubs had already affiliated to the centre and were going to make use of the premises. It was a good thing that all youth clubs in the neighbourhood should have a common meeting ground, for no matter what individual interests the various clubs were following the ultimate problem was the same: trying to make good citizens of the young people of Prestwick.

After a gymnastic display by Monkton and Prestwick 11th Ayr Boys' Brigade, and country dancing performed by members of Prestwick 12th Ayrshire Company G.T.C., Mr G. Nethercut, Prestwick Athletic and Boxing Club, Scottish amateur muscle-control champion, gave a demonstration of muscle control and ju-jitsu.

Provost Milligan recalled that this was the second time in a quarter of a century he had come to an opening of these premises. They had come to a time of life when they felt they wanted to do something for the young people. He hoped the boys and girls would make use of the arts and crafts they could learn there and would join this youth movement which had come to stay. He paid tribute to ex-councillor Mrs A. Crawford, who was so very much concerned with the origination and development of the youth club.

A table tennis exhibition was given by Messrs J. McLean, H. Martin, B. William and W. Clark, and indoor aeromodel flying staged by Prestwick Aeromodellers' Club aroused much excitement amongst the younger spectators. The final item, a gym. display was contributed by the younger members of the Monkton and Prestwick 11th Ayr Boys' Brigade.

Afterwards, the young people over fourteen joined in dancing and games led by Miss Nan Donald, who was assisted by Miss Joan Little.

PRESTWICK PROVOST

There was unanimous approval at the statutory meeting of Prestwick Town Council in the Council Chambers on Friday to the appointment of Mr Frank M. Milligan, 1 Allanvale Road, to the provostship of the Burgh.

Bailie Flanigan who presided at the outset, moved the appointment and was seconded by Bailie Black. The oath having been administered, Provost Milligan took the chair, and thanked them for the honour they had bestowed on him. At the same time he said he realised the responsibilities that had been placed on his shoulders, and looking back over the years at the men who had occupied the office before him, said he could not hope to maintain that standard in the management of municipal affairs without the co-operation of each one on the council.

There was one advantage, said Provost Milligan, that he did enjoy and that was that this council was made up of young men and that they represented almost every phase of local industry. "It is quite true to say that never in the history of Prestwick has such an excellent cross-section of the community been serving Prestwick at the same time". It would be his endeavour, he continued, to carry on the policy and programme initiated by the previous council and he would listen to their deliberations with judicial interest.

In expressing appreciation for the way the staff had been encouraged to give of their best during the election, Provost Milligan said he saw from the press that it was a question whether Prestwick had not created a record in counting votes.

Prestwick's new Provost is 64 and was educated at the High School in his native Dublin. He lived for some time in the southern states of America and was in central Africa as agent general for Lever Bros. Immediately prior to the first world war he was in West Africa where he was interested in several Palm Oil estates. As a journalist he travelled to Canada where he was editor of "Successful Agriculture" and is the author of a book, "Cultivation of the Palm Oil" published in 1913. He relinquished his interests in Africa in 1914 and returned to Great Britain and served in the Royal Naval Armoured Car division in France. Later he was appointed director controller of munition stores for Scotland.

During the Boer War he served with the 74th Coy. Dublin Imperial Yeomanry and among his decorations holds the Queen Victoria Medal with five bars.

Provost Milligan took an active interest during the last war in the formation of the L.D.V. and later served with the Argyll and Sutherland Home Guard in Glasgow. He transferred to Prestwick Home Guard Coy. in 1941 and was eventually given command of H.Q. Coy. of 7th Ayr Bn. (R.S.F.) Home Guard and retired with the rank of Major when war finished.

He was president of the United Services Club from 1932-35 and numbered among his other interests are membership of St. Nicholas Golf Club for the past 27 years and the Royal Automobile Club for even longer. He is also a director of Ayr Greyhound Stadium and Mount Vernon Sports Stadium.

He was elected to Prestwick Town Council in 1930 and promoted a Bailie the following year and served until 1938. He was re-elected to represent the first ward in 1945 and became Police Judge and Bailie in 1946, having thus completed ten years' service.

Mrs Milligan has also taken keen interest in local affairs and is especially well known for her activities in connection with the Girl Guides Association.

Provost and Mrs Milligan have two daughters and one son, Major Andrew F. B. Milligan, R.S.F., who saw three years' active service overseas. He received the M.B.E. whilst attached to the Somaliland Scouts.

Three vacancies in the magistracy were filled with the appointment of Mr John D. Young, 14 Caerlaverock Avenue, as second Bailie. Bailie Young, who has conducted his own draper's business in Kilmarnock for 25 years, has resided in Prestwick for 12 years and is well known in musical circles. He is church organist in Craigie Parish Church.

Mr Alexander B. McNair, proprietor of the Beach House Hotel, who was elected third Bailie, came to Prestwick in 1941 from Motherwell and was born in Paisley where his father was a magistrate. As a member of a family connected with road transport for many generations he was engaged in that until 1941. He joined Prestwick Town Council in 1945 for the first time and was convener of the entertainments committee.

The fourth Bailie is Mr John Kerr, 8 Whinfield Avenue, who was elected for the first time in 1945 and re-elected the following year. He served as convener of the Parks Committee this year and took a keen interest in the activities of Howie Bowling Club and St. Ninian's Golf Club. He is a member of Ayr County Council representing Town Planning, Highways, Police and Law, Social Welfare and is convener of Prestwick High School. Bailie Kerr is the local manager for the Petroleum Board and the Anglo American Oil Company Ltd.

Under the provisions of the new Local Government (Scotland) Act, 1947, Prestwick for the first time has an honorary treasurer of the Burgh. Provost Milligan, in proposing Bailie Black, who has been convener of finance, said he could think of no one better qualified to carry out these duties and the appointment was agreed to unanimously. Under the same Act the appointments of Bailie Steele as Dean of Guild was unanimously agreed to.

As with the other nominations put before the meeting by the Provost, the appointment of conveners of the various committees, were all agreed.

1948

British railways were nationalised.

The Soviet Union blockaded West Berlin; supplies to the city were airlifted in.

The free National Health Service began operating in Britain.

The British Citizenship Act became law; making Commonwealth citizens British subjects.

Chinese Communists announced that a North China People's Democratic Republic was established in North Korea, claiming the whole of Korea for Communism.

Mr and Mrs J. Johnston

Featuring 'lately in the local news when he broke his neck in a pit mishap, Mr James Johnston, 56 Glenburn Rows, Prestwick, celebrated, with his wife, their golden wedding at Hogmanay. Still recovering from the effects of his accident, the 74-year-old miner has spent 66 years in the pits, since he followed his father underground at the age of 8. He later worked in Lanarkshire, Ayrshire, and Lothians pits before coming back finally to Ayrshire 22 years ago. Almost a year ago, on New Year's day, he hoisted the N.C.B. flag at Glenburn colliery, being the oldest miner on the pay-roll, and having an unbroken record of service in the coal industry. Mr and Mrs Johnston were married at Airdrie, the bride's home town—Mr Johnston is a native of Dalkeith— and Mrs Johnston, then a girl of 20 and unconnected with mining, dedicated herself to being a collier's wife. The celebrations took the form of a small family gathering, for the couple have no children of their own, although they have living with them three nieces, one of whom is manageress of the Prestwick Laundry.

2nd January 1948

AIRPORT BORN IN ADVERSITY

From Outset Prestwick Met Official Opposition

Interest in the future of Prestwick Airport has been maintained at a very high pitch over the past few years, and at present expert views as to the proper development of the aerodrome vary in private and in official quarters.

While studying the two main proposals put forward as future plans for Prestwick, it is enlightening and of value to review events and incidents in the history of the airport since its construction by Scottish Aviation towards the end of 1935. Some of these are still vivid in the public memory; others were little noted, but their cumulative effect was important.

In August, 1935, the objection of the Air Ministry Airfield Board to the construction of the airfield on the grounds of unfavourable weather conditions was overcome, and construction was commenced in September. Scottish Aviation opened the airfield in February, 1936.

It is interesting to compare the reasons for the Air Ministry Airfield Board's original opposition with their proposal in March, 1938, that Prestwick Airfield should be acquired for an R.A.F. Station, on the grounds of exceptionally favourable weather conditions. This proposal was opposed and subsequently withdrawn.

Transatlantic Terminal

Shortly after the Heathfield site was acquired by the Air Ministry for R.A.F. Fighter Command, in September, 1940, Prestwick Airfield became a Transatlantic air terminal, and nine months afterwards it was requisitioned for war purposes by the Air Ministry and the management of the airport transferred from Scottish Aviation to the R.A.F. Construction of the main runway was completed in September, 1941, and the secondary runway six months afterwards.

Between April and August, 1942, Scottish Aviation submitted to the Director-General of Civil Aviation, a detailed target plan for the development of the airport as a combined landplane and flying-boat terminal. This plan was later approved and recommended by both the Clyde Navigation Trust and the Scottish Council on Industry.

One month after Scottish Aviation offered to the Secretary of State for Scotland to place their holding in the airport so that a Scottish public utility corporation might be formed to own, manage and develop Prestwick Airport, the Air Ministry Airfield Board reported, in January, 1944, that "careful investigation shows that Prestwick will not provide even an aerodrome of local dimensions."

This was refuted by submission of complete details and costs of the target development plan, and in May, Ayr County Council met with the Department of Health for Scotland in an endeavour to obtain the acceptance of the target development plan and, in conjunction with it, the housing, industrial and other planning for the neighbourhood.

Sea and Air Ports

At the end of November, 1944, the Cooper Committee considered premateur the recommendation by the Scottish Regional Port Director that a deep water, fog-free passenger port for North Atlantic steamship services should be constructed at Prestwick in conjunction with the Trans-atlantic airport.

Scottish aspirations suffered another severe set-back in March when Sir Stafford Cripps stated that we could afford to have only one really first-class airport, and added, "As the House knows, it has been decided that Heathrow Aerodrome which is in course of construction and will cost a very large sum of money, is to be utilised as the main central Transatlantic airport of this country."

The Ministry of Civil Aviation intimated in December, 1945, that they would assume position of landlords of Prestwick Airport as from January of the following year, and would compulsorily purchase the airport holding of Scottish Aviation. It is surprising to note that at November of this year, assumption of ownership still continued without purchase.

Scottish unanimity on the subject of aviation was shown by a resolution unanimously passed by a meeting called by the Scottish Council on Industry at the beginning of 1946 to discuss the future of Prestwick Airport.

The meeting which was attended by members of Parliament, peers, representatives of local authorities, chambers of commerce, and trade unions resolved that both in the administration of airports and the operation of internal and external air services an adequate devolution of the powers of initiative and management should be guaranteed to Scotland.

The Council emphasised those points because it believed that if denied the opportunity to do so the structure of economic life in Scotland would be seriously undermined.

New Runways

February, 1946, saw a meeting between representatives of the Ministry of Civil Aviation, the Scottish Office, Scottish Aviation, B.O.A.C., the Admiralty, and the section of the Air Ministry Works and Buildings Department attached to the Ministry of Civil Aviation, decide to replace the unsatisfactory war-time secondary runway; rule out the proposed construction of a new third runway; and agree that the extension of the main runway should be considered in the light of a further survey to be carried out.

Prestwick Town Council resolved to co-operate in the development of the proposed new secondary runway by "freezing" a portion of their Marchburn and St. Quivox Road housing schemes, but, in June, the Air Ministry Works and Buildings reported that the line for the new runway was impracticable on the grounds of the cost of grading. Scottish Aviation disagreed that costs would be excessive.

The Scottish Aerodromes Board announced in October, 1947, that work would commence between the spring and autumn of next year on laying a three-inch carpet of tarmacadam on both existing runways at a cost of approximately £300,000.

Of the existing runways, the main one was planned in 1940 on the line suggested by the wind conditions experienced since 1935, and provided for maximum extension; but the present secondary runway was introduced merely as a war-time expedient and was the best available under war conditions. Its disadvantages include an approach over the town of Prestwick, hills to the north-east reduce the gliding angle, and as it crosses the main runway there is an element of risk. It was this runway which Prestwick Town Council described as a menace at its November meeting.

Targets Compared

Up to November, as far as could be ascertained the existing proposals of the Ministry of Civil Aviation for the development of Prestwick Airport were for a three-runway system retaining the present secondary runway and providing a new third runway on a northerly line from Redbrae towards Prestwick. Thus both the secondary and the new third runway would have approaches over Prestwick.

The three runway system would have the main airport buildings in the area now occupied by Scottish Aviation factories, would involve the diversion of the Glasgow, Irvine and Troon roads, and the retention of Heathfield Aerodrome. In some quarters it is felt that this retention would be undesirable owing to the possible danger of collision. These proposals appear to be similar to those rejected by the meeting in February, 1946.

The Ministry of Civil Aviation's proposals appear very modest when compared with the Prestwick Airport Target Development Plan which, as previously mentioned, was submitted by Scottish Aviation in 1942, and subsequently was approved by most of the Scottish authorities to whom the development was a matter of concern. It aimed at developing the existing main runway by doubling it in width to 200 yards and lengthening to seven thousand yards. The main airport buildings would be in the centre where they could also control and serve a flying boat area. The main road and railway line would eventually be carried by cut and cover under the main runway. It was felt that seven thousand yards would probably be the final limitation of runway lengths. The proposed secondary runway in this scheme would be sited in line with the direction of the south-west gales, and would have a direct approach over the sea from the south-west through a gap in the residential areas between Ayr and Prestwick.

23rd January 1948

PRESTWICK SKIPPER IN SEA ORDEAL

Caught In The Ice

With the bulwarks of their ship strained almost to bursting point through ice pressure, a blinding snowstorm and 55 degrees of frost making escape over the ice impossible, Captain Thomas Fairweather, 4 Newdykes Road, Prestwick, who is skipper of the Glasgow steamer Thelma (2880 tons deadweight), and his crew of 28 were rescued on Friday from their perilous predicament by the Ymer, largest ice-breaker in Scandinavia.

The ship's company, mostly from the West of Scotland, had spent two nerve-wracking days and nights in constant danger of their vessel being crushed by the thickening ice and their going down with her, after the ship had been caught and held fast in the ice off Haernosund at the northern end of the Bothnian Gulf, just below the Arctic Circle.

Cargo Of Timber

The Thelma, owned by Glen and Co., Glasgow, left Glasgow on December 15 to pick up a cargo of timber and wood props from Sundsvaal, North Sweden, for Dublin, when they ran into a sudden and unexpected cold spell.

Captain Fairweather, who has resided in Prestwick for 10 years and who was awarded the M.B.E. for his war services, said in Stockholm after the rescue, that they were handicapped by the heavy cargo which kept the ship very low in the water and this gave the ice a grip. At last they could make no headway and he was obliged to wireless for immediate help.

The blizzard that swept the area at the time made it impossible for other ice-breakers to find them, and the Ymer, despite the newly installed British radar, had great difficulty in locating the stricken vessel and took a whole day to come alongside and open a sea passage.

Intense Cold

Their greatest enemy, said the captain, was the intense cold which seemed to pierce right through their balaclava helmets, but fortunately they had sufficient provisions, fresh water and spirits to last them for some weeks. If their ship had broken up, which had seemed likely, they would have been obliged to take to the ice, but in Capt. Fairweather's opinion they would not have had a chance of reaching shore safely. The crew made great efforts to try and free the ship and in doing so some of them got frost-bite.

The captain of the rescue ship said that they had had to leave 30 other stranded vessels in order to reach the Thelma in time.

When interviewed at her home, Mrs Fairweather said she had received a radio message from her husband in Wick on Saturday, but he had made no mention of his narrow escape. His ship, she said, was due to arrive in Dublin on Monday and she was hoping to have him at home for a few weeks.

30th January 1948

CO-OPERATIVE YOUTH CLUB

Parents and friends joined the Ayr Co-operative Youth Club in the Co-operative Hall, Prestwick, on Friday, to celebrate the anniversary of the birth of Burns.

"The Immortal Memory" was proposed by May Tavendale, who said they were gathered as a youth club to pay simple homage to Robert Burns as Scotland's most illustrious son. Youth dictated that sentiment be simple but sincere, and she went on to paint a word picture of the poet's life. Although Burns despised the practices of snobbery and slave-driving, he gave honour where honour was due, and had among his friends some of the highest ranking men in the country. She asked them to pay tribute to this brilliant personage as he would have liked it; not merely by meeting on the anniversary of his birth, but by singing his songs, reading his poems, and contributing towards reaching the goal of Burns' brotherhood of man.

The chairman for the evening was Bill McAlpine, and Michael Porter piped in the haggis which was addressed by William McAlpine. A toast to "The Lasses" was proposed by Freddie Burdon, and reply was made by Dorothy Lees. "Bonnie Jean Armour" was submitted by Bill McAlpine, whilst Elizabeth Sim replied to Bailie John Pollock's toast, "The Ayr Co-operative Youth Club." Accompanied by May Graham, Elizabeth Sim and Rena McFarlane sang Burns' songs during the evening, whilst readings were contributed by Beryl Ferguson.

13th February 1948

Prestwick Public Park

In giving consideration to the desirability of amending the layout of the public park it appeared to the Prestwick Town Council that it was entirely used by the schools in the town and by members of the various youth groups. They suggested to the Ayrshire Education Committee that it might be more convenient to everyone concerned if the park could be made available to the schools and youth groups to a much greater extent that it was at present.

The Council therefore asked the Education Committee if they would be willing to take over the park for the use of the schools and youth groups on payment of a nominal rent of £1 per annum. If this were done it would, it was pointed out, probably result in there being less interference through outside parties playing on the pitches at a time when these were desired by the school children, etc. A five years' lease of the ground was suggested, and the Authority would have the right to alter the layout of the various pitches to suit their own convenience.

At their meeting on Tuesday the Ayrshire Education Committee agreed to accept a lease of the park on the terms stated on condition that it be used solely by the schools and for organised youth group activities.

Prestwick

ROWDY FUSILIERS.—Two soldiers from Fairfield Camp, Monkton, appeared in Prestwick Police Court on Monday, following a scene at a dance in the Town Hall on Saturday evening. Fusilier William Glancy, H.Q. Company, charged with assaulting Thomas McGhee, miner, 32 Marchburn Avenue, Prestwick, by butting him in the face with his head and severely cutting his lip, and also with breach of the peace, was sent to prison for thirty days. Bailie Kerr imposed a fine of £3 on Fusilier Allan Gray, Administration Group, R.S.F., for a breach of the peace.

27th February 1948

N.C.B. CRITICISED

Soon As Bad As M.C.A., Says Prestwick Councillor

An appeal for a very strong attitude to be adopted towards the National Coal Board with regard to the houses at Glenburn was made by Mr T. J. Ross, at the monthly meeting of Prestwick Town Council, on Tuesday.

The Town Council requested the National Coal Board to take steps to put these houses in reasonable condition and to install electric lighting in place of the existing gas lighting.

Mr Ross asked if the town clerk had communicated recently with the N.C.B, regarding the houses and if he had received any reply.

Mr John L. Jones, town clerk, said he had written following the last committee meeting, and had received a very interesting reply to the effect that the general area manager of the N.C.B. was away on business and would not be available until the middle of March.

Bailie McNair—Is he here for a pastime?

"It is a year past in January since this matter was first referred to the National Coal Board in Edinburgh," declared Mr Ross. "We were promised at that time our request would be given consideration, and for 13 months they have stalled and stalled, and we have never had one letter in the least degree satisfactory."

Mr Ross said they would soon be as bad as the Ministry of Civil Aviation on Prestwick Airport, and added, "I suggest that we take a strong attitude towards the N.C.B. in view of the fact that these houses are not sanitary. It was from a public health point of view that I raised the matter over a year ago."

Housing Points Scheme

A recommendation for the adoption of amendments to the existing housing points scheme for the allocation of council houses was remitted back to the Housing Committee.

Treasurer J. B. Black said he wished to enter his dissent to the proposed scheme, as the scheme as detailed was open to many criticisms. He was not disposed to detail or specify these criticisms then. Mr Ross had criticised the previous scheme and he thought it only right that Mr Ross should be given an opportunity to show that, as housing convener, the plan he now proposed was workable. He (Treasurer Black) thought the scheme was unworkable.

Dean of Guild Steele thought they had plenty of time before the scheme came into operation, and if Treasurer Black had some points to bring forward it should be remitted back.

Mr Ross said that Treasurer Black had not been present at the meeting when the scheme was discussed, and if he had any suggestions to make to improve the scheme he (Mr Ross) had no objection to a remit back.

Sand from the Foreshore

The Town Council considered the question of removal of sand from the foreshore and agreed to request the co-operation of Mr Hector Macarthur in preventing sand being removed from the foreshore at the south esplanade through this ground.

Treasurer Black said he was greatly concerned with the amount of sand being removed with the sanction of St. Nicholas Golf Club. During the week he had noticed the shore at that particular point was almost void of sand. He suggested that the town clerk be asked to write to St. Nicholas Golf Club pointing out the damage to the foreshore through selling or giving away sand, and asking them to desist from doing so in future. It was a danger to the golf course as well as to the foreshore.

Provost Milligan said that in May they would not be given permission to carry out sand.

5th March 1948

Prestwick Septuagenarian Fined For Assault

At Prestwick Police Court on Saturday, a 71-year-old retired Prestwick man, George Smith, 17 Station Road, pleaded guilty through an agent to assaulting two coalmen, delivering coal to a neighbouring house, by striking them with a stick.

The fiscal, Mr R. M. Gardiner, said that there had been some difference with regard to a lane to the rear of Regent Park Terrace, Prestwick, and accused had put up a gate. The two men, John Moffat, 67 Walker Road, Ayr, and John Scott, 61 Lochside Road, Ayr, were delivering coal to a nearby house and asked him to open the gate, when an altercation took place and he struck them with his stick.

Smith's agent stated that dispute over this lane had been going on for a matter of 20 or 30 years. His information was that the coalmen threatened to remove the gate from its hinges if it was not opened, and although accused flourished his stick, he did not know whether any severe blow was struck. Accused had repeatedly complained to the police about this right-of-way, but had been always put off by a question of title.

He was sure the Town Council knew that the dispute had been going on for about 25 years.

The fiscal—It is not a public path. It is a lane provided for access to the eight houses, and it has been so used for more than 40 years. I don't think that the legal question of right should enter into it at all—as regards legal rights, they can go to a civil court. Mr Smith has no right to forcibly restrain them.

Showing photographs of the lane to the presiding magistrate, Bailie Flanigan, who was accompanied on the bench by Bailie Kerr, the agent said that he had taken a look at it that morning, and that it was in a dreadful state. He emphasised that the accused was well on in years.

"He should have more sense, then," remarked Bailie Flanigan, imposing a fine of £2 or 20 days' imprisonment.

26th March 1948

Prestwick Rotary Club Inaugurated

The inauguration of a Rotary Club in Prestwick took place in the Parkstone Hotel on Thursday evening of last week, the new club being sponsored by the Rotary Club of Ayr.

Mr George C. Allan, Kirkcaldy, chairman of Districts 1 and 2 of Rotary International of Great Britain and Ireland, presided, and among those present were Mr William D. Blanche, district extension convener; Mr W. M. Buchanan, secretary and treasurer of Districts 1 and 2; Mr Henry A. Rankin, district vice-chairman; Provost Frank M. Milligan, Prestwick; the Rev. G. McLeod Dunn, and representatives of Glasgow, Paisley, Kilmarnock, Ardrossan-Saltcoats, Hamilton and Ayr clubs. Greetings were read from a large number of clubs in Districts 1 and 2, which cover the whole of Scotland.

An Important Town

Mr Blanche, in inviting the chairman to inaugurate the new club, said Prestwick had as foster club one which was outstanding in Rotary work in the Scottish districts. He congratulated the Ayr club on this extension effort. Prestwick was not a large burgh but it was one of the most important towns in Scotland. It had the airport, and it was disappointing that the mentality of the Government was not so clear as the atmosphere round Prestwick (laughter) because they did not appear to rank Prestwick the same way as Scotland did

But the future held something very fine for Prestwick, because he did not think any Government could prevent the development of Prestwick Airport. The responsibility on the members of this new club would be heavy because they would be the nearest Rotary Club to the landing point of many thousands of American tourists. They had direct contact with the United States of America, and it was interesting to have

these contacts with the country where their great movement was founded.

Mr W. Nicol Watson, president of the Ayr club, seconding, said the Ayr club had also initiated the Ardrossan-Saltcoats, which had been very successful. He regretted the severance with Past President Thom, but Ayr's loss would be Prestwick's gain.

The chairman accepted the proposal that the Prestwick club should go forward, and declared it an interim club under the rules of R.I.B.I.

First Office-Bearers

The formal resolution to found the Prestwick club covering the burgh of Prestwick and the parish of Monkton and Prestwick was moved by Mr J. B. Black and seconded by Mr David Graham, and the following office-bearers were appointed: president, Mr R. H. Thom; vice-president, Mr J. P. Livingstone; secretary, Mr John L. Jones; treasurer, Mr James A. Kinghorn; council, Mr Graham, Mr James Melrose, Mr Black, Mr Thomas H. Greig, Mr William S. Moir and Mr John Paton.

Fellowship and Understanding

The chairman, addressing the members of the new club, said Rotary had no secrets and no fancy handshakes, but it had high ethical aims. Rotary was founded on fellowship and mutual understanding. They should not be afraid of Rotary because it came from America: almost simultaneously Baden-Powell had given us the Boy Scouts! If the Rotary motto "Service above Self" was practised by everyone we should have reached the millenium. It involved duties which were definitely personal and could not be passed on to someone else.

The greatest problem which concerned Rotary to-day was the international situation. The Hitler regime put a stop to many Rotary clubs, although some had carried on underground and had received their charter back. Some were in Czechoslovakia, and they had not heard from them for over a fortnight, but one of the founder members there was Jan Masaryk. Continuing, Mr Allan said he brought to the Prestwick club the greetings of Rotary International, and he welcomed them as part of a great world fellowship of business and professional men.

President Thom, acknowledging, said the Prestwick club hoped to make contact with representative people from abroad and to give them a good impression

Provost Milligan expressed his pleasure at the formation of a Rotary Club in Prestwick.

The chairman was thanked for his services on the call of Mr Livingstone.

Provost Milligan, Mr J. P. Livingstone, Mr George C. Allan, Mr R. H. Thom, and Mr H. A. Rankin at the inauguration dinner.

26th March 1948

ROBES AND CHAINS

Gift To Prestwick Provost And Magistrates

Prestwick Town Council at its meeting on Tuesday evening unanimously agreed that the Provost and Magistrates should have robes and chains of office, sketches of which had been submitted.

The matter was raised when Treasurer J. B. Black asked if any action had been taken regarding the suggestion made in November of last year by Mr R. R. Stalker, Broughty Ferry, that a fund should be started to provide a chain of office for the Provost of Prestwick, and offering to contribute 10 guineas.

The town clerk, said the Provost, had obtained a sketch of the proposed chain, which was now submitted for the Council's approval, and, he added, "A local gentleman has offered to join issue with Mr Stalker and make a gift of the chain to the town." The question of robes for the Provost and magistrates, and town clerk had also been raised, he continued, and a few local people including several past provosts had offered to contribute the provision of these. It was likely a few other public spirited people in the town would be willing to contribute to the cost. At any rate the offers they had received made it almost certain that the ratepayers need have no qualms about the cost of the robes being put on the local rates.

"I suggest we accept these gifts offered to us," said the Provost, "and that we record our grateful appreciation of the generous action of the donors I feel sure an order for the supply of the robes could be placed now in the almost certain knowledge that the balance of the cost required will be forthcoming at an early date."

Repair Of A Lorry

A minute of the General Purposes Committee recommending that a tender amounting to £108 submitted by Messrs. Seatons Autos (Prestwick) Ltd., for the repair of the bodywork of the Council's Morris Commercial lorry was carried by 8 votes to 4.

Treasurer Black had moved that a lower estimate be accepted. Two offers had been considered and the one of £64 6s. 6d. by Mr John Limond, Ayr, rejected. As a Council, he declared, they had to consider themselves as trustees for the community. Here they were accepting for no reason at all an offer of £108 against £64 6s. 6d.

Mr T. J. Ross seconded.

Bailie McNair said that the more costly estimate allowed for the replacement of mudwings instead of merely patching up as suggested in the other offer. The higher offer promised to be a lasting job, and he proposed that the minute be approved. This was seconded by Mr T. C. Clarkson.

Marchburn Bus Service

It was carried by 7 votes to 2 that no action should be taken with regard to suggested changes in the present route and terminus of the Marchburn bus service.

Dean of Guild Steele had moved as an amendment to a Streets and Works Committee minute that the terminus should be altered to its previous position at the junction of Marchburn Avenue and Outdale Avenue. He claimed that the use of the old stance would be fair to all who used the service.

Supporting the minute, Bailie McNair said that people on the route could easily catch the bus by walking 200 yards. On the shore they had to walk 300 or 400 yards, and they had no bus service.

Treasurer Black said that to suggest they ask the bus company to alter what they had already decided on—for the sake of people walking 200 yards—was ridiculous.

An Excise Claim

The Council approved payment to the Customs and Excise the claim for the duty payable on vaporising oil used in the golf course tractor from 1938 to December 31, 1947. This was agreed when the town clerk, Mr John L. Jones, revealed that as the Town Council had been under a misapprehension the Customs and Excise were prepared to waive the claim for vaporising oil used on the golf course, and to restrict it to the amount used on the roads. This meant that the amount claimed was reduced from £430 9s. 2d. to £206 13s. 4d. Treasurer Black, who had taken up the matter, had agreed that this was a very reasonable attitude for the Customs and Excise to adopt.

[During the period in question, the oil had been supplied free of duty in error. As the tractor was a road vehicle on which a full road fund licence had been payable, duty should have been paid.]

Summer Accommodation

The town clerk said that he had a great many applications from people seeking accommodation in hotels and houses in the burgh. As he did not have sufficent information to give he had to turn most of these people away with no satisfactory answer, and he asked persons with summer accommodation to let him know so that it could be entered in the official guide.

Bailie McNair said he was sure that the town clerk would not use information so received for any other purpose.

28th May 1948

Glenburn Miners To Be Sued

The Scottish Division of the National Coal Board is to take action against twelve Glenburn miners who went on strike on Tuesday and also against about 360 who stopped work on Wednesday, and will sue them for breach of contract. Almost 1000 tons of coal were lost by the stoppage at the Prestwick pits, it is stated.

The statement issued by the Scottish Division of the Coal Board on the Ayrshire dispute said:

"There have been a disquieting number of unofficial disputes this year at Auchincruive Nos. 4 and 5 Collieries, Prestwick (locally known as Glenburn Colliery), most of them of a sectional nature involving comparatively few men in each section. The lack of discipline prevailing, however, has not been confined to any one section.

"Between the beginning of the year and May 18. 20 stoppages took place representing a considerable loss of output. On the latter date a notice was posted at the colliery reminding the workmen of their terms of employment and warning them that those who took part in any further unofficial stoppages would be held to have broken their contract, and would be sued for damages by the National Coal Board

"On Tuesday 12 men struck. When they presented themselves for work to-day they were offered re-employment only on the understanding that the National Coal Board made such an offer without prejudice to any rights to sue for damages. The 12 men and all the remainder of the day shift (about 360 men) then went home.

"Summonses are being served on the 12 men who struck work on Tuesday and similar action will be taken in due course against the other strikers."

14th May 1948

SECOND THOUGHTS

Prestwick Town Council And House Allocation

At the end of two and a half hours' full and frank discussion round the table by members of Prestwick Town Council and representatives of the Joint Wards Committee, the Council agreed to suspend the standing orders and call a special Council meeting on Tuesday to investigate the allocation of a house to Mr David Bannerman, cashier in the burgh chamberlain's department.

At Monday's meeting presided over by Provost Milligan, Mr T. J. Ross, the central figure in the dispute that aroused Prestwick ratepayers to protest en masse at a meeting on Wednesday of last week, was absent. Was Mr Ross still a member of the Council? asked a wards representative, to which the town clerk replied that he did not want to answer that question there.

Asked when they were likely to hear the decision of the Council one way or the other on the house allocation, the Provost said no time would be lost and that the next meeting would take place in two weeks' time.

At the back of some minds was the thought they were going to see Mr Ross an ex-Councillor, said a wards representative, whereupon Bailie McNair said it would appear that this resignation or the withdrawal of it was dependant on the Council's reversal of the decision on the house. If Mr Ross so desired there was nothing to prevent his going to the town clerk and withdrawing his resignation, but he (Bailie McNair) could not see that the resignation should be conditional.

Treasurer Black said he could understand it if Mr Ross had resigned in the heat of the moment, but he had had a typewritten resignation all ready to hand in at the end of the Council meeting.

What is a Key Worker?

Asked what were the main points of objection to the allocation of this house, a delegate said that in Prestwick they had a points scheme, and in this case the Council went outwith that scheme and had no right to do so with people depending on it for their houses. Here was a glaring example of preferential treatment. They objected to any person being housed outwith the points scheme, was the reply given to a question by the Provost as to whether there was any objection to the corporation housing its key workers. That seemed to be the crux of the whole matter, said Provost Milligan.

A lengthy discussion ensued as to what was a key worker during which Bailie McNair by replies from Mr James A. Kinghorn, town chamberlain, brought out that in answer to an advertisement in the press, 12 replies had been received, two from local people, and that none had been found suitable. The information given to the ratepayers, said the Bailie, was that twelve to fill the post could be found in an hour, when in fact they had received no replies from local people suitable for the job and had to go outside.

A wards member replied to that by saying that irrespective of qualifications or where he came from, the key man in the chamberlain's department was the town chamberlain.

Various figures had been put out as to the numbers of people in Prestwick on the list for houses, and the burgh factor stated the number of live applications was 533.

This was not the only house allocated to key workers in the corporation and the Provost wondered why the Joint Wards Committee did not raise objection to the other allocations.

Three Houses For Officials

All houses built in Prestwick, said Mr J. L. Jones, town clerk, were subject to allocation by the Council. There were three houses allocated to town officials of which only two had been occupied, leaving the third available for a Town Council worker.

The wards representatives submitted that once the house was vacated it automatically reverted to the housing committee for re-allocation. The Council did not, in their submission to authority for permission to build so many hundred houses, ask for, in addition, a stated number of houses for burgh officials. Was this to remain a tied house to be played about with by the Council, to be let to whoever they wished, or was it free? By no stretch of the imagination could this cashier be called a key worker.

The Council was the authority for the letting of houses, said the Provost and if they considered a man was a key worker their opinion was just as good as that of anyone else.

Bailie McNair remarked that he and Treasurer Black, in the first instance, had objected to officials getting houses in the burgh. Instead he had suggested they ask the Secretary of State if something could not be done in that respect. It had been the decision of the Council about two years ago to let houses to burgh officials and as that had not been altered that was why he and Treasurer Black fell in with the proposal.

Mr Cooper, one of the delegates, said all could make mistakes and he could think of nothing worse than being "bellowed" into changing a decision, but he assured the Council there were a good few thousand people in Prestwick who did not think this man was sufficiently important to get the house. If it went to a poll vote he felt sure 95 per cent. of the people would not think his name was justified at being even on the bottom of the list. They should bear in mind that the majority thought they had made a wrong decision.

Prestwick Town Council Adamant Over House Allocation

By six votes to five Prestwick Town Council at a special meeting on Tuesday refused to suspend the standing orders to allow further discussion of the question of the allocation of a house to the cashier in the Town Chamberlain's department.

Proceedings were brief, about five minutes sufficing to reach a decision. It will be recalled that Mr T. J. Ross resigned from the Council over the allocation of a house to this employee, and hundreds of ratepayers were turned away from a protest meeting n the Town Hall on May 5 after approximately 700 had been admitted.

Mr Ross was not present at Tuesday's meeting, and the town clerk (Mr J. L. Jones), in answer to Mr Clarkson, said Mr Ross had not been invited as he ceased to be a member of the Town Council on April 27.

2nd April 1948

MILK FOR BABIES

(To the Editor, "The Ayrshire Post")
Prestwick.
March 16, 1948.

Sir,—I wish to make a complaint but unfortunately do not know to which authority it should be made.

Prestwick mothers who give their babies National Dried Milk can obtain this food from the clinic only and the hours of collection amount to the large number of four per month. These are on the first and third Tuesdays of the month between 2 p.m. and 4 p.m. Should a mother be unable to attend the clinic during these times she must go to the Food Office in Ayr.

Why cannot this food be obtained from the chemist where it could be purchased as required? To add insult to injury, the clinic was closed today at 3.50 p.m. leaving at least eight mothers to go without.

I should also like to add, and I know that in this I have the support of most mothers, that the manner of those ladies who sell the milk, orange juice, etc., leaves much to be desired.

Prestwick Mother.

28th May 1948

Prestwick Beauty Contest

Prestwick Town Council on Tuesday—Provost Milligan in the chair—heard Bailie McNair give details of the £600 bathing beauty contest which is to be held on July 17 at the bathing lake, and which was launched at the meeting with the blessing of the council.

The contest, said Bailie McNair, would have a very wide appeal and would quite possibly attract entries of young ladies from all over. It might therefore be necessary to operate it in heats and it was hoped to give prizes to the first four in each. A great amount of work had been involved in making the arrangements and he paid tribute to the cinema trade who are to supply film stars as judges. The Tourist Board had also indicated their willingness to assist and had it been possible to arrange an air trip to Canada as a prize, which they had been offered, the board would have undertaken to play their part at the other end through some of the Caledonian societies. Bailie McNair also warmly thanked the town clerk (Mr John L. Jones) for the real assistance he had been in getting the project under way.

Winners of this beauty contest, which is included in a long list of other summer attractions at Prestwick this year, will have a "dream" holiday. The first prize winner will be presented with a free air trip for herself and a companion to Copenhagen, Stockholm, Oslo, Amsterdam or Paris, and a cash prize of £80. The runner-up can relax with a companion in Amsterdam in the knowledge that she is £60 richer and the third lady placed has a choice of destination from Oslo, Stockholm or Copenhagen with £40 in prize money. There will be other prizes in the contest.

11th June 1948

NO BY-ELECTION
Divided Opinion At Prestwick Council

Prestwick Town Council decided, by seven votes to four, at a special meeting on Tuesday, to fill the vacancy in the Second Ward by co-option, and deferred selection of the co-opted member for two weeks.

A by-election, said the Provost, would put back the rota in that ward by at least one year and would put out Dean of Guild Steele a year earlier than he would normally have retired through no fault of his own. What was there to stop a councillor resigning near the end of his three-year term, fighting a by-election, and coming back in for another three years? He thought it might be as well to postpone this for another two weeks so as to give the matter further consideration.

Bailie McNair moved they co-opt someone and that they continue for two weeks to consider whom they would co-opt.

Mr Clarkson seconded.

25th June 1948

PRESTWICK'S NEW COUNCILLOR

Mr James McGinty, M.A., 1 Queen's Terrace, Prestwick, the new councillor, took his seat at the monthly meeting of Prestwick Town Council, on Tuesday, after it had been carried by nine votes to two that the Council should accept Mr McGinty's nomination by the Second Ward Committee to fill the vacancy in the Town Council caused through the resignation of Mr T. J. Ross.

The town clerk (Mr John L. Jones) read a letter from the secretary of the Second Ward Committee intimating that the committee had discussed the matter fully and after taking all the circumstances of the case into consideration, it had been decided to agree to fill the vacancy by co-option. They nominated Mr McGinty.

Provost Milligan moved that the nomination be accepted, and this was seconded by Dean of Guild Steele, who said that while he had always felt that a representative in the Town Council should reside in the ward he represented, he thought it had always been the habit in the Council to accept the nomination of the ward committee.

Lost An Election

As an amendment, Bailie Kerr moved that the nomination be not accepted. Stating that while he did not know Mr McGinty at all, there were one or two considerations which the Council ought to take into account. Firstly, Mr McGinty did not reside in the Second Ward, but in the First Ward. Secondly, he had fought an election on a previous occasion, "and the electors had no confidence in him to such an extent that he only polled very few votes as compared with other nominees put forward."

Provost Milligan—"I want you to be quite fair. I do not think it is right to say because a man did not top the poll his neighbours had no confidence in him."

Continuing, Bailie Kerr said he did not wish to bring in political matters, but Mr Ross had been a Moderate member, and he thought he should be replaced by a Moderate. From information he had received Mr McGinty had not changed his position from being on the Labour side. The Bailie continued: "I have nothing against the Labour side in the slightest—my own position in the Council is non-political, and I will maintain that to the very end—nevertheless, I think it is only right that the Second Ward should have put forward at least a Moderate member to represent them in this Council."

No Labour Connection

Rising on a point of correction, Dean of Guild Steele declared emphatically that Mr McGinty was not a member of the Labour Party, and had not been for a long while.

Treasurer Black said he resented very strongly the suggestion that no man should be elected for a particular ward unless he happened to reside in that ward. His own opinion was that wards were formed for convenience, but the interest of the whole community was involved. When a person was appointed—no matter for which ward —it was his duty to see he considered the burgh as a whole and not as a part. "I think for once the Second Ward Committee must have been inspired to suggest that Mr McGinty should be elected," he concluded, "because I can think of very few more erudite, educated, and intelligent men, and I am quite sure his presence on this Council will be a tremendous asset."

To put the matter to a vote, Mr Allan said he would second the amendment, and on a division the motion for acceptance was carried by nine votes to two.

Mr McGinty was present in the Council Chamber, and he was asked by Provost Milligan if he was prepared to make the declaration that night. He replied in the affirmative, and on being invited, went forward, made and signed the declaration.

THE NEW MEMBER

Mr McGinty is at present assistant headmaster in St. Mary's School, Abercrombie Street, Glasgow, and, after the summer vacation, becomes second master at St. Robert's School, Househillwood, Glasgow. A graduate of Glasgow University, Mr McGinty, who is 45 years of age, has taught in St. Ninian's High School, Kirkintilloch; St. Paul's Secondary School, Whiteinch; St. Michael's School, Parkhead; and Lourdes School, Cardonald. He is a native of Glasgow, and came to live in Prestwick in 1940. Six years later he unsuccessfully contested the First Ward against Provost Milligan and Bailie McNair. He is church organist of St Quivox Church, and he has undertaken considerable youth group work.

23rd July 1948

BUSIEST POST-WAR "FAIR"

The Ayrshire coast towns had prepared for the annual invasion from Glasgow, and caterers, shopkeepers, hotels, boarding houses, and transport authorities were ready for the Fair folk on pleasure bent.

This has proved to be the busiest "Fair" since the war, and whatever attractions might be offered elsewhere Ayr, Prestwick, Girvan and Troon all appear to have a larger quota of visitors than for some years past.

The railway has had its busiest time since the war years, and the bus companies have run so many duplicates that it has been hardly possible to maintain a count. The police, however, have had an unusually quiet time for this part of the year, and this may well be connected with the widely acknowledged fact that there is comparatively little money to be disbursed freely.

Many Day Trippers

There has not been the same clamourous demand for apartments as has been seen formerly, and although hotels and boarding houses have been fully booked up, it is thought that a large proportion of those crowding the street are day trippers unwilling or unable to expend a large portion of their holiday money on accommodation.

The railway found it could cope adequately with the traffic and this has been attributed to the greater availability of trains and officials have felt that if prices had compared more favourably with bus fares, this would have attracted a larger number to travel by rail. The system could have transported many more without difficulty. There was little rail traffic on Friday morning, but this swelled in the afternoon, and the real rush developed on Saturday morning. Sunday was practically normal, but since then there has been a heavy programme of day excursions.

On such a week as this, it did seem peculiar that the provision of special cheap fares was limited to the two race days only, and the persons taking advantage of these facilities had to travel back by the early trains. The only incident of any consequence at Ayr station was on Monday when officials had to persuade a party, who appeared to have been at the bar as well as the races, that the nationalisation of the railway companies did not mean they could travel first class on third class tickets.

Air Flights Popular

Probably the busiest spot on the coast on Sunday was Prestwick Airport, where nearly 400 holiday-makers took advantage of the pleasure flights flown by Scottish Airlines.

Whether from lack of accommodation or the necessary funds fifteen young men decided to spend Monday night in the shelters on the Ayr seafront. First casualty at Ayr was eighteen-year-old Katherine Farrell, 145 Coburg Street, Glasgow, who fell to the sands from the esplanade wall on Monday, and was admitted to Ayr County Hospital with a back injury. Ayr police had their regular daily quota of anxious parents searching for missing offspring, and wailing "weans" weeping for absent guardians.

Prestwick Smash

A large number of thirsty people in the vicinity of Main Street, Prestwick, suffered a shock on Monday morning when they heard the crash of broken glass, and on looking round saw a brewer's lorry had become involved in an accident with a car, resulting in a large number of bottles being strewn over and shattered on the main road. The casualties were all empties. A line of cars and buses about 200 yards long formed as the traffic was held up for some time until the roadway was cleared.

At The Races

With Ayr race meeting, the second of the series which forms the summer circuit in Scotland, traffic Ayrward was particularly heavy on Monday. Whereas the weather on the opening day last year "washed" out the attendance to a great extent, on this occasion more favourable conditions obtained with the result that the attendance at around 24,000 showed a big increase. On the Tuesday the crowd was in the region of 17,000.

Some of the fields were disappointingly small, yet curiously enough the chief event on Monday which had only two runners provided the closest finish of the two days. One of the big disappointments was the defeat of Heads of Ayr, owned by Miss Baird, which failed to get a place in the last event on Tuesday after being soundly supported. There were cheers for the eleven-year-old The Pale, when he cleverly beat a good field of sprinters for the Rozelle Handicap.

Prestwick

HOUSE RENTS.—After giving consideration to the financial loss on housing schemes, Prestwick Town Council agreed, on Tuesday, that the rents of council houses be increased to the extent necessary to meet the deficiency on the Housing Revenue Account. The rent of 2-apartment flatted type is to be increased to £21; 3-apartment flatted type to £26; 3-apartment cottage type to £28; 4-apartment cottage type to £32; and 5-apartment cottage type to £36. The increase takes effect from November 28.

6th August 1948

THUNDERSTORM CUTS ELECTRICITY SUPPLIES

Heat-Wave Ends

The violent thunder storm which swept the countryside on Saturday night following the oppressive heat-wave, caused considerable interruptions in electricity supplies throughout the county.

Fortunately it side-stepped the main supply flow into Ayr, but the area along Main Street, New Road, and Prestwick Road was affected.

The principal interruptions in the district occurred shortly after nine o'clock on Saturday night when consumers in Ayr and Prestwick were without lights for about half-an-hour. Two local cinemas, The Orient, and The Ritz, were blacked out. At the Orient, the manager had a hectic few minutes distributing about a thousand complimentary tickets for re-admission this week. At the Ritz, however, the audience made the best of the circumstances and sat patiently until the programme resumed.

Cause of Black-Out

The interruptions in the Ayr district, it was explained by an official of the South Western Electricity Board, were due to the opening by lightning of the feeder circuit-breaker at Kilmarnock. Alternative currents were brought into play and the circuits were closed again in about half-an-hour.

The south-west districts of the county had their share of the "breaks", Dunure and Girvan being blacked-out for some time.

An overhead line at Hurlford was struck by lightning and this caused breakages in supplies into the Cumnock, Muirkirk, and Mauchline districts and these places were without light for some time. Though the storm was severe, stated the official, these were the only areas affected in the county and the main supply circuits into Ayr, Ardrossan and Largs were kept free.

Earlier on Saturday afternoon distant thunder was heard in Ayr and district, but shortly after eight o'clock the storm broke with great severity, and vivid flashes of forked lightning were followed by crashing peals of thunder. Rain fell in torrents, and holiday-makers were compelled to seek shelter in any convenient place.

Heat Affects Railways

On Thursday and Friday Ayrshire railways suffered set-backs through the very high temperatures, the heat of the sun causing over-expansion of the rails, resulting in the lines buckling at four places. Near Newton-on-Ayr station trains to and from Glasgow had to run on a single line on Thursday. Buckling also occurred at a point between Ayr and Alloway stations, between Ayr and Patna, and near Kirkconnel.

Squads soon put the matter right, and nowhere was the delay more than two hours. British Railway officials, who pride themselves on taking preventive measures before anything dangerous happens, felt that the small irksome delays were worth while in order to prevent anything of a disastrous nature occurring. The exceptional heat (Prestwick on Thursday recorded an all-time high record of ninety degrees) came suddenly after a comparatively cold spell.

Trouble With The Points

The delay at Newton Station on Friday was also caused through the excessive heat (the meteorological station at Prestwick showed a drop of only two degrees from the previous day) creating trouble with the points.

Saturday, dull and oppressive, culminating in the violent thunderstorm and heavy downpour, was a poor ending to the Glasgow Fair fortnight, and Paisley holidaymakers, who began their annual fortnight's vacation, did not have a very good inauguration. From Thursday the temperature tumbled down almost thirty degrees until Tuesday at midday when it was hovering around the sixty mark, with a chance of better and warmer weather to follow.

8th October 1948

CHILDREN AND SCHOOLS

To the Editor, "The Ayrshire Post"
13 Caerlaverock Avenue,
Prestwick,
September 30, 1948.

Sir,—Since hearing of the unfortunate accident which occurred at Prestwick Toll last week, as the result of which a little girl lost her foot, I cannot help feeling that, had the education authority used a little discretion, this tragedy might never have occurred.

That child, I understand, was approximately six years of age and in the second class at Prestwick Public School. My daughter will be six years old next month and is in the second class at Heathfield School.

It would be interesting to have an explanation as to why a child living within a few hundred yards of Prestwick Public School must travel to Heathfield and why a child living within a few hundred yards of Heathfield must travel to Prestwick.

I think we parents have worries enough without additional ones such as this which could easily be avoided.

I sincerely hope that the education authority will bear this in mind for future reference **A. M. McWhirter.**

7th August 1948

"NO JOKE"

AT PRESTWICK

Two Glasgow visitors returned to Prestwick on Saturday to give evidence at the local police court, which led to Bailie Kerr imposing a fine of £2 on George McCreadie Reid, taxi driver, 30 Sandgate, Ayr, after finding him guilty of committing a rather unusual breach of the peace.

The Glasgow couple (Mr and Mrs John Branks, 4 Littleholm, Dalmuir West) explained that on July 21, while passing under the railway bridge in Grangemuir Road, Prestwick, they saw a car coming towards the shore from Main Street, travelling fast. The tunnel was flooded at the time with rainwater, and as they did not have time to pass through before the car reached them, they decided to turn back. "But the car simply went flying right through, and the water came over us," said Mr Branks. "We had to turn our backs to it, and it passed right over our heads. My wife's coat has the marks of the water."

A detective-constable stated that from a distance of 30 or 40 yards he heard the car's horn being blown, and took it that the driver saw some obstruction or people at the bridge. He then noticed the couple trying frantically to get out from underneath it, for there were only about six inches of surface under the bridge on which one could walk, the rest being flooded. A Rolls Royce taxi came through, showering a "terrific spray" up in the air, and he saw the driver and his passenger laughing. "I assumed they were laughing at the discomfiture of the foot passengers."

A police sergeant, who made inquiries before charging accused, stated that Reid replied: "I did not realise the water was so deep," and accused repeated this in the witness box, adding that it was a very wet day and his windscreen was blurred by rain. The 15-year-old message boy who had been his passenger said that they had been laughing because he remarked that if the car windows had not been closed, they would have been drenched themselves.

22nd October 1948

Airport's First Civil 'Plane Disaster

NOTED PILOT KILLED

THIRTY-EIGHT PEOPLE ARE DEAD IN THE FIRST CIVIL AIR DISASTER IN THE HISTORY OF PRESTWICK AIRPORT.

IN THE EARLY HOURS OF YESTERDAY MORNING A CONSTELLATION, ON A FLIGHT FROM AMSTERDAM TO NEW YORK, BELONGING TO K.L.M. ROYAL DUTCH AIRLINES, CRASHED AT AUCHINWEET FARM, A MILE AND A HALF FROM TARBOLTON VILLAGE. IT WAS PREPARING TO LAND AT PRESTWICK.

The aircraft was carrying thirty passengers and ten of a crew, and 34 of the total complement were killed while two of the six survivors died later in Ballochmyle Hospital, and two in Kilmarnock Infirmary.

The Constellation had made an approach run into the airport at 12.35 a.m., but regaining height sharply circled over Tarbolton, when the crash occurred.

Preliminary official details indicated that during a ground control approach, the commander of the aircraft sent a radio message saying "I have hit something. Going on fire. Climbing away." The machine crashed a few minutes later.

Lights Dimmed

Shortly after 12.30 a.m. yesterday electric light in Ayr lowered suddenly, but immediately resumed full illumination. It is believed that it was associated with the aircraft having struck the transmission lines of the British Electricity Authority, which are carried on pylons near the scene of the crash.

Two Survivors

An official statement issued by K.L.M. at Prestwick Airport later gave the name of the Chief Pilot as Captain Koened Dirk Parmentier, and among the thirty passengers were the vice-president of K.L.M., Mr H. Veenendaal, and a member of the board of control, Mr E. Fuld.

Captain Parmentier, who was 48, was a well-known figure at Prestwick Airport and other airports in many parts of the world. He had been a regular visitor to Prestwick ever since K.L.M. started their transatlantic service just after the war. In pre-war days he earned fame as the co-pilot of the K.L.M. passenger aircraft which came in second in the Robertson £10,000 air race from London to Melbourne in 1934.

The survivors of yesterday's disaster were: Flight Engineer J. Y. Feukenkamp, and Mr W. H. Philippo, Holland.

From the passenger list issued later by K.L.M. officials the names of the dead were learned to be:

Mary Badir, U.S.A.; Henry Finnie, U.S.A.; Paul C. C. Catselides; W. M. Katharina Fuld, Dutch; Edgar Fuld, Dutch; Maria Gamanova, Czech; David Heumann, German; William Hilarius, South African; Alfred Hohenlohl, Austrian; Austin F. E. MacInerny, British; Abraham K. Deleeuw, Dutch; Arie Philippo, Dutch; E. Pinto, Dutch; and Mrs Pinto, Dutch; James Rampas, U.S.A.; John Reichel, U.S.A.; Maria Reichel, Austrian; F. L. Rohts, U.S.A.; Mrs Mathilde K. Rohts, U.S.A.; Lily Marie Fuld, Dutch; J. G. Sas, Dutch; F. Schulmtf, Swiss; H. F. Tol, Dutch; W. F. Gale, U.S.A.; Hendrik Veenendaal, Dutch; Rupert Wedermeyer, U.S.A.; Emma Wedermeyer, U.S.A.; Rudbin Radzanowicz, Polish; Hena C. Radzanowicz, Polish.

Members of the crew who are dead in addition to Captain Parmentier are: First Officer J. K. O'Brien, Canadian; Second Officer Humphrey W. W. Parks, British; Wireless Officer H. P. P. Hurts, Dutch; First Steward J. C. Mink, Dutch; Second Wireless Operator Willem Bleuze, Dutch; Second Flight Engineer B. Timmer, Dutch; Second Steward H. H. van Overbeek; Air Hostess Elsie Anna M. Fey.

22nd October 1948

Jumped From Aircraft

In a despairing attempt to save his life a male passenger apparently jumped from the crashing aircraft seconds befor it struck the field. Police early on Thursday morning found his broken body about 150 yards from the wreckage and the spot where he landed was clearly marked by a deep indentation in the ground and his shoes.

Mr Thomas Neil who farms the 220 acres of Auchinweet Farm told *The Ayrshire Post* that his 'phone was put out of order when the plane brought down the telephone wires after it had struck and broken three of the 132,000 volt high tension wires at Langlands Farm, Tarbolton. Mr Neil's family were all asleep in the farmhouse which lies about a mile and a half from the village and a slight noise was all they heard but it was sufficient to let them know that a 'plane was in trouble.

Blazing Furiously

Rushing out to the door they saw the aircraft down in the field and Mr Neil went by car to Tarbolton police station and gave the alarm. The moans of the injured were clearly audible from his door, said Mr Neil, and the 'plane which was blazing furiously was ringed round with other smaller burning piles as the scattered wreckage caught fire. In the field where the wreckage lies Mr Neil had, until Thursday night, bedded down 50 cattle, but they for the first time had been housed in the byre.

Mr James E. Poli, 40 Montgomery Street, who said he was first on the scene, had a dramatic story to tell. He had heard the 'plane go overhead about 12.30 making a strange sound. Looking out he saw flames coming from the aircraft, and it was obvious it was in difficulties. He himself did not hear the crash, but realising that something was seriously wrong, he ran for a friend, Mr James Wilson, Craigie View, and they went by car to the scene.

Rescue Efforts

Dead and dying were lying scattered about the blazing inferno, but he saw that four men and two women were still alive and he plunged into rescue work. It was with the greatest difficulty that he was able to get near enough to pull away to safety one woman, who despite a broken left leg and her clothes and hair being alight, was still conscious and able to speak to her rescuers. They managed to drag her clear, put out the burning hair and then completely stripped her of her burning clothing.

By that time farmers, farm labourers, miners and villagers were arriving in ever increasing numbers and Mr Poli who was unaware of the identity of the lady, did not know whether she had been taken to Ballochmyle Hospital or not.

Of the burned-out wreckage only the tail assembly seemed to have suffered the least damage. The blackened debris extended for over two hundred yards while across the road from the field where it lay were a pair of landing wheels standing upright and with their pneumatic tyres apparently undamaged.

Beside pieces of aircraft mechanism were such delicate things as watches and suitcases some of which were undamaged by the fire.

12th November 1948

PRESTWICK'S CIVIC ROBES

The Provost, Magistrates and town clerk of Prestwick are now equipped with robes and insignia of office, which have been given to the town by various donors.

The robes were presented to the civic chiefs at a function held in the Queen's Hotel, Prestwick, on Friday evening, and on that occasion the opportunity was taken to present to four former provosts of the burgh medallions to mark their services to Prestwick.

A colourful garment in scarlet superfine, the Provost's robe is richly trimmed with white fur and ermine tails; his chain of office is formed by a series of gold rectangular plates, bearing a heavy medallion carrying the burgh arms. Some of the links are inscribed with the name of former provosts, the terms of office of all civic leaders back to 1903 being so commemorated.

The four robes for the magistrates are of dark purple, trimmed in a fashion similar to that of the Provost's, but for the fact they are not trimmed along the foot. Mr A. A. Hunter, manager of the ceremonial robing department of R. W. Forsyth, Ltd., Glasgow and Edinburgh, the firm which provided the robes, attended the function to assist in the initial robing.

An Ancient Burgh

After dinner, Provost Milligan remarked it was strange Prestwick had not taken steps before in all its history to provide these insignia of office. The charter had been granted in 1601 by James VI, and that stated that the history of Prestwick dated back some further 600 years. From that document it seemed the town was something over 1000 years old, and it had progressed from generation to generation, making a name for herself in modern times as a weaving town, a famous resort, golfing centre, and in more recent years it was known by every country that used

the sky as a means of transport. It was only fitting a town of such importance in the development of the world should have some recognition for its civic administrators.

The presentation of the insignia had arisen from a tiny seed planted ten months before by a visitor to the town. The Provost went on to tell how Mr R. R. Stalker had written to the town clerk on November 8, 1947, suggesting that a scheme be formulated to purchase a chain of office for the first citizen, and offering to forward a cheque for such a fund as a symbol of the many happy times Mr Stalker had spent in Prestwick.

This had been noted in the local newspapers, said the Provost, and several gentlemen had come forward wishing to identify themselves with such a scheme. Soon they had sufficient offers to give the Council confidence to place an order for the robes.

Testifying to Dignity

The robes and chain were dedicated by the Rev. Donald M. Caskie, Monkton and Prestwick. After giving a resumé of the town's history, Mr Caskie declared: "There are certain hasty people who deprecate the wearing of robes. They profess to see no need for them, and in condemnation they think themselves too advanced and enlightened." But the wearing of robes was a mark of civilisation in east and west, and was a custom which, far from being outmoded, was gaining in extensiveness. Robes of office were far more than mere decoration. They were symbols testifying to the dignity and sanctity—not of the wearer—but of the office which he discharged.

Surely, he added, the dignity and importance of the various offices of local government could not be too strongly represented and upheld today in a time when our affairs were becoming increasingly subject to remote and, therefore, largely impersonal and not always too wise

Provost Milligan was then presented with his robe of office by the donor, Mr J. F. Crichton. and the same gentleman also fitted the chain of office in the absence of the donor, Mr A. W. Berkley.

In the absence of Mr R. R. Stalker who was to have presented the magistrates' robes on behalf of the donors, Mr Caskie carried out this ceremony, and soon Bailies M. B. M. Flanigan, J. D. Young, A. B. McNair, and John Kerr were arrayed.

Wig and Gown

On behalf of the donor, ex-Provost Robert H. Dunsmore, Mrs Dunsmore presented the town clerk (Mr John L. Jones) with his wig and gown

Provost Milligan and Mr Jones expressed the community's gratitude to the donors for their generosity, and assured them it would never be forgotten. The Provost trusted that in years to come the robes "will be an emblem and mark which will keep the Provost and magistrates to the high pitch which has been laid down by our predecessors since 1903."

Provost Milligan then presented to ex-Provosts D. Bryson, T. Howie, and A. Ferguson, and to Mrs Dunsmore, acting in her husband's stead, medallions similar to that borne on the Provost's chain of office.

After the senior magistrate, Bailie Flanigan, had called for a vote of thanks to the donors, Bailie McNair visualised Prestwick doubling its population within the next ten years The town's future depended on the type of men and women sent into the Town Council Even though they were "hemmed in" by an international airport, he could see a very bright future for Prestwick.

During the evening the company was entertained by Mr Clifford H. Westcott (bass-baritone) and Miss Margaret Gibson (soprano), who were accompanied by Mr E. C. Keir; and the Rae Welsh Trio

26th November 1948

"PRESTWICK'S GREATEST ASSET"

Town Council And Condition Of Beach

A "hunch" that dredging operations in Ayr harbour were responsible for shingle being brought up on the Prestwick fore-shore, was expressed by Bailie A. B. McNair, at the monthly meeting of Prestwick Town Council on Tuesday.

Other members intimated fear that Prestwick's greatest asset would eventually disappear through the constant un-authorised lifting of sand from the beach. The Council agreed to appoint a small committee to examine these matters, and empowered it to take action to bring the deterioration to an abrupt halt.

Provost Milligan was in the chair, and was wearing for the first time in the history of Prestwick his chain of office.

Remarking that the question was an old one, Bailie McNair reminded the Council that at one time they had taken what were considered strong steps in connection with the removal of sand from the foreshore. In recent times this had been going on until it had come to the stage of being a very flourishing business. He believed the burgh surveyor had been doing all he could to stop it, but this did not seem to be succeeding.

Illustrating his point, the bailie revealed that as soon as the beach chalets had been removed from their summer places and put into their resting place, within two days carts were along there and the sand dug out at the spots where the chalets had stood.

Their Greatest Asset

"We must do something about this," he urged. "The foreshore of Prestwick is possibly the greatest asset we have. I feel certain if we don't look after it it is going to go—in fact it is going."

The burgh surveyor, Mr James Melrose, reported that until recently certain of the local contractors had permits to lift shingle from the central part of the beach which was heavily inundated with shingle in the early parts of the year. When it became obvious they had taken the amount of shingle wanted and had started to make raids on the sand, he had withdrawn permits completely. The only occasion on which permits had been issued in recent months had been for one or two cases where it had been the annual custom for such items as the dressing of a bowling green.

During the past few days he had tried to see if there was some permanent solution to this business, and at the next committee meeting he proposed to make certain suggestions to the Council. He thought they had gone into the possibility of an action of interdict before, and Mr Jones could possibly give some idea of the difficulties in that.

"I have found certain of the contractors are quite co-operative. They have had a very good crack of the whip from the beach throughout the years. But there are some who just defy all forms of appeal, and fairness does not seem to enter into it. It is a completely commercial business, unscrupulous. The depredations on the sand do not confine themselves to the beach. We are having similar trouble at the municipal golf course." They had the co-operation of the police, but it seemed to be a fairly easy thing to get away with a cart-load of sand between four or five in the morning.

Better Than A Fine

Remarking that he had actually caught a man that afternoon with a cart-load of shingle, Mr Melrose said this man had no authority from his employer. He had thought it would be more punishment for this man to make him about turn and take it all back. He had given him this as an alternative to reporting to the police, and he thought it would be better than a five shilling fine.

Mr Clarkson suggested that for the next few weeks no carts be allowed on the beach, so that anyone seeing a cart there would know it was illegal and could telephone the police.

They had tried that before, replied Mr Melrose, and it debarred them from using the sand at all, even for some very useful purpose.

"This is a very serious thing, because in a very short number of years we shall probably have no foreshore at all," said Treasurer Black. An indication of that was very pronounced at the south end of the promenade where at certain periods of the day there was no foreshore where the children could play. He could recollect when there had been a splendid fore-shore there. This had probably been caused by the continuous carting of sand from the Bellrock area. He had understood this was to cease in May, but there was a number of carts regularly employed there.

One remedy would be to have an action of interdict raised against anyone carting sand from the foreshore without permission. Regarding Bell-rock, he would like to have the town clerk go into the matter and keep before him the view that one person could not utilise his property to the detriment of another person's. That was what was happening at Bellrock. "I suggest that a small committee be formed with powers to get on with it and put a stop to this notorious business of wrecking our foreshore."

Hunch About Ayr Dredger

Raising the question of shingle on the foreshore, Bailie McNair said by watching he was getting the idea they would find the shingle was brought up with a south-west wind or tide, but never with a north-west wind. "I have a hunch," he declared, "which I cannot prove at present. I feel the dredger at Ayr Harbour has something to do with it." He feared a considerable amount of shingle might be in Ayr Harbour bottom, and continuous dumping of this might have created a soft bed which the tide was bringing up to their foreshore.

Provost Milligan said this was a difficult question which he had discussed in London with surveyors of the Government research department. They were unable to give any cause as to why they should lose sand and bring up shingle. Unless they were in a position to make a model of the shore and scientifically cause tides, they were unable to give an indication. They had suggested the use of sleeper barricades, and the Town Council might consider that. The surveyor could show where suitable barriers could be put out.

1949

The North Atlantic Treaty Organisation (NATO) was founded for mutual assistance against aggression.
Britain recognised the Irish Republic.
Apartheid was introduced in South Africa.
British dockers went on strike and railway workers mounted a 'go slow'.
The pound was devalued from $4.03 to $2.80 causing devaluation of other European currencies.
Nationalisation of the iron and steel industry came into force.

NEW PRESTWICK BAPTIST CHURCH, 192 Prestwick Road.

DIAMOND JUBILEE CELEBRATIONS.
LORD'S DAY, 27th February
11 a.m. — INAUGURAL SERVICES — 8 p.m.
Rev. WALTER J. MAIN, Dundee.
Preceded by MEETING for PRAYER and COMMUNITY SINGING at 7 p.m.
MONDAY at 7 p.m.   SOCIAL MEETING.   Tea Ticket, 1s 6d
Speakers—
Revs. JOHN A. PRICE, M.A.; W. D. BROWN; BEN BRIDGES;
JAMES SCOTT, M.A., Ph.D.; WALTER J. MAIN, and others.
Soloist—Mrs N. MOSS, Prestwick.
NOTE.—Owing to unprecedented demand for tickets, it is regretted that
ticket holders can be admitted.
TUESDAY, 1st MARCH, to FRIDAY, 11th MARCH (inclusive), at 7.30 p.m
CHRISTIAN CHALLENGE CAMPAIGN.
Rev. WALTER J. MAIN will speak and sing.
Come and hear a Man with a Man's Message.

THE PRESTWICK PLAYERS present
THREE ONE-ACT PLAYS—
(Drama, Tragedy, Comedy)
in the TOWN HALL, PRESTWICK,
on TUESDAY, 1st FEBRUARY, 1949
Doors open at 7 p.m.   Curtain 7.30
Tickets (Front Area and Balcony) inc.
tax 3/-, Back Area 2/-. May be had at
the Burns Emporium, 51 Main Street, or
from members of the club.

PRESTWICK THIRD WARD SOCIAL WELFARE ASSOCIATION

GRAND PANTOMIME   "ALADDIN"   By Members of
St. Quivox Youth Group
in
TOWN HALL, PRESTWICK, on SUNDAY, 30th JANUARY, 1949
Doors open 7.15 p.m.   Commence 7.45 p.m.
Balcony 3s, Area Stalls 2s 6d, Back Stalls 2s; Children Half-price for Stalls only.
Tickets can be had at W. S. Muir, Grocer, Main Street, Prestwick; Allan's Garage,
Main Street, Prestwick; or Members of Committee.

PROCEEDS IN AID OF THE FUNDS OF THE ASSOCIATION.

21st January 1949

AIR CRASH INQUIRY

Medical Assistance

Dr Arthur M. Brown, house surgeon, Kilmarnock Infirmary, said that between 1.15 and 1.20 a.m. (he told the chairman he was using "B.B.C. time") he received a dramatic call from the control officer at Prestwick: "For God's sake send an ambulance and rescue party to an air crash." The message went on to say they had tried to get aid from Ayr and Prestwick and nobody could come and that the crash was near Mauchline.

Dr Ralston, who had just finished an operating session, accompanied witness and the surgeons and nurses in an ambulance which set out about fifteen minutes after the phone call. En route they were delayed by fog and also as they did not know the exact location. They arrived in the village, saw no sign of fire or wreckage, and had finally to knock up a farmer before being directed to Auchinweet Farm, some fifteen minutes after arriving at Mauchline. There were no other doctors present at that time, said Dr Brown, and he and the Kilmarnock party attended to six living casualties in various parts of the field. Two of the injured were taken by ambulance to the infirmary, arriving there about 3.35 a.m. Later, witness had learned that 30 minutes after the rescue party left, the hospital received another phone call giving the exact location of the crash.

Both casualties, said Dr Brown, were conscious and could talk, an American lady, Mrs Walls, being able to state her religion, but the second patient, a young lady, could only speak Dutch, and she died before it was known she was a Roman Catholic. Had this been known, witness assured Mr Leslie, the services of a priest could have been procured.

Electric Clock Stopped

Other medical evidence was given by Dr P. J. Hanafin, medical superintendent, Ballochmyle Hospital, Mauchline, who said he noticed a flickering of the lights in his own house and his electric clock stopped at 24 minutes to one that morning. Four people died in the hospital primarily from burning.

Dr William L. Kennedy, Westcroft, Tarbolton, said he had been awakened by the "tremendous" sound of the engines of an aircraft—his wife remarked she thought it was a jet engine. He had thought it would crash into the house. A bluish white light had been seen advancing through his bedroom window and the sound of the aircraft, which appeared to be passing right over the house, died away, to be heard possibly a few minutes later though only faintly.

Sometime later he was contacted by his assistant who told him the plane had crashed. While they were getting dressings ready, Inspector Halliday

---

The Ayrshire branch of the National Union of Journalists has communicated with the sheriff clerk regarding the acoustics of the Sheriff Court and the difficulties experienced by newspaper reporters, and suggesting consideration of the installation of sound reproduction equipment. In doing so, appreciation is expressed of the courtesy and consideration always shown by court officials at Ayr.

---

phoned. Dr Kennedy gave several injections at the scene of the accident, but thought the possibility of their survival was very slight.

Miss Margaret Onions, operator V.H.F. receivers at Prestwick, was recalled and asked by Mr Leslie about erasures in a log book. A word "drift" on a message, said Mr Leslie, appeared to have been written on an erasure. Miss Onions replied that the controller had dictated "cross wind" to her as she took down the message, then changed his mind and she altered the entry.

POLICE CALLS ELUCIDATED

There was no appeal made to Ayr Burgh Police for assistance. This was made evident on Wednesday and helped to clear up any misunderstanding over the use of the term "Ayr police" heard in previous evidence.

Constable William Halliday, on duty in Sandgate, Tarbolton, about 12.15 a.m. (local time) heard the sound of an aircraft coming, as he described it, from the direction of Ayr. There was nothing abnormal about the approach, but having passed over his position he spoke of a "vivid flash" which he agreed could have been the plane striking the overhead cables. In the vicinity of Droystone Farm it appeared to him that the engines cut out. He heard no crash and on going down to the new housing site could see no flames. He returned to the police station and tried to 'phone Prestwick police, but got no reply. He then decided to 'phone County Police headquarters at Ayr and it was then that the lights flickered. Instead of calling their number he dialled "O" and the operator put him through to Ayr Burgh Police who immediately switched him through to the County Police to whom he reported.

In reply to Mr Campbell, witness said the telephone to Prestwick station was in order and gave out a ringing tone.

Constable Robert Cruickshank, Ayrshire Constabulary, Ayr, on duty that night, said he took the call from Halliday and undertook to get the message to Prestwick. Later there was a query from the airport asking if they had any word of a plane crash. He could not at that stage give any particulars and referred the caller to Prestwick police.

Constable David Struthers, Prestwick, said Constable Cruickshank phoned him the information received from Tarbolton and at approximately 1.10 a.m. Prestwick controller telephoned, and it was then that the airport official had been told about getting services from Ayr police.

Cross-examined by Mr Campbell whether he meant Ayr Burgh Police or Ayr County Police, witness explained that the ambulances on call were kept in the hospital which came under the Burgh Police.

Inspector Robert Halliday, Ayrshire Constabulary, Prestwick, said he had received a report from Constable Struthers that a plane was apparently down in the vicinity of Droystone Farm, Tarbolton. He went there immediately and found that Constable Halliday had not returned from the scene at Auchinweet Farm. After contacting local doctors, the Inspector gave orders to have more doctors, nurses and ambulances sent for and took up his position at Tarbolton Cross from where he directed rescuers to the field.

First on the Scene

John Alexander, 39 Southfield Crescent, Tarbolton, said he was first to approach the blazing plane while his brother who had assisted him in locating it, went into Auchinweet Farm. He had been in bed when a dull thud attracted his attention and the aircraft, he said, was ten or eleven feet above the roof of his house as it passed over the first time. The wing on the starboard side was on fire and all four engines were spluttering. As it came into his view again, about 50 yards from his house, after making a sweep round, it seemed to have lost height. He heard no crash nor did he see flames, but after speaking to Mr John R. Main, superintendent of ground services, Scottish Aviation, Prestwick, he started to search for the aircraft, flames from the ground finally guiding him to Auchinweet Farm.

John L. Milliken, barman, Black Bull, Tarbolton, was just putting his car away when he first heard the aircraft, which he did not see at any time in the air. There were three distinct flashes which he described as being similar to bombs dropping. It appeared to him that the Constellation formed a loop over the northern end of Tarbolton and when it came back a second time the engines cut out. There was a lull, then a red glare sprang up in the sky. He was at the field about 12.45 a.m. having overtaken Constable Halliday on the way, and did what he could for six survivors. There were no fire tenders when he arrived, but ambulances were there when he returned from Tarbolton where he had gone to get medical help.

The Court adjourned on Wednesday afternoon to visit Auchinweet Farm and Prestwick Airport.

Witnesses were recalled for re-examination when the inquiry was resumed yesterday, and evidence was still proceeding as we went to press.

28th January 1949

PRESTWICK BAILIE FEARED HOUSING DICTATOR

Recommendations by a sub-committee appointed to go into the matter of repairs, supervision and management of Council houses at Prestwick gave rise to considerable discussion at the monthly meeting of the Town Council on Tuesday night—Provost Milligan presiding.

Bailie J. B. Blark asked that the report be remitted back for further consideration. The report not only made the burgh surveyor director of housing but he feared it also made him dictator in their housing scheme. For that reason he thought they should consider the report very carefully. He also took exception to one of the items in the report which gave the sub-committee "fairly wide powers." He would not be a party to his powers as a councilor being delegated to a sub-committee; fairly wide powers could be anything or nothing.

Bailie McNair, while characterising the report as a good one, seconded, as he had a suspicion that it gave too much power all of a sudden. The question came in here also of the collection of rents and as to who was to be responsible.

Moving the approval of the minute, Dean of Guild Steele referred to the long time spent on the matter before the report was brought in. He disagreed with the fear expressed that the surveyor was being made a dictator. There was one point he wished to criticise himself and that was "that the burgh surveyor will be the sole judge of the extent of the repairs necessary." He pointed out that the sub-committee had no powers as their findings would be subject to the Housing committee and the Town Council.

The Provost said if the minute was passed they were not handing powers to the sub-committee. He pointed out that there was a great lag of time between the factor's report and his authority to take action, and he thought this accounted for the fact that powers were asked to take action on matters that might be automatic. If the management committee (suggested in the report) met regularly these matters could be dealt with without delay.

Mr James McGinty seconded the approval of the report. He pointed out that there was no creation of a department suggested as the sub-committee would be under the jurisdiction of the whole council. He failed to see that any councillor would be delegating his duties.

In the course of further discussion the Provost indicated that the surveyor was being given no more powers than he already held, and he suggested that the lines dealing with fairly wide power be deleted.

This was agreed to, as also was the deletion of the lines that the surveyor would be the sole judge of the extent of the repairs.

No Pitch For Football

It was intimated that a request by the Town Council that football clubs in the New Prestwick area might have the use as a temporary measure of the pitch at Heathfield school had been refused on the ground that further use would be detrimental to the pitch. Applications from the Education Committee's youth groups had been refused for the same reason.

Bailie Flanigan said the football pitch available existed in name only because every Saturday the game had to be put off. There was water on it at all times and he suggested another part opposite the golf club house.

The burgh surveyor said that if they did that they would be interfering with something for which they had obtained a grant. A pitch and putt site could not be suitable for a football pitch.

It was agreed, on the suggestion of Bailie McNair, that having regard to the facilities the Council had afforded at the public park that the Education Committee should again be approached on the matter of making available their play ground.

25th February 1949

Mr ROBERT L. ANGUS

The death took place in a Glasgow nursing home, on Friday, of Mr Robert L. Angus, of Ladykirk, Monkton, a deputy-lieutenant of the county of Ayr, and a well known industrialist. Mr Angus had been ill for over two months, and was removed to the home about three weeks before his death. He was the younger surviving son of the late Robert Angus, and was born at Cragston, Lugar, his father at that time being closely identified with the important Lugar Iron Works. Mr Angus was educated at Fettes College, Edinburgh. Ladykirk House, where he resided, was built by his father in 1906, and besides the estate of that name, which he inherited. Mr Angus owned property in Berwickshire. He was best known, however, because of his association with the heavy industries, and particularly coal mining. He was chairman of William Baird and Co. Ltd., and of Bairds and Dalmellington Ltd., and he was also a director of Bairds and Scottish Steel Ltd. and the North British Locomotive Co. Ltd. As a member of the Central Committee he took an active interest in the affairs of the Mining Association of Great Britain, and he was also for thirty years chairman of the Ayrshire Coal Owners' Association, succeeding the late J. B. Thorneycroft, of Hillhouse, in that position. For many years also

he was a prominent member of the Conciliation Board, which dealt with disputes in the coal fields. Mr Angus took a keen and kindly interest in the Kirkmichael Welfare Home for miners and the Troon Home for the wives of miners and their daughters. He had been chairman of the Ayrshire District Joint Welfare Committee since its inception, and was a generous contributor at all times to the Troon home. Baths for miners, and the extension of mining instruction under the aegis of the Welfare scheme, also appealed to him, and in many and diverse ways he was a good friend to the mining community of the county.

Mr Angus was deputy chairman of the Clydesdale Bank, and a director of the Midland Bank, and he was one of the original directors of Scottish Aviation Ltd. In his younger days he used to ride with the Eglinton Hunt, and he was joint M.F.H. for two seasons prior to the war. He was a member of the Western Meeting Club and of the committee of that body, and some years ago had several horses in training. Mr Angus was chairman of the Monkton Unionist Association for a number of years, and he was

hon. president of the Ayr Choral Union.

His interests extended to the breeding of Ayrshire cattle, and he was a director of the Ayrshire Agricultural Association, and for a term president. He won numerous prizes, frequently had exhibits well forward in the "derby" at Ayr, and in 1938 had the satisfaction of winning the female championship for Ayrshires with Ladykirk Snowflake, which had stood reserve in the two previous years to the rather famous Mid Ascog Moss Rose. Mr Angus, some years ago, gifted a fine trophy to the Association for the winner of the derby.

Mr Angus, who was 66 years of age, is survived by his wife, two sons and two daughters.

The interment took place on Tuesday in the family vault in Monkton Churchyard, prior to which a funeral service was held in St. Cuthbert's Church of Monkton and Prestwick, and conducted by the Rev. D. M. Caskie.

4th February 1949
Boxing

Hopes For Prestwick Flyweight

Experienced Scottish amateur boxing officials thrilled on Friday evening to one of the hardest fought contests ever seen at the Grove Stadium, Glasgow. From the third round to the end the crowd were caught in a fever of excitement and there were no protests when the home boy, Jim Quinn, Grove A.A.C. lost the verdict to young John McCulloch, Prestwick A.B.C. After the bout, "old hands" at the game forecast a bright future for the Prestwick flyweight, and he is now in great demand for the many shows being arranged in the West of Scotland.

At the show run by Kilmarnock A.A.C. in the Grand Hall, Kilmarnock, on Monday, in aid of Kilmarnock Old Folks Fund, McCulloch boxed splendidly to gain a second narrow points win over F. Fernie, Greenfield Pals, just about the cutest flyweight in the Scottish amateur ring.

That same evening David Dunsmuir, Ayr Y.M.C.A., N.C.B. British heavyweight champion, gained a third round k.o. win over J. McVicar, Greenock Victoria, who went down to a short hook after being sickened by two successive jabs to the solar. A. Sneddon, Kilmarnock A.A.C., gained his first victory this year when he out-pointed a not-too-fit W. Young, Ayr Y.M.C.A.; and a young Ayr boy, J. Ross, now with the Grove A.B.C., yielded a lot of weight and the verdict to E. Munn, Kilmarnock. For the fifth time there was a keen clash between welterweights A. Anderson, Ayr Y.M.C.A., and N. McMillan, Kilmarnock A.A.C., and the Kilmarnock lad showed considerable improvement in gaining his second win in the series. The Scottish featherweight champion, H. Gilliland, Kilmarnock A.A.C., was floored once in the fifth round by his predecssor in the championship, W. Taylor, L.M.S. Although Gilliland clearly won the decision, his form has slipped badly from the crest that has carried him so far.

John McCulloch of Prestwick A.B.C. tops the bill at the L.M.S. Hall, Glasgow, on Saturday, against F. Parks, L.M.S.; and in addition to the other local lads (reported in these columns last week) entering for the Scottish amateur championships, McCulloch will compete in the flyweight division in Edinburgh on February 12. A. Anderson, Ayr Y.M.C.A., is taking part in the welterweight competition the same night. The Prestwick club are running a special bus to Edinburgh, and anyone wishing to see the show should contact **Mr T. McGillvary, 57 Berelands Road, Prestwick,** or the boxing organiser at Ayr Y.M.C.A.

Jock Todd is sure of a strong local support when he meets Bert Gilroy, Scottish light-heavyweight champion, for the latter's title, at the Kelvin Hall, Glasgow, on Wednesday. The 52 tickets at 10s 6d, allocated to Ayr Y.M.C.A., have been sold out, though a few guinea tickets are still available. There are still a few vacant seats in the special buses to leave the Y.M.C.A. at 6 p.m. on the evening of the fight.

25th February 1949

Prestwick

MUNICIPAL ELECTIONS. — Polling is to take place on May 3 in the municipal elections when contests are to be fought in all four wards. Bailies McNair, Young and Flanigan retire by rotation in the first, third and fourth wards, and Mr James M. McGinty who was elected *ad interim* in place of Mr Thomas J. Ross in the second ward.

RAILWAY SLEEPERS. — At a cost of £175 it has been agreed to purchase 500 railway sleepers for groynes on Prestwick shore. Treasurer Black said that while it was expensive it was worth it if it would improve the front.

BATHING LAKE. — Approval was given to a sub-committee minute dealing with proposed alterations to Bathing Lake which would entail the reduction of the water area; removal of the diving platform to the centre of the lake, and the provision of additional seating. A consulting engineer may be called in to give an estimate of the cost and the sub-committee are empowered to visit other burghs for first hand information regarding certain of the suggested alterations.

18th February 1949

Attractions For Prestwick

At a public meeting held in Prestwick Council Chambers, on Tuesday, it was agreed that a development council should be set up to consider, along with the Town Council, any schemes for the improvement of the amenities and trade of the burgh.

There was general agreement that the immediate aims of the council should be to concentrate on attractions and amusements which would bring summer visitors and tourists to the town, and an interim committee was set up to explore in greater detail the establishment of the Development Council, how it would function, and to report back to another public meeting.

There are ten members on the interim committee of which Provost Milligan will act as chairman *ex officio*. Three members of the Town Council are on the committee—Bailie A. B. McNair, convener of the Parks and Attractions Committee; the vice-convener, Mr W. S. Moir; and Mr T. C. S. Clarkson, vice-convener of the General Purposes Committee. The following were elected to fill the remaining seven vacancies: Mr W. Crane, 44 Kirk Street, and Mr J. Ross, manager of the Broadway Cinema, to represent ordinary ratepayers as distinct from either hotel and boarding-house keepers, or merchants; Mr James McFarlane, Queen's Hotel, and Mr J. W. Michael, Strathdevon, 10 Queen's Terrace, representing hotel and boarding-house keepers; and Mr G. M Hogg, fishmonger, Main Street, and Mr John Paton, radio engineer Boyd Street, representing the merchants. A representative of the Joint Wards Committee, Mr David Armstrong, was also elected.

The interim committee is to meet in the Council Chambers on March 1, and before then the town clerk, Mr John L. Jones, is to prepare a tentative draft constitution to be submitted to the members.

At the outset of the public meeting, Provost Milligan, who presided, urged that recommendations coming from a council made up of merchants and others in the town would be a great support and help to the Town Council in introducing innovations. There were, of course, difficulties at present with regard to certain development, especially where capital expenditure was concerned; but the town clerk would keep them right in that direction.

Bailie McNair suggested that the Development Council could do much in the sphere of winter social activity in the town, by arranging such things as whist drives, a Sunday evening cinema club, Sunday concerts, and by maintaining a high standard of dancing at the Town Hall. Other suggestions put forward by members of the public were for "decent music" for holidaymakers, provided during the day by an orchestra which might also play for dancing in the evening; further amenities on the shore front, including greater facilities for purchase of sweets, newspapers, and tea; more children's days; a roller-skating rink; and a model yachting pond at Boydfield.

A note of sober restraint was added by Mr Jones when he remarked: "Don't think you are to have all these things before the summer." Where capital expenditure was involved they would have to make out a very strong case before any priority would be granted. He suggested that the Council should categorise proposed developments into sections listing those which could be put into operation immediately, those which could be contemplated within five years, and the others which could be tackled in the dim and distant future.

18th February 1949

Bonnets On The "Pitch" At Prestwick

Prestwick Town Council's decision to erect 30 four-apartment Blackburn prefab. houses of the permanent type on the open space at Crandleyhill Road has brought a storm of protest from residenters in the ward.

A petition, signed by 120 people, has been forwarded to the Town Council against such a proposal. It states that the minutes of the last statutory meeting of the Council contain no reference to the proposal, and it is their understanding that the matter was dealt with in private after that meeting.

The protest is on the following grounds:—(a) the present use of the ground is beneficial to the residents of the southern part of Prestwick. The Pitch and Putt course is a popular amenity and a source of revenue to the burgh; (b) there is no open ground suitable for recreational use by the residents of the Fourth Ward other than the remainder of the old municipal golf course. It has been understood that it was the Council's policy in the past to preserve this land as open ground for recreational use. The present proposal involves an encroachment on the open ground.

It is contended further that it is a principle of town planning that open spaces are as necessary to the amenity of a community as are houses, and that the proposal loses sight of this principle. The Blackburn type of house, it is maintained, is ugly and barrack-like in external appearance, is unsuitable to the neighbourhood and would not be an adornment to Prestwick. Several local authorities had refused the type of house on these grounds.

A copy of the petition has been sent to Mr A. M. Rosie, planning officer for the county, and it has also, it is understood, been forwarded to the Department of Health.

Loss Of Six Holes

A residenter told the "Post" that the encroachment will mean the loss of six of the eighteen holes that were formed for putting on what was formerly the old St. Ninian's golf course. In existence for over a year and a grant received towards it, the putt and pitch course was so popular, it is asserted, that the demand was limited only by the number of clubs that were available for players.

Council Decision

It is understood that the Town Council, meeting in committee, heard the petition but have decided to do nothing about it, and the petitioners have been apprised of the finding, so that, subject to the approval of the Department of Health, the scheme is to proceed.

25th March 1949

"Down Your Way"

To the Editor, "The Ayrshire Post"
Glasgow, March 22, 1949.

Sir,—We do not usually have the chance of seeing "oorsels as ithers see us", but on Sunday afternoon, we had, at least, the opportunity of hearing "oorsels as ithers hear us", and a humiliating affair it was.

One morning last week, I had a note from a friend in Ayr, telling me to be sure to listen in on Sunday afternoon at 4 p.m. The name of Mr McMynn, appearing on the programme, lent enchantment to the hour as I settled myself in an armchair by the fire, to listen to what would be, at least, pleasing to a Scottish ear, for Ayrshire with all its loveliness, its Doon and Afton Waters, and its rich memories in song and story, could surely produce a programme second to none.

Alas, "Down Your Way" proved to be the best bit of burlesque I have heard for a long time, and I feel aggrieved, as I do not like the quiet of a sabbath afternoon to be broken by such rubbish

Thank you, Mr Milligan, yours was a splendid effort to take us "down your way", and I can just visualise you planting the gardens around Ayr with flowers so that visitors who rove by Bonnie Doon may also pronounce them fair.

Thereafter the programme deteriorated, and we had to listen to the most awful mixtie-maxtie of songs and tunes, interposed with silly questions, and answers.

"Down Your Way". What way? Whose way? Well, you can guess anything you like, and you won't guess correctly, for we had Paul Robeson, Bing Crosby, the Rhumba, Chopin. I wonder if the contributors to the programme were excluded from choosing Scots songs; if not, it's a sad reflection on Ayrshire. Have they never heard such lovely songs as "Afton Water",

"Of a' the Airts", "The Bonnie Lass of Ballochmyle" and last but not least, that gem of Burns songs, "Mary Morison"?

I like the music of Chopin immensely in its proper place, but not when I am watching the clock, and noting that only a few minutes are being left for Mr McMynn to speak—yet, here was the man that could have taken us "Down Your Way" for the whole hour himself. I wonder what he thought about it all. He remained what he is—a dignified Scotsman. Shade of dear departed Rabbie, if you were listening, forgive us our transgressions.

Scotland Yet.

Prestwick

FOOD PARCELS. — The Rotary Club of Prestwick a fortnight ago received 62 cases of foodstuffs from Rotary Clubs in Queensland, Australia, who asked that the 30 cwts. of tinned goods be distributed to residents in Prestwick. Suggestions as to suitable recipients, bearing in mind the claims of people living alone or widows with children, were received from the churches and professional men in the town, and last week 350 11lbs. parcels were delivered with the best wishes of the Queensland clubs, to whom a letter of appreciation is to be sent by Prestwick Rotary Club.

1st April 1949

Prestwick Parents' Protest Treated "With Contempt"

A protest from 278 Prestwick parents was dismissed by Area No. 3 Education Sub-Committee at their meeting held in the County Hall, Ayr, on Tuesday afternoon.

The chairman, Bailie Andrew Gemmell, Ayr, produced the letter to which were attached the signatures of the 278 people, many the parents of pupils attending Glenburn School, Prestwick, protesting against the appointment of Roman Catholics as conveners to Prestwick schools. In the words of a member, the committee decided to "treat it with the contempt it deserved", and it was agreed that no action be taken on the matter.

When he produced the protest, Bailie Gemmell said he was sorry it had ever been raised. He took it that the only answer they could give was that the people protesting had had the opportunity to attend the public meeting when the appointment was made; and that the only action they could take was to attend the next public meeting to appoint members to the committee and take the necessary steps then. The protest had asked for an explanation regarding the appointments and for action to be taken towards the removal of the Roman Catholics. "We can take no action nor do we desire to take any action."

Mr A. Graham, Prestwick, remarked that the committee were a democratically elected body and that the people protesting had had their opportunity.

Monsignor T. A. Hayes, Troon—There is no Iron Curtain here yet.

Bailie Gemmell—I hope not.

"I have done my duty conscientiously as convener of one of the schools in question," Mr Edward Hamilton, Prestwick, said, "and I would only ask the Committee to deal with the protest in the contemptuous manner it deserves. I do not think it should be recognised as correspondence at all."

Bailie Gemmell—It is just being reported, that is all. I think we had better tell them straight that they had their opportunity.

Monsignor Hayes thought that the matter should be merely reported and allowed to lie on the table, and after a short, but lively discussion, it was unanimously agreed to take no action.

Mr Graham said he would like to ask a question, but the chairman thought that the least said the better.

New Primary School

Earlier the committee discussed the proposed new Roman Catholic Primary School at Prestwick, which had been approved before the war. A letter from the county clerk said that this matter had to be considered in relation to education in the whole county. The Education Committee had remitted this to the director of education for suggestions and for an order of priority for the replacement of the six least satisfactory Roman Catholic schools in the county. He was preparing this priority list and then they could see whether it was right to have a new school in Prestwick.

"Meanwhile there is no Roman Catholic School in Prestwick," said Treasurer Peter Boyle, Ayr. "That is land we have held since before the war, so it will wear us out unless we wear it out."

Mr Hamilton thought Prestwick had a big roll, and these children had to travel eight miles outside their own area to school. Irrespective of denomination, all available school space in Prestwick was overcrowded, so in assessing priority in the Prestwick case he would be very pleased if that were borne in mind.

PRESTWICK WARD GRIEVANCES

New Prestwick houses which were being reduced to slum conditions through lack of proper administration were described by Councillor James McGinty at the annual meeting of the Second Ward ratepayers, held in the O.E.S. Hall, Prestwick, on Monday— Mr Andrew Graham, chairman of the Ward Committee, presiding.

Throughout the length and breadth of the burgh there were scandalous conditions, said Mr McGinty, instancing a case where "a squad of children" were playing round bare electric wires hanging from a wall. He complained that it was impossible to obtain information from the tenants, and asked why there was no Tenants' Association in the ward, or in Prestwick. Rents had been raised, and while other counties had contested this through their tenants' associations, the people of Prestwick were doing nothing about it.

It seemed that Prestwick as a burgh was neglected by the County Council— it was sandwiched between Troon and Ayr, and "got the leavings." This was because the people of Prestwick had not made themselves heard.

The Airport Runway

In two years' time, the new runway at the airport was going to encircle the town. It was not so much a matter of geography as of geometry, and he could not see where houses were going to be built. There was an application list of 800, and as a teacher he knew that this did not mean 800 people, but, on an average, five times 800. He had been told that when the runway was in position, the airport was going to bring a great new industry to Prestwick. This he did not believe, for he could not see K.L.M., for instance, going to Prestwick Town Council and asking for 500 men.

Dean of Guild Gilbert Steele spoke of the work done so far in the management and repairing of municipal houses by the House Management Committee, and of the levelling-up of rents. Criticising the latter, he mentioned tenants who had paid rent on their houses for twenty years, practically buying the houses which were not up to the standard of the new houses, and yet they had suffered the largest increase in their rents. When a report on the expense of repairs was asked for, it was strange to see that the old houses had the lowest cost.

Glenburn Lighting

He described the negotiations with the Coal Board regarding the installation of electricity in Glenburn, and said that while a reply was being awaited, some people had taken it on themselves to go round Glenburn and get a petition signed, stating that the electricity board was quite willing to install electric light if the tenants were willing to pay for it. "They took this petition in to the area general manager, and he agreed right away—he was getting the job done for nothing, and he was also having a hit at Prestwick Town Council. This, I think, was dirty tactics."

The prospective Labour candidate, Mr Hugh Boyd, suggested that in his opinion St. Nicholas Ladies' Golf Course was the ideal place for houses, when sites were being looked for. The rents of municipal houses should be reduced, for the burden was becoming too great for a working class family.

Touching on the subject of houses for "key men," he described this as "too much of a racket." The only cases in which houses should go to people outside those on the housing lists should be in such cases as sufferers from tuberculosis. The phrase "key man" would need to be more finely defined to have any justice.

13th May 1949

PRESTWICK MAKES SALVAGE PAY

Steadily refusing to take part in stunts but concentrating on convincing the public that salvage collection is a necessary routine very gratifying results have been obtained in Prestwick, according to the annual report of the sanitary inspector, Mr James Melrose.

Waste paper collection averaged 25.7 cwts. per 1,000 of population per month last year, compared with 15.4 cwts. averaged in burghs throughout the country and 20 cwts., which is the Board of Trade target.

There was also a good increase in the weight of kitchen waste collected through the partial adoption of a scheme of individual waste containers, which is being extended. Already the weight of kitchen waste has doubled, and it is expected that 12 to 15 tons a month will be obtained.

The scheme, says Mr Melrose, has the advantage that it will allow the removal of that most unsightly and often objectionable war-time necessity —the street pig-bin.

The pig producer to whom the kitchen waste is sold has stated that the quality of the waste pig food has improved greatly since the introduction of the scheme.

The cash value of salvage has increased from £883 5s. in 1946 and £996 9s. in 1947 to £1,313 17s. 7d. in 1948, and in addition the increased salvage figures attracted bonus payments by the Board of Trade amounting to £150.

The Board of Trade director of salvage and recovery in a letter received by Mr Melrose since the report was published, says: "The continually good salvage efforts of your Council have not passed unnoticed, and these reflect credit on the members and officials concerned and indicate a high degree of co-operation by householders of the district."

With regard to kitchen waste he remarks that the figure of 13.2 cwts. per 1,000 of population, whilst below the official target of 1 ton is not overlooked that the rate of collection may possibly be affected by the kitchen waste retained for domestic poultry keeping, etc., which but for this might be collected by the Council.

"The Council and the householders" he adds, "may rest assured that these high level rates of salvage recovery represent a material contribution both to the paper-using industry and agriculturists, and that this, in turn, contributes an important factor in the restoration of the national economic position and food supply."

Details of the weight of salvage recovered in 1948 compared with the two previous years are:—

	1948	1947	1946
Waste Paper	152 tons 11 cwts.	119 tons 13 cwts.	99 tons 9 cwts.
Rags, etc.	19 tons 4 cwts.	18 tons 8 cwts.	9 tons
Kitchen Waste	87 tons 15 cwts	61 tons 19 cwts.	67 tons 12 cwts.
Light Scrap	2 tons	3 tons 5 cwts	4 tons 16 cwts

13th May 1949

INJURED IN BERLIN AIRLIFT CRASH

"I would not go through yesterday again for anything in the world. It was terrible!" Mrs. Braney, 5 New Dykes Road, Prestwick, told a "Post" reporter on Wednesday morning.

Her husband, Mr Hugh B. Braney, was injured in a British Lancastrian tanker plane that crashed early on Tuesday in the Russian zone. The plane left Tegel Airport, in the French sector of Berlin at 6.30 a.m. and crashed 25 miles south of Schwerin, the capital of Mecklenburg.

Mr Braney and other three members of the crew were rushed to a Soviet zone hospital to be treated.

It was his first trip to Germany from Bournmouth for some time. He has two children, a boy and a girl. He is 35 years old and served in the R.A.F. for several years as a navigator and after the war he was employed as an engineer but disliking the job he became runway controller at Prestwick Airport and studied for a civil navigator's licence which he received in March. He is very keen on gardening, but his chief interest is in his home and family. He had been looking forward to coming home in about ten days' time. He likes Germany and is very keen and happy in his work there.

Mrs Braney received information on Tuesday that he was not seriously injured, but she was still very worried and at the time of her interview with the "Post" reporter she was hoping for some more news of her husband.

13th May 1949

Prestwick May Have Housing Gap

Though public health conditions in Prestwick are good, there is no room for complacency, said the sanitary inspector (Mr James Melrose) in his annual report.

Far too many people continue to live in other people's houses as subtenants, with consequent overcrowding and lack of opportunity for family life. At the end of last year the number of houses required to meet immediate needs was slightly below 600.

Thirty new houses were completed and occupied in the Council's post-war programme, bringing the total of permanent houses built since the end of the war to 134, with 60 likely to be completed by the autumn. The rate of completion was rather disappointing, and was mainly due to labour shortages, particularly plasterers.

The refusal of the Department of Health last July to grant permission to start a limited number of houses in order to preserve continuity, he fears, will result in a long gap between the completion of the present building programme and any future houses.

Another factor likely to complicate the provision of future houses is the inability of the Authority to plan sites, while all the undeveloped land lies frozen by the Ministry of Civil Aviation. This ground was first denied to the Council in February, 1946, and after 3 years it is still under the dead hand of sterilisation. One of the most irritating aspects of this matter is that it seems virtually certain that the runway proposals which caused the hold-up will never materialise on that particular line.

The water supply to the burgh was ample and excellent, the daily average consumption in that part of the town supplied by Prestwick being 637,500 gallons. (New Prestwick is supplied from Ayr Corporation Waterworks.)

The disposal of household refuse is by tipping on the north shore, the tip forming an embankment which gives protection to valuable golf course property. At the end of the year St. Cuthbert's Golf Club asked the Town Council to consider tipping to the depth of a few feet over an area of low-lying fairways constantly subject to flooding, and with the approval of the planning authority and the Department of Health this is being done.

13th May 1949

AIRCRAFT TECHNIQUE IN BUS BUILDING

PRESTWICK

Scottish Aviation Ltd., engaged solely in the aviation industry since 1935, decided that the facilities at Prestwick were ideally suited for similar types of constructional engineering.

During the past two years they have been turning their activities to other industrial markets and have carried out extensive design and development work on coach and bus bodies. Their single deck buses are already in operation and the company have now completed their first double decker which only awaits the finishing touches of the paintwork and it will be ready for its tests. There are also 130 orders on the books for more vehicles.

For years, an official stated, body building has lagged behind chassis construction in the country, and as it was felt that additional capacity was still necessary throughout the British Isles for the construction of all types of bodies for passenger vehicles, the workshop facilities which the factory organ-

sation have available amounting to approximately 500,000 square feet of floor area and fully equipped with the most modern tools, backed by an experimental department, could make a real contribution to a major industry. Moreover the engineering principles associated with aircraft construction were adapted with advantage to the manufacture of light alloy bodies of varying types.

It was decided not to follow normal coachbuilding practice but that there would be an adaptation of the company's aircraft experience to the building of bodies of stressed skin monocoque construction, now standard practice in modern aircraft engineering.

The first of the prototype coaches left the workshop, which has the biggest floor area devoted to body building in Scotland and is indeed equalled by few in England, some 15 months ago and has been in service ever since with satisfactory results. In addition the high strength characteristics of the light alloys have made it possible to give comparable strength to steel and the substantial weight reduction—as much

as 15 cwts. on the smaller vehicle or about 30%—has in turn, it is claimed, resulted in considerable fuel saving.

Aware that in certain circles light alloy construction has until recently been regarded with some trepidation on the grounds that fatigue failures are greater than normally experienced in composite construction, it is not considered that these doubts are borne out any longer particularly in view of the experience the company gained during the war in the aircraft industry.

In fact it is generally conceded that the time has now come when the light alloy group will fulfil an important place in the body building industry, particularly in view of the shortages of steel and timber.

Since the inception of Scottish Aviation's new industry a considerable number of single deck buses of the luxury and service coach type have been turned out and Glasgow Corporation Transport Department have already placed an order for ten double-decker bus bodies.

13th May 1949

PRESTWICK'S BAILIES

At Prestwick Town Council on Friday, the appointments were: (left to right) Mr John Kerr, senior bailie; Mr M. B. M. Flanigan, second bailie; Mr A. B. McNair, third bailie, and Mr W. S. Moir, fourth bailie.

PRESTWICK

Of the two new Prestwick members, Mr H. Boyd (Labour), who is 35, was born in the burgh and has lived there all his life, being educated at Prestwick Public School, and now a mechanical engineer at Glenburn Colliery. He is married, with two children, and has had nine years' experience of committee work, having been a member of Glenburn Colliery consultative and production committees.

Mr A. M. Brown (Moderate), a native of Glasgow and educated there, has lived in Prestwick for the past ten years, and is secretary of the Ailsa Shipbuilding Company, Ltd., Troon. He is widely travelled, with secretarial experience in Cardiff, Calcutta and Colombo, and held a commission in the H.L.I. during the first world war, in which he was twice wounded.

10th June 1949

BABIES BARRED

(To The Editor, "The Ayrshire Post")
Prestwick,
June 2, 1949.

Sir,—I would like to ask what there is in a pink, 8 lb scrap of humanity that is so abhorrent to Prestwick landladies.

I am led to ask this because we are expecting our first baby at the end of this month, and we have been told that we will have to find another place to live. I have been all over Prestwick and I cannot find anyone who will let rooms to us. Is it because it might interfere with the serious business of soaking holiday-makers? I have been offered rooms at sums up to £30 per month, but as I am neither able nor willing to pay such an outrageous sum, we are still faced with the prospect of having no roof above our heads at the end of the month.

Perhaps if these people went to Church and got a grounding in Christian principles they might eventually say "Suffer little children to Come unto Me".   Frantic

10th June 1949

GOLF CLUB JUBILEE
Prestwick St. Cuthbert Had Humble Beginnings

Members of Prestwick St. Cuthbert Golf Club had a field day on Saturday when they celebrated the club's 50th anniversary. Following a series of competitions, including a special Jubilee Medal Competition, members gathered in the clubhouse for a social evening over which the Captain, Mr Alex. Hay, presided.

Among a number of veterans present was Mr William McLellan, who retired only two years ago after having served 47 years as secretary. Another, Mr John Murray, aged 82, took part in the singles competition and won a prize with a round of 88.

Those who entertained were: Miss Frances Mansbridge, Miss Mary Blue, Miss Myra Murray, Mrs M. Cameron, Mr Tony Yandall, Mr G. F. Horn, Mr J. Lambie, Mr W. Dunlop, Mr J. Walker, Mr D. Johnstone, Mr R. Gemmell and Mr R. McFarlane.

The St. Cuthbert Club had an unusual origin. It arose from a discussion among a number of workmen who were assembled in a mason's shed on a job in Prestwick. These men had long been associated with the game, either through acting as caddies on the championship links of the Prestwick Club, or in watching giants of the game play there in the championships.

A Cut-down Cleek

In Victorian days golf clubs were almost unknown in working-class homes, and most of the younger Prestwick boys learned to play their golf by using a "cleeked" piece of wire for a club and a cork for a ball. Older boys were more fortunate and often could take up the game in luxury style by playing with a cut-down cleek and an old gutta ball over the muirlands which surrounded the then village.

Having determined that working men could have a golf club just as easily as any other class the workmen arranged a public meeting and as a result the new St. Cuthbert Club was born.

Primarily responsible for the whole organisation that created the club was the late Mr Robert McWilliam.

Ground sufficient to cover nine holes was obtained from the Fairfield Estate, and an old house on West Orangefield Farm, colloquially known as Beenie's Bower, became the clubhouse. It is notable that the rich man's club across the railway helped to make the new artisan's club possible by loaning a mower.

During the years the St. Cuthbert club has weathered many difficulties. There was, at one time, a problem of loss of membership through the state of the fairways. The shrinking club coffers were raided to the extent of the purchase of a horse mower and the situation was saved.

Famous Names

From time to time St. Cuthbert's has produced players of the highest order. Among those who attained international status were the late Bobby Andrew, who became just as famous in the U.S.A. as he was in Scotland; John Wilson (better known as a St. Nicholas player because as such he became the first Scottish Amateur Champion and a Walker Cup player); Gordon Lockhart, now professional at Gleneagles, and W. C. Gibson.

A remarkable number of the members took up the game professionally and most went to Canada or the U.S.A. Among names still revered among the older school at Prestwick is that of the late Henry Wright, who has been described as one of the best working-class players that Ayrshire has ever produced.

Improvement Plans

The course was confined to nine holes only for the first few years. Today it is undergoing the first stages of a big scheme of improvement. The immediate objective is to end difficulties which have been experienced from time to time through flooding particularly by the overflowing of the Pow Burn during heavy rain. Matters in this respect came to a head during last winter when the flooding was the worst in living memory.

That this big scheme should be possible reflects the highest credit on the succession of committee men who have managed the St. Cuthbert's affairs. Despite higher costs of maintenance the annual subscription of the club stands at its pre-war figure of 30s. per year which may well be a low record in this respect. And the club has a substantial credit balance in the bank. The majority of members are either artisans or business and professional men.

Prestwick

OLD FOLKS' SOCIAL.—The Glenburn District Welfare Association held their fifth Old Folks' social in the Town Hall, Prestwick, on Thursday of last week, Mr William Campbell presiding. Addresses were given by Provost Milligan, the Rev. Father Breen and the Rev. D. Caskie, and the programme was contributed to by Mrs Vera Barrie, Miss Marion Graham, Mr W. Cameron, Mr R. Davidson, Master Rowan and the Andrews Sisters (songs), Miss Graham (dancer), McAvennie and Partner (comedians), Miss Frew (dancer) and Miss McLaughlin (dancer), Mr James Murray being accompanist.

PRESTWICK HIGH SCHOOL.
EXHIBITION OF ART, HANDWORK and NEEDLEWORK
on
FRIDAY, 24th JUNE, in the HIGH SCHOOL from 2.30 to 4 p.m. and 7 to 9 p.m.
Presentation of Prizes in the BROADWAY CINEMA on THURSDAY, 30th JUNE at 10 a.m. Musical Items by Senior Choir.

17th June 1949

FORMER PRESTWICK PROVOST'S GOLDEN WEDDING

"A very gallant gentleman and a very graceful lady," ex-Provost and Mrs Thomas Howie, Maxwood, St. Ninian's Road, Prestwick, on the occasion of their golden wedding were entertained at dinner in the Queen's Hotel, Prestwick, on Friday, by Howie Municipal Bowling Club.

Members took the opportunity of expressing by way of a presentation their gratitude for the many benefactions which Mr Howie has bestowed on the town of his adoption.

Mr R. N. Smith, past president of the club, who welcomed the 64 members and friends to "this Howie family gathering," said they sometimes called Mr Howie the father of the bowling green. He was certainly the father of the Howie bowling club, and all who had enjoyed the facilities provided there would join in congratulating the couple on their golden wedding, an occasion reached by less than one per cent.

The benefactions of Mr and Mrs Howie to the town of Prestwick were innumerable, and he mentioned the pleasure it gave to look at the flower-beds of St. Nicholas Church which were presented by Mr Howie. But best of all was the Howie bowling green.

The Best Game

Bowls was the best game for promoting good fellowship and a happy pastime and the Howie members were proud of the fact that it was there that about 25 per cent. of Prestwick's bowlers had been trained. Many visitors also had arrived in the town ignorant of the joys of bowls and had departed with a hearty appetite for the game.

Mrs R. Don, president of the ladies' section, on behalf of the club, presented to Mr Howie a richly adorned book of names, signed by almost every member of the club in gratitude for their many kindnesses, and Mrs Smith presented Mrs Howie with a bouquet of flowers.

In his reply Mr Howie drew prolonged applause when he offered a cheque which had also been handed over to him, to buy a prize to be played for annually on the Howie green. He was afraid they were not worthy of all the nice things which had been showered upon them but they appreciated the gathering and all it stood for in the bowling club.

Doing His Duty

Nothing pleased him more than to go to the green and see so many people enjoying themselves, and he did not know what would have happened to the many visitors to Prestwick if the club had not been there for them to amuse themselves. Of his other gifts, he was happy to have been able to give these and felt that he was doing nothing more than his duty to his fellow citizens. He would look through the book of names and recall afresh the number of times he had played with them all.

"Our Guests" was proposed by the Rev. S. Stewart, Lochside, who said that it would have been a slur on Prestwick and especially on the name of the

Left to right: Mrs Howie, ex-Provost Howie, Mrs Don and Mr R. N. Smith.

Howie bowling club if this occasion had been allowed to slip past without expressing to Mr and Mrs Howie their thanks.

Replying Bailie W. S. Moir said he had known ex-Provost Howie for nearly 25 years, and in addition to being a good and true friend he had been a great asset to the town of his adoption. Mr J. B. Aird, past president, who said he joined in 1942, proposed the "Howie Bowling Club," and President W. D. Bruce replied.

During the evening songs and duets were rendered by Mrs Don, Mrs Thomson, Miss Gibson and Mr Cameron.

Public Activities

Mr Howie was born on the 300-acre holding of Maxwood, Galston, which was on the Portland estate and had been tenanted by his father from 1854. After his marriage at Kilmarnock on June 7, 1899, by the Rev. J. A. Hogg, minister of Galston Parish Church, Mr Howie became joint tenant of Maxwood with his father, and continued to farm there until November, 1919, when the Duke of Portland transferred the farm to the then Board of Agriculture for the constitution of fifteen small-holdings.

On relinquishing the tenancy of the farm Mr Howie was appointed by the Board a sub-commissioner of the Lands Division, and took up residence in Prestwick as being central for the area he was to supervise, which included Arran, Ayrshire and Wigtownshire, where he was responsible for the laying out of many smallholding schemes.

While still at Galston, Mr Howie had commenced practising as a land valuator, and has continued for nearly fifty years in that capacity. He was also on the Ministry of Agriculture's panel of arbiters before the setting up of the Board of Agriculture, and still acts under the Department of Agriculture, carrying out many arbitrations, some of which are accepted as standard decisions by the Courts.

On coming to Prestwick he took an interest in public affairs, and in 1925 was elected to the Town Council. He was re-elected in 1928 and 1931, and in the latter year became Provost, his

term of office, although covering the years of economic depression, seeing the promotion of many schemes in the town. In 1934 he gifted the Howie bowling green to the burgh, and it has formed one of its attractions since, being largely patronised by the visitors who spend their summer holidays in Prestwick. He also gifted to the burgh the shelter at the south end of the esplanade. In his association with St. St. Nicholas Church, Prestwick, he has been for some years convener of the Finance Committee and of the Fabric Committee, and has been responsible for the laying-out of the flower beds around the church, which have been so much admired.

With his close interest in farming matters, Mr Howie has been prominent in agricultural councils, and was president of the Scottish Chamber of Agriculture in 1934, and president of the Ayr County Executive of the National Farmers' Union in 1944, and also president of the Ayr and Monkton branch. He was also president of the Central Arbiters Association for Scotland and is still a member of its council. He is a life member of the Highland and Agricultural Association and the Ayrshire Agricultural Association. Since the purchase by Ayr Corporation of Craigie estate and Dalmilling and High Thornyflats farms he has supervised their cultivation with profit to the Council, and was also in charge of the cropping of Belleisle during the war years and of laying it down to grass for the golf course since. He has been for 52 years agricultural correspondent of the "Post."

Mrs Howie is a daughter of Mr Adam Currie, merchant, Galston, and throughout her adult life has taken great interest in church work in both Galston and Prestwick, possessing the long service badge of the Woman's Guild.

The anniversary was celebrated at a family gathering at Belleisle, Ayr, on Tuesday evening of last week, Mr and Mrs Howie receiving many messages and telegrams of congratulation as well as many presents.

24th June 1949

Crackers To Replace Falcons As Airport Bird Scarers

Reporting to Prestwick Airport Consultative Committee in the Council Chambers, Prestwick, on Saturday on efforts to control bird infestation of the runway, Group Captain J. A. McDonald, Airport Commandant, said Prestwick was included in a series of trials of peregrine falcon hawks for six weeks at the beginning of the year and the use of these hawks had reduced infestation to the lowest known figure. Of the seven hawks brought to Prestwick two had been shot by unknown persons, one was found with a broken wing and had apparently been beaten and two went wild. The trials had succeeded, however, in completely clearing the airport of birds. Prestwick at certain times of the year was covered with migratory stock in addition to what he called the "permanent staff," mainly seagulls.

Because of the difficulty of obtaining falcon hawks on a large scale, the same experiment would probably not be repeated but in October or November something like a large Chinese cracker would be tried out. This, he explained, consisted of rope-like fuses set up on poles at intervals on the airfield and as the crackers went off irregularly it was hoped that the noise would frighten the birds away.

Group Captain McDonald also reported that the public response had been magnificent to conducted tours of which there had already been 170 this year. School children of 14, 15 and 16 who were to write an essay on the airport, for which small prizes would be given, were coming along in ever-increasing numbers.

Entrances To Be Closed

It was agreed to recommend that, in the interests of public safety, "short cut" entrances to the airport at Shaw Farm, Shields Farm, Sandyford and Brieryside should be closed.

Asking for a definition of the airport boundary, Mr William Howie, Ayr District Council, said that Mr Smith, of Shields Farm, said that if he was refused access to the 'drome he could stop traffic going up his road-end.

Bailie McNair, Prestwick, said the committee appointed to inquire into this had recommended that these entrances be closed, but he thought that in an emergency application could be made to the Airport Commandant for passes. What the Commandant was after was the number of people going through the airport who had no real need to go that way.

The question before the Consultative Committee, said the chairman, was the closing of these entrances on the perimeter of the airport, and it was up to the airport authorities to decide who to let in. He thought the greatest hardship would be to miners who had used these entrances.

The war-time system of passes was mentioned, but Mr Thomas Paterson, Ayr, thought this would be a continual source of annoyance.

The committee agreed to recommend closure of these entrances to the airport authorities, the effect of which will be that vehicular and pedestrian traffic who previously used these entrances to the perimeter of the airport will have to detour about a mile and a half.

1st July 1949

11 YEARS' PERFECT ATTENDANCE

When Ayr Academy closed this week for the summer holidays, 18-year-old prefect Nancy Smillie, 169 Main Street, Prestwick, had only one regret and that was that she had been prevented from attending everyday since she started school. As it was she got off to a flying start with a compete attendance during her first session at school, but five days off with

tonsilitis the next year spoiled her attendance card though she has made up for it since for from then on until yesterday she had never missed a school working day during the eleven years, even though on occasion she did not feel too fit.

Some students may welcome the severance from lessons—and exams—with a sigh of relief but not so Nancy who passed her "highers" last year and is going to the university to take an Arts degree.

During her scholastic career she has made her mark in the various athletic activities of the Academy and was girl champion golfer last year and the year before in addition to winning the senior girls' swimming championship two years running, a title which she was hoping she would retain at Prestwick bathing lake on Monday.

Nancy's father, Mr James T. Smillie, shoemaker, is a golfer of note for on his home course, St. Nicholas, as well as on Troon courses he has holed out in one on some thirteen or fourteen occasions.

1st July 1949

BIGGART HOME OUTING

Organised by the Ayrshire branch of the Scottish Commercial Travellers' Association, the children of the Biggart Home, Prestwick, numbering 100, were given an outing to Dalrymple on Saturday. The company made quite an imposing cavalcade as, preceded by an A.A. scout, the 26 cars carrying the little guests made their way to the village by the Doon. Glorious weather prevailed, and the hosts entered with zest into the games arranged for the children. The Glebe field proved ideal for the sports, and in addition to the prizes provided for the successful competitors, each child received a gift. The prizes were donated by Mrs T. Andrew. Tea was served to the company in a nearby hall. Friends outside the Association provided toys and other gifts.

1st July 1949

"IN A BAD STATE"

Prestwick Town Councillor And Public Morals

It was high time every encouragement was given to religious bodies to try and further religion in this country. We had now got to the stage where, because of the lack of religion, the morals of the people were in a bad state, said Treasurer Black at the meeting of Prestwick Town Council on Tuesday, Provost Milligan presiding.

He moved that a decision of the Parks and Attractions Committee on Bute Hall open-air services be over-turned. Mr W. Allan seconded the amendment to the minute which bore that the committee had recommended that permission be not granted an application by the Bute Hall Brethren to hold open-air meetings in Boydfield Gardens should the weather prove un-suitable for the summer open-air gospel meetings on the shore front which had already been agreed upon.

Bailie McNair, convener, said he had no alternative but to move the minute. They all appreciated what had been taking place in recent years, and realised that it was up to us to do every-thing possible to improve the moral out-look of the people. The Bute Hall mem-bers had their own hall within 70 yards of the ground under discussion to which they could go to hold their meetings if inclement weather prevented these taking place on the shore. That was why permission for their latest proposal had not been recommended by the committee.

Bailie Moir seconded, and on a vote the minute was carried by seven votes to three.

Bathing Lake Crowds

During the heat wave on Sunday Prestwick Bathing Lake had housed a crowd of 3,000, over 2,000 of whom had been in the water. There had been the chance to make pounds not just shillings, said Mr Allan, who asked what time the lake closed on Sundays and when told by the town clerk, Mr John L. Jones, that it was closed at six p.m., expressed the opinion that surely this could be a more flexible matter and adjusted to suit the extraordinary conditions of last weekend when it might, with profit, have been open until later in the evening as during the week. There was no reason why discretion should not rule when there was the opportunity of extracting extra revenue from the pool.

Bailie McNair, convener, explained that on Sunday he had been in the lake about 4 p.m. and the bathmaster had reported to him that with so many people inside he could not be responsible for any accidents that might take place unless the doors were closed. A mem-ber of the bathing lake staff had to be posted high up on a vantage point where he could see under the water in case any bather got into difficulties. Bailie McNair described the place as "a seething mass" and had agreed with the bathmaster as to the advisability of closing the gates. There had been another 3,000 crowd on Saturday and a day or two of these figures would mean a contaminated pool if there was not a great deal of work done after the place was closed. The bathmaster did not finish at 6 o'clock as there was much to be done after the bathers had left the water.

Money-Making Chance

Treasurer Black said they needed revenue from the lake and there was no use throwing away the chance when it presented itself of making some. He also referred to the lack of indication as to the opening and closing times of the lake. Two youths had gone in and were no sooner in the water than they were told the lake was closing.

The burgh surveyor (Mr James Melrose) said the crowds were told an hour before it was closed and yet people still came in ten minutes before it was shut and tried to make their time spin out.

Bailie McNair said that discussions were to take place in a few days be-tween himself, the burgh surveyor and the bathmaster to review the position at the lake.

The bathing lake superintendent re-ported that on the night of June 9-10 the lake premises had been broken into and a number of articles stolen in-cluding cash amounting to £21 15s 6d. The town chamberlain reported to the Parks and Attractions Committee the arrangements in operation for the lodging of cash in his department from the lake and other premises. The com-mittee decided that the superintendent be severely reprimanded for his action in this instance in allowing cash to remain in the premises overnight and that he be given explicit instruction in writing as to such arrangements for the future.

Matter of Courtesy

Mr Boyd, who said he had visited the burgh yard, complained about the sprays for burgh employees. It should be the first consideration of the Coun-cil that their own employees could get a wash at the end of the day's work before going home.

The burgh surveyor said that if Mr Boyd had visited the burgh yard it was without his permission or know-ledge to which he took strong objection. "I am the responsible official and I will not have any person going into the place without my con-sent."

Mr Allan thought Mr Melrose was taking up the wrong attitude. He was an official of the town and they were the elected representatives of the rate-payers whose interests were their con-sideration.

Mr Boyd said the question of the sprays had been lying on the Council table for years.

This matter was already under con-sideration by the burgh surveyor, said Provost Milligan, and so far as Mr Boyd's visit to the yard was concerned, out of courtesy alone, it would, per-haps, have been better if he had noti-fied Mr Melrose, though on this ocasion no great harm had been done.

Roadway Charge

Mr Allan, convener of the Housing Committee, asked for a remit back of a housing minute which showed that Mr Robert Craig, 4 Kirkhill Crescent, had asked for assurance with regard to the Town Councils' proposal to erect houses in Crandleyhill Road and the formation of a new road off Kirkhill Crescent, that he would not be called upon to bear any part of the cost of making either the roadway or the foot-path adjoining his boundary wall. The committee agreed to recommend that he be called on to pay the proportion of the cost of the road and footpath *ex adverso* his property.

If there was any reason for such an exception then the Council should be made aware of it, said Bailie McNair, though Provost Milligan thought no harm would be done in remitting the minute back.

There were plenty of examples, said the town clerk (Mr John L. Jones), replying to Mr Allan, who said he would like to know of a stated case. He also wanted to know if any cases had gone the "full distance" and a man forced to pay by order of the Court.

Dean of Guild Steele said this man had put up frivolous objections and had done everything possible to keep them from building this housing scheme. All adjoining proprietors had to pay a share of the roadway and he did not see why they should depart from precedent.

He moved the minute which was carried by seven votes to three against Mr Allan's amendment.

Tennis Facilities

Treasurer Black raised the in-adequacy of Prestwick's tennis facili-ties. There were only four clubs operated by youth groups and this number was totally inadequate for a watering place like Prestwick. He sug-gested that an effort should be made to construct another six at least. There were only two places so far as he could see where they could be erected and he said they might get ground on the municipal golf course or a site off Links Road.

Bailie McNair welcomed the interest by other members of the Council in the provision of tennis facilities which, he said, had been giving him a head-ache for a long time. So far as Links Road was concerned the only objection might be that it was too near the sea breezes and would perhaps put players off their game. He would be delighted to explore all possibilities and it was agreed to remit it to the Parks Com-mittee.

1st July 1949

Prestwick School Conveners

A protest made by Prestwick parents four months ago against Roman Catholics being appointed conveners of Prestwick schools was the reason given by two members of Area No. 3 Education Sub-Committee for declining re-nomination as conveners of Glenburn Public School and Prestwick Public School.

The matter arose at a meeting of the sub-committee on Tuesday when new conveners of schools were being appointed. Mr Andrew Graham, Prestwick, declining the convenership of Glenburn Public School, recalled that in April a petition of protest had come before the committee signed by 278 Prestwick parents because of his denomination.

"I live with these people," said Mr Graham, "I have got to work with them, my children have got to play with their children, but when it comes to personal and family insults it is going a bit too far. I am not duty bound to take this convenership so I wish to decline it."

Mr Edward Hamilton, Prestwick, who declined convenership of Prestwick Public School for the same reason, regretted that anything like that had ever turned up as his relationship with the school had been very happy. "I resent having to pander to these people," he said, "I maintain that that is what it looks like on the face of the thing, but it is the children I am thinking about. I am convinced that if we were appointed conveners of these schools again some of these people would keep their children from school."

Bailie John Kerr, Prestwick, and Mrs M. Turnbull, Ayr, were appointed conveners of Glenburn and Prestwick public schools respectively.

The committee also decided that a special bus from Ayr taking children to St. Patrick's School, Prestwick, should alter its route to uplift children from Whiteside and Adamton camps. Normally these children had to walk to Monkton to get the school bus.

1st July 1949

PRESTWICK HIGH SCHOOL EXHIBITION

The third of Prestwick High School's annual art exhibitions comprising the work of pupils from the infant classes to the junior secondary was held in the school on Friday, and was notable for the high standard shown, especially that done by the third year pupils.

Colourful woven wool slippers made by the boys of Primary III. and skilfully made rugs by Primary IV. boys were noteworthy features in that particular section, and an unusual chord was struck by a "wedding anniversary" wool bag also in the Primary IV. class. An attractive display of needlework and knitted articles done by the girls from the infants upwards is also on view, and this ranges from grey flannel skirts and cotton blouses to knitted gloves and jumpers in all shades and colours. Notable in the woodwork show is a carved lamp-stand, although it is possibly equalled by some of the smaller lamps and bookends made from walnut and other woods, and a well-constructed little book-case with an attached smoker's cabinet. A strongly made little table and stool also deserve mention.

A very high level is reached in the art sections, especially in a colourful and well-drawn portrayal of St. George and the Dragon, and a lively painting of the "Derby", while sketches contributed by former pupils add a professional touch to the whole. Drawings of circus performers and of scenes depicting sport are much in evidence, and a number of these are well done, obvious care having been taken, particularly in the colouring.

15th July 1949

Windfall For Prestwick Poor

Following the annual meeting of the Monkton and Prestwick Nursing Association on Friday—Mrs Connal presiding—a special general meeting was held to consider the position arising from the National Health Service Act and the steps to be taken by the Association.

Mr J. B. Clark, solicitor, Ayr, explained that where an association owned a nursing home the property was purchased by the County Council. Ellesmere, 7 Allanvale Road, Prestwick, had been gifted to the Association under special conditions, one of which was that if it became advisable to terminate or liquidate the Association the property should be sold and the proceeds handed over to the minister of St. Nicholas Church for the benefit of the deserving poor of the parish. He stated that the County Council had made an offer of £2100, the price fixed by the district valuer, and that the Council had compulsory powers to purchase at that figure.

Market Value

The minister and session of St. Nicholas Church, the only people interested in the price, had pointed out that this sum did not represent the true market value of the house but had decided to accept the offer under protest.

It was agreed that, as it was no longer possible to carry on the work for which the Association was formed, steps should be taken to wind it up, and the Executive Committee were authorised to sell to Ayr County Council the heritable property and to dispose of the proceeds in accordance with the conditions laid down when the property was gifted by the late Mrs Anderson, Parkstone, Prestwick, to formulate a scheme for the disposal of the funds of the Association to some charitable object or objects, and pending the disposal to continue to hold and administer them on behalf of the Association.

The financial statement, submitted by Mr M. Mitchell, the hon. treasurer, showed that the total funds in the hands of the Association amounted to £5671. The office-bearers were re-elected to carry on meantime.

1st July 1949

PRESTWICK BOATING FATALITY

While out rowing with a male companion on Saturday, 21-year-old Ian S. K. Cleat, eldest son of Mr and Mrs William M. Cleat, 45 Marina Road, Prestwick, was drowned within a few hundred yards of the crowded shore.

When one of the oars of their boat was lost, Cleat, a fitter employed by Scottish Aviation Ltd., immediately dived over the side in an attempt to retrieve it, but while he was in the water the boat drifted away from him and he got into difficulties. The other young man tried to manoeuvre the boat round to save him, but it was only after a search lasting about 25 minutes that the body was recovered and brought ashore by the occupants of another rowing boat.

Attempts at resuscitation were immediately made on the beach, and in Prestwick Police Station and on the way to Ayr County Hospital artificial respiration was applied without success.

29th July 1949

COUNCIL HOUSES

Prestwick Warning To Careless Tenants

"Tenants of council houses ought to have it brought home to them that they just cannot occupy these houses and use them in any way to suit themselves. They must realise they have some responsibility to the Town Council in the way they keep the houses and gardens."

This was stated by Treasurer J. B. Black at Tuesday's meeting of Prestwick Town Council, Provost F. M. Milligan presiding. The Council were discussing a report by Mr James Melrose, sanitary inspector, on the condition of a council house at 45 Newdykes Road which, according to the report, was much below a reasonable standard. Stating that the unsatisfactory condition of the house was the result of years of general neglect, the report continued: "The tenant and his family appear to have had little idea of the elementary rules of housekeeping and hygiene, and no sense of responsibility towards the premises, including the garden, or towards the rights and enjoyment of their neighbours." Supervision for some months would be required to obtain a reasonable standard which the tenant would be expected to maintain thereafter.

In the event of another tenant going into the house, said Mr Melrose, the cost of repairing it would amount to a considerable sum. Apart from structural difficulties there would be the question of complete redecoration. Without allowing for the replacement of fittings and chipped sinks he estimated the cost of repair to be in the region of £80 to £100.

The matter was referred to the House Management Committee.

Pedestrian Crossing

Discussing the refusal by the County Council to provide a pedestrian crossing in Main Street, at the junction with St. Quivox Road, Mr A. M. Brown asked on whose instruction their request had been turned down. He thought that the reason for the refusal of that and other applications by the Town Council was that traffic through Prestwick must not be impeded and the safety of the citizens—particularly the younger inhabitants — was secondary. He said he would like to see traffic light signals at the Cross, not so much with a view to regulating the Cross vehicular traffic as to setting up a pause in the lateral traffic so that pedestrians south of the Cross could have breathing space in which to cross the busy street. Throughout the whole length of Ayr Road traffic was practically continuous and anybody trying to cross there had little chance. Traffic lights would set up a pulsation in the traffic to give people some semblance of a chance to get over safely.

Provost Milligan assumed that the question of a St. Quivox Road cross-

DIRTY BOOTS BREAK JANITOR'S HEART

Glasgow school children who had their summer camp in Prestwick High School this year have left behind them a black mark. The mark, in fact, is on the floor of the school gymnasium.

The matter was raised at a meeting of the Area No. 3 Education Sub-Committee on Tuesday when Mr James W. Scott, headmaster of Prestwick High School, said in a letter that although the gymnasium was excluded from the let of the school, the gym. certainly had been used. Every year, explained Mr Scott, the floor of the gymnasium was oiled. This had been done in the summer and the floor left for six weeks to let the oil dry. But grit had been ground into the oiled surface and it would not recover until the floor was oiled next summer.

"I wish to protest against those in charge doing this after being specifically told that they could not have the use of that gymnasium," said Mr Scott, and added: "My firm conviction is that it is not fair to our children in this school that it should be used day and night all winter and spring and then let again in the summer."

Not only had the gymnasium floor been abused, but according to Mr Scott cupboards which had been left locked and barricaded with desks for protection had been forced open.

Enlightening the committee further, Mr Robert Brown, headmaster of Annbank J.S. School, said he had seen the gymnasium. "It is the finest in Ayrshire and was the apple of the janitor's eye," he said. "Now the man is heartbroken that his wonderful floor has been damaged." The damage, said Mr Brown, had not been caused by proper gym. shoes; dirt that was carried in must have come from outside shoes. There was grit right along the edges of that fine gymnasium, he said, and also on the wall bars. "They must have opened a locked door to go into the gymnasium."

Another committee member, Bailie John Kerr, Prestwick, confirmed that there was much dirt left about the floor of the domestic quarters and that cupboards were open. The rooms, he said, were left in a scandalous condition.

The headmaster had negotiated with Glasgow Education Authority for compensation, said the chairman, Mr T. Paterson, Ayr, but next year's arrangements for letting schools for this purpose would be looked into. "Perhaps our staffs will have to have a marching-out inspection before the children go away."

ing had been reviewed by the road authorities of the County Council and by the Ministry of Transport. Regarding the position at the Cross, he said that for ten years they had been suggesting traffic lights at that point. They had had visits from the police and Ministry of Transport at various times and these experts had given consideration to their application, but apart from that he could give no further information.

Motor Cycling On The Sands

Objection to the times arranged for motor cycle racing on Prestwick sands was raised by Bailie A. B. McNair, convener of parks and attractions committee. Bailie McNair recalled that when the Town Council granted permission for motor cycle racing on the sands it was agreed that the times of the meetings were to be arranged between the promoters and the parks convener. Up till then, said Bailie McNair, no approach had been made to him or to the town clerk. The last meeting, some weeks ago, had started at 3.30 p.m., during a show in the bathing lake. According to advertisements, he said, the next meeting would take place on August 6, at 2.30 p.m. That afternoon there was a show in the bathing lake at 3 p.m. which was revenue-producing to the town.

Provost Milligan thought the first step should be to notify the cycling club. "We don't want to discourage them," he said, "because Ayr Cycling Club are doing exceptionally well. They have to select their times according to the tides, but they must toe the line." It was decided to write to the motor cycling club to try and co-operate with them.

A Petition

A petition, signed by 27 residents in the area comprising McNeill Avenue, Weir Avenue and part of Berelands Road, objected to the annoyance caused by parties who took their meals in Gardiner's Coffee Room, McNeill Avenue, and also in the O.E.S. Hall, Berelands Road. On one occasion, stated the petition, police had to be called in to restore order. The petition suggested that failing reasonable precautions being taken the magistrates recommend that the catering licence be withdrawn; that in the meantime supervision be exercised by the police; and that the parking of vehicles taking these trips be prohibited "in and around this coffee room."

Bailie McNair thought it was just too quick to give a decision immediately without having a report on the matter by themselves, and it was agreed to make an investigation with the help of the police.

ESPERANTO.—The opening meeting of the Esperanto Class was held in Prestwick High School on Tuesday evening when 21 students enrolled. first lesson by the direct method led to the end of the lesson to students answering simple questions in Esperanto and taking dictation.

9th September 1949

WOMEN'S VOTE

Prestwick Conference Reminded Of Its Power

Almost 200 women attending a Labour Party conference in Prestwick on Saturday heard Mr John Pollock, prospective Labour candidate for the Ayr parliamentary division, tell them: "There are more women than men in this country, and while one vote may not seem important, a united vote on the part of members of your sex could put a Government into power and, what is of more concern to us at present, it could put a Government out of power."

Women, he said had proved themselves during the six years of war. Now they had a valuable contribution to make to what we were pleased to call peace. They were living in a man-made world and they had to do something about it. Was the housewife not concerned with politics? Things like gas, electricity, transport, street lighting, hospital arrangements, and education, were politics and were administered by councillors who were elected by the community. The housewife, as a ratepayer, had no right to grumble if she did not take a part in politics

Laundered Political Thinking

They must not send their political thinking to be done in the same way as they sent out their laundry. They must find out things for themselves The woman who said "I don't see how politics affect my daily life" had no argument. That was the task the women of the Labour Party had to perform. They had to go out to meet that attitude of mind and seek to persuade women that they were wrong in holding that view.

The meeting was the first to be held under the auspices of the Ayr Labour Party (Women's Section) and was followed by a "question time" and social.

"Nothing To Apologise For"

Mr William Ross, M.P. for the Kilmarnock division, said that he had not the slightest doubt that if, in 1945, in Prestwick they could have had a meeting half the size, of women who were sincerely anxious to get and do things, then a man who was harassing him with letters to the papers would not be putting "M.P." after his name.

Labour, he said, had nothing to apologise for as a party or as a Government. They went to the people in 1945 with a programme that had now become famous. They had carried out their promises to the people against an Opposition that was slow to start and only now was beginning to realise how an Opposition should behave and fight.

A Measure of Success

"Recently," he said, "the severity of the strength and loudness of their criticism is, in my mind, a measure of the success of the Labour Government. They are not talking in thousands for election fights, they are talking in millions."

Amid applause he continued: "If it is worth ten millions or even more to keep the Labour Government out of Westminster surely it is worth the work of all the labour women in the country to see that the Tories are kept out. What you have got to lose is the future of the ordinary people of this country."

Ayrshire, he said, after four years of Labour Government had been able to throw itself open for exhibition and inspection. There was the Scottish Industries Exhibition—if one would listen to the political pundits of the Tory party one would have thought that Scotland was dead industrially. Instead, Scotland had been industrialised.

It had been the Labour Government that had toiled during these four years for a future which promised a better and more dignified life for Scotland The Government had never shirked unpopularity but had gone ahead with the support of the people.

American Papers Copy

Mr Ross criticised the "little papers with their little columns, the local daily press, and the national press." It was little wonder, he said, that their counterpart had been taken up in America. The same people in America who were today criticising Britain were the same people who prayed and worked for the defeat of Mr Truman. But the fame of the Health Service had spread and the people of America wanted the same kind of health service.

"There is no need to apologise for what we have done but resolutely go ahead with what we started," he continued. They would face their new task in a new Government with the slogan that production must rise and that the Government would ensure that it had adequate power properly to control the industrial life of the people.

18th November 1949

BIRTH OVER THE ATLANTIC

Remote control from Prestwick enabled an accouchement to be carried out successfully in a plane over the Atlantic on Tuesday.

Not long after a trans-Atlantic airliner had left Prestwick for Gander, Newfoundland, the pilot radioed that a woman passenger was about to give birth to a child. The first message received at Prestwick asked for a doctor to be available to give instructions, and Dr. John Rowell went to the airport and the instructions he gave were transmitted from Redbrae trans-atlantic control point to the air liner.

The woman, Mrs Łeokalia Rolbieki, a Polish refugee, was safely delivered of a baby daughter, her fourth child. A laconic message came to Prestwick: "Baby born; mother and child doing nicely—it's a girl." The mother was one of 60 D.P.'s travelling on a specially chartered flight from Bremen to New York. Her husband and the other children were also on the liner.

Pictures taken of the mid-Atlantic baby arrived in Prestwick on Wednesday by the same liner on which the child was born, the aircraft having made the return flight in 8 hours 53 minutes, a record. The child is to be christened Sverre after the Viking aircraft.

11th November 1949

PRESTWICK MEMORIAL UNVEILED

For two minutes on Sunday Prestwick was hushed as ex-servicemen and women, school-children and members of youth organisations paid homage to the fallen of two world wars.

Despite the chilling winds a large crowd gathered at the war memorial to take part in the service of remembrance conducted by the Rev. D. M. Caskie, St. Cuthbert's. Following the scripture reading, Provost F. M. Milligan unveiled the memorial to which had been added the names of those who fell in the last world war.

In his address he said that after the first world war people thought that they could at last live at peace with their neighbours, but they had failed to recognise the Nazi reptile raising its ugly head. It was now our duty to unite with every people living in a democracy throughout the world. The cenotaph would be a reminder for all time of the need for justice, peace and liberty. "The warriors of the last war have joined the ranks of their fathers of the first world war—in honour they lie side by side," he said.

Wreaths were laid by Provost Milligan on behalf of the Town Council; by the Army Cadet Force; the Royal Air Force Association; the Red Cross; the Boys' Brigade; the Boy Scouts; the Girl Guides; Prestwick High School; Prestwick Public School; Glenburn School, and Prestwick Rotary Club.

28th October 1949

HOUSING PLANS FOR PRESTWICK

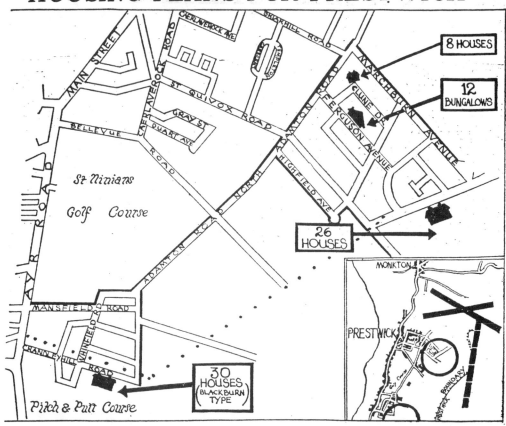

SIGNING THE COVENANT

A piper helped to attract attention to the Covenant at Prestwick Town Hall where, during the day, 610 signatures were obtained.

9th December 1949

S.A.L. Employees Reply To Sir Patrick Dollan

Reply has been made by the employees of Scottish Aviation Ltd., to statements made by Sir Patrick Dollan, chairman of the Scottish Advisory Council on Civil Aviation, in which he referred to Mr Thomas Johnston's speech at the dinner held at Prestwick on Tuesday of last week to mark the ninth anniversary of transatlantic air services to Prestwick.

The employees point out that throughout the period in which Sir Patrick Dollan was a director of British European Airways Corporation, which appoints him as chairman, and, in fact, all those who comprise the Scottish Advisory Council on Civil Aviation, he has issued a steady stream of fulsome statements and glowing promises as to what was happening in civil aviation affairs in Scotland or was going to happen next month or next year, many of which have either been inaccurate in the first instance or later been contradicted by his own statements or subsequent events.

Some of his statements, including his latest one, appear to us to display a certain vindictiveness towards our efforts at Prestwick to create employment and skill in the several branches of the aviation industry, which probably reflects the views of those for whom he speaks and which, we feel, has accounted for some thousands of our colleagues losing their employment at Prestwick and the steady reduction in industrial employment which is still taking place.

Prestwick's Opportunity

Sir Patrick Dollan implies that no company or individual in Scotland has the capital, experience, personnel or the aeroplanes to operate air services, nor have any schemes been submitted.

At the end of the war, Prestwick, and the organisation there, had handled a greater volume of trans-Atlantic aircraft than any other organisation in the history of aviation. Consequently there was the airport, the technical capacity, the finance, some 6,000 of us, and everything which goes to make for the successful operation of modern airline services.

As compared with this, the Dutch had not a single building standing on their airport at Amsterdam and had just got rid of enemy occupation. Today the Dutch airline company is one of the most efficient in the world, and parallels Dutch shipping as a factor in the National economy, whereas, thanks to the policies which Sir Patrick Dollan so strongly advocates, the Scottish airline, which was so fully equipped in every sense and which could have encouraged our aircraft industry, has had to seek an opportunity of keeping its capacity exercised to a minor extent, by forming several airline companies in foreign countries, and is doing around the highlands and islands of Greece and on international services from Greece, precisely what it ought to have been doing in and from Scotland.

Filling the Gap

In our opinion had the Liberator conversion, to which Mr Johnston referred, been permitted by the Ministry of Aircraft Production the gap in British trans-Atlantic aircraft would have been filled and in the process of doing so a very large and prosperous aircraft manufacturing industry would have continued at Prestwick.

Sir Patrick Dollan has, in various ways, endeavoured to disparage the fact that the company at Prestwick, of which we are the employees, had any part whatsoever in creating Prestwick Airport.

From the day Prestwick Airport was started in 1935 the employees have been aware that the intention of the company and everyone in it was that Prestwick should one day become a great trans-Atlantic airport and a great centre of the aircraft manufacturing industry and that the sole policy of the company and ourselves has been to create employment and skill in an industry which offered such tremendous scope for generations to come.

An Aircraft Industry

It is perhaps barely worth referring to, but it would appear from Sir Patrick Dollan's statement that there is no aircraft industry in Scotland and never has been, and that there will not be one until another large flat area of ground is discovered somewhere in Scotland. This statement is not dissimilar in some respects to one made recently by the Secretary of State for Scotland in which he also appeared to be unaware of the fact that there was an aircraft industry at Prestwick, as he appeared to be still seeking the means of establishing one.

Clearly, the whole planning of Prestwick from the commencement has been that of a large trans-Atlantic airport which would also be the site and testing ground for a large Scottish aircraft manufacturing industry, the seeds of which, and the employment in which, were started well before the war.

Finally, we feel that everyone in Scotland is well aware that there has been no lack of requests to the Scottish Advisory Council, the Scottish Office and to every Ministry concerned for the encouragement of the various branches of the aircraft industry at Prestwick, and it is quite pointless of Sir Patrick Dollan to imply that any lack of approach is the cause of present difficulties.

We are vitally concerned that the sad depletion of employment at Prestwick should cease and that some measure of official encouragement should be given to the industrial position at Prestwick instead of the continual discouragement which has been its lot for the past four years. It may not be generally known, and we think it should now be made known, that, apart from the general discouragement and the denial of the background of a Scottish airline company, industrial capacity at Prestwick has been undermined since December, 1945, when the Ministry of Civil Aviation assumed the position of landlord of Prestwick Airport and all it contains, without purchase. This has meant that all security of tenure of factory buildings, all the basis on which to plan post-war work, all landlords' repairs, all terms of tenancy as and when compulsory purchase became a fact, have been completely lacking and, apart from all other reasons, this is a major cause of the reduction in industrial employment at Prestwick.

What industry could develop properly when left for four years in a state of complete uncertainty as to its future home?

NATIONAL PARTY PROTEST

The Ayr Branch of the Scottish National Party at a special meeting on Tuesday passed the following resolution: "That no one can have any confidence in the Scottish Advisory Committee on Aviation so long as Sir Patrick Dollan remains its Chairman." Indignation was expressed by members from Prestwick at the untrue and unfair allegations made by Sir Patrick Dollan about the aircraft industry in Prestwick.

THE LATE MR A. ORR. — For many years a costing clerk with Messrs Glenfield and Kennedy, Kilmarnock, and the first post-war proprietor of the Towans Hotel, Prestwick, Mr Allan Orr, died at his home, 3 Allanvale Road, on Christmas Eve. He took over the hotel in 1946 on his retirement but gave it up owing to ill health. He was an expert in the growing of ferns. Mr Orr is survived by his wife and two of a family.

30th December 1949

PRESTWICK AIRPORT PLANS

Scottish Chamber Of Commerce Not Satisfied

Criticism of the proposed plan of the new main runway at Prestwick Airport is made in a letter which has been sent by the Central Committee of the Scottish Chamber of Commerce to Lord Pakenham, Minister of Civil Aviation.

The committee are to seek the aid of the Scottish Council (Development and Industry) in their campaign for the adoption of a satisfactory long term policy for the airport.

The following is the text of the letter:

"The Central Committee of Scottish Chambers of Commerce, having circulated to their members particulars of your Edinburgh statement of October 13 and received their reactions to it, and having since given it very full consideration, regret that they cannot accept your statement as providing a satisfactory answer to the points raised in our letters of July 16 and September 23, 1949. These points were:

"(1) Our fear that the plan then proposed by your Ministry for the development of Prestwick Airport might prove to be a short-term one which might prevent the adoption of a long-term plan on the lines of the original target development plan for the airport, and which made provision for the possibility of Prestwick being developed as a combined land 'plane and flying boat transatlantic air terminal in the future.

"(2) That your Ministry's proposed development plan included a new main runway 7,000 feet in length in a direction which had not been found necessary on account of the prevailing Prestwick wind conditions during nine years' intensive use by transatlantic traffic, and in a direction which precluded further extension.

"(3) That housing and other local planning in the neighbourhood had been frozen on account of your Ministry's rejection of the original target development plan without having defined any alternative to it, and that this condition had existed for several years.

Millions for Heath Row

"(4) That your Ministry had found it possible to spend many millions of pounds on the development of Heath Row Airport, near London, during the same period in which they had not found it possible to agree on a development plan for Prestwick Airport.

"(5) That Prestwick Airport was still without the primary facility of air feeder services.

"(6) That your Ministry's interpretation of the terms of reference of the Prestwick Airport Consultative Committee was such as prevented that committee from serving any useful purpose.

"(7) That consideration should be given to the possibility of bringing Prestwick Airport under the ownership and control of a Scottish public utility corporation through which its use and development could be encouraged in the same way as has been done by the Clyde Navigation Trust in the case of the harbours and ancillary industries of the Clyde.

"Your statement refers to the above points only in so far as it intimates that you have now officially adopted the proposed plan of your Ministry and your conviction that there is no justification for the development of a flying-boat base in Scotland.

Joint Action

"The Central Committee of Scottish Chambers of Commerce consider that the Scottish trade and industry which they represent are so vitally concerned with the adoption of a long-term plan for the development of Prestwick Airport that they cannot accept the official adoption of a short-term plan at this stage or one which does not make provision for the possibility that the handling of large flying boats will become a requirement of Scotland's international air terminal at some time in the not distant future.

"Your statement that limitations on capital investment will prevent work from being carried out until at least 1953 is regretted in view of the capital expenditure incurred during recent years and still being invested in other airports. The statement means that there will continue in use for another three or four years the temporary south-west runway, which was due for replacement at the end of the war as being below the safety standards for civil use and as presenting a danger to the town of Prestwick which it adjoins and with which it is directly in line. This we consider is deplorable.

"We are therefore making representations to the Scottish Council (Development and Industry) with a view to endeavouring to have the action and intention of your statement brought into line with the future of trade and industry in Scotland, and to having action taken with regard to the other points which we raised and to which you made no reference."

Prestwick

DANCE. — The Prestwick Players held a Christmas dance in Parkston Hotel, Prestwick. The prizes for the speciality dances were, in the unavoidable absence of Mrs. Milligan, presented by Mrs Clarkston.

OPEN SPACE.—Following a request from the Fourth Ward Committee requesting that a portion of the ground at the corner of Waterloo Road and Afton Avenue be laid out as a public open space, it has been agreed to carry out an inspection of this, and certain other areas, in the spring.

PRESTWICK OLD FOLKS PARTY

Formed just over a year ago the Third Ward Social Welfare Association of Prestwick, held its first Old Folks Christmas Party on Wednesday evening of last week in the Town Hall. Over 100 old people spent an enjoyable evening. Mr R. W. Purdie, chairman of the Association, presided, and welcoming the guests, outlined the activities which the Association intended to carry out. Among others present were Mrs Milligan, wife of the Provost, who was himself unable to be present; Bailie Moir and Mrs Moir; Councillors Brown and Allan, who represent the ward and their wives; Mr J. L. Jones, town clerk, and Mrs Jones; the Rev. G. McLeod Dunn, St. Nicholas Church; and the Rev. Father Breen, St. Quivox R.C. Church, who said grace before supper was served. The programme was sustained by Mr James Parker (baritone), Master R. Hamilton (boy soprano); Miss M. Keenan (girl soloist), Miss N. Bell (violinist) accompanied at the piano by Miss Janet Moscardini, Mr Johnstone Woods (accordionist), Miss Joy Graham (dancer), Miss Betty Wilson and her troupe, and Rev. G. McLeod Dunn (recitation). Mrs McKean played the accompaniments for the singers. At the close Mrs Pettigrew, on behalf of the old folks, returned thanks for the treat. Guests over 80 years of age, who received special gifts were Mrs Gillespie, "Granny" Aitken and Mr A. Samson, Broompark Road.

YOUTH FELLOWSHIP.—The combined Youth Fellowships of St. Cuthbert's, St. Nicholas, and South Churches, Prestwick, held their first annual dance in Western House, Ayr, on Tuesday of last week. The guest of honour was Miss Primrose Milligan, one of the stars from the Scottish radio show "It's All Yours". Miss Milligan entertained the company with a few impersonations which were well received. On Christmas Day the combined fellowships of St. Nicholas and the South Church held a Christmas Service in the South Church. St. Cuthbert's fellowship attended the service of the Nine Lessons held in their church in the evening. The lesson for the fellowship was read by Mr A. Andrews. St. Cuthbert's fellowship have now no further meetings until the second Sunday of the New Year when they meet in the Church Hall at 7.45 p.m.

INDEX